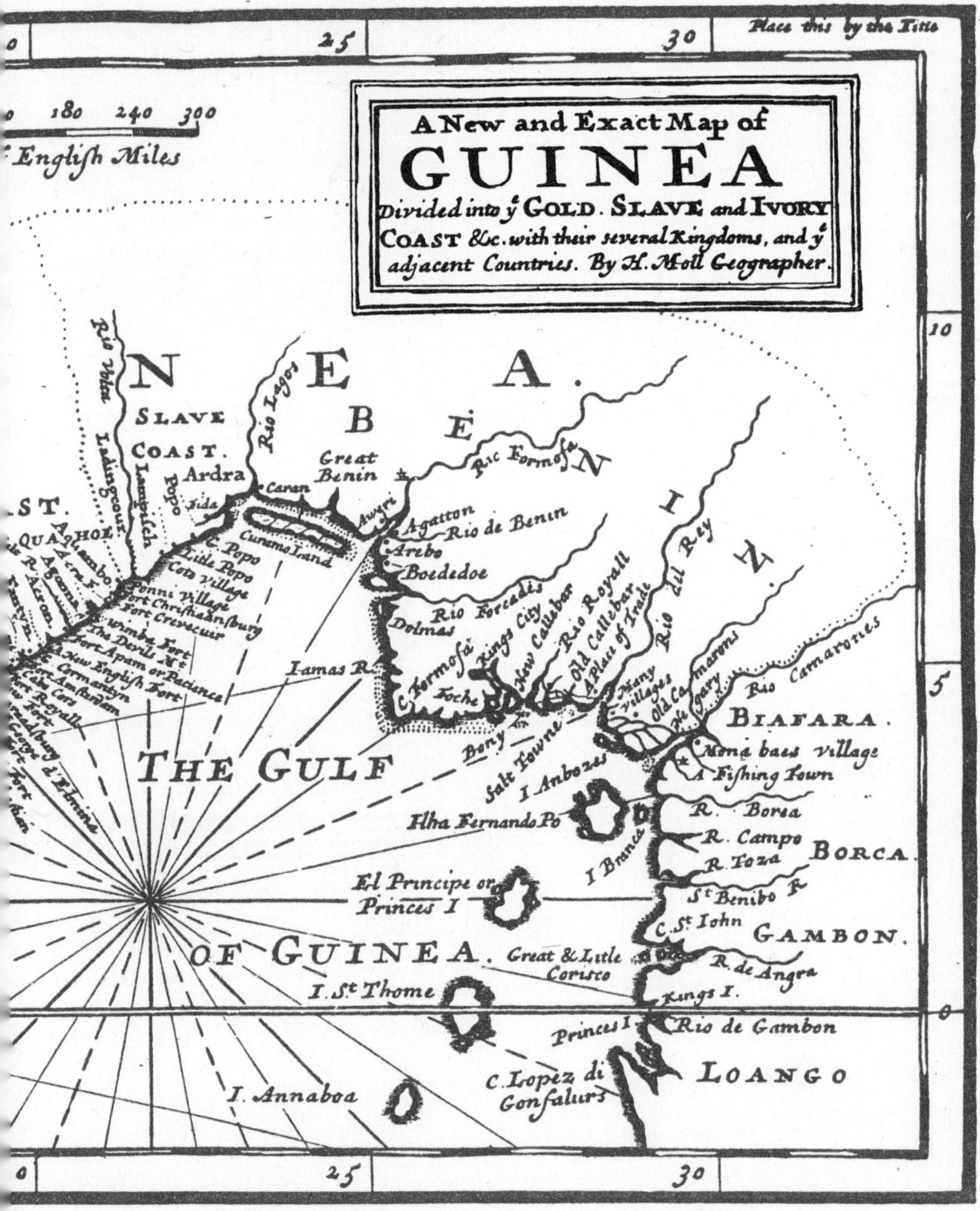

A New and Exact Map of GUINEA

Divided into y^e GOLD, SLAVE and IVORY COAST &c. with their several Kingdoms, and y^e adjacent Countries. By H. Moll Geographer.

180 240 300
English Miles

THE GULF OF GUINEA

SLAVE COAST
Ardra
Great Benin
Rio Volta
Rio Lagos
Rio Formoso
Agatton
Rio de Benin
Arebo
Boededoe
Rio Forcados
Dolmas
Kings City
C. Formosa
Foche
New Callebar
Rio Royall
Old Callebar
A Place of Trade
Rio del Rey
Many Villages
Old Callemar
Rio Camarones

BIAFARA
Mona baes village
A Fishing Town
R. Borea
R. Campo
R. Toza
BORCA
St Benibo R.
C. St Iohn
GAMBON
R. de Angra
Kings I.
Rio de Gambon
LOANGO

Ilha Fernando Po
I. Anbozes
I Branco
El Principe or Princes I.
Great & Little Corisco
I. St Thome
Princes I.
C. Lopez di Gonsaluus
I. Annaboa

Iamas R.
Bony
Salt Towne

N E B E N I N

QUAQHOE
Popo
Little Popo
Cota Village
Bonni Village
Fort Christiansburg
Fort Crevecuir
The Devils Mt
Fort Apam or Patience
New English Fort
Fort Ormonon
Fort Amsterdam
Caen

In 1907 the book was reprinted by Sir Alfred Jon̄[...] object of showing the Merchants of the present da[...] hundred years ago by the enterprising people of th[...]

RICHARD FRY

Bankers in West Africa

THE STORY OF THE BANK
OF BRITISH WEST AFRICA
LIMITED

HUTCHINSON BENHAM
LONDON

Hutchinson Benham Ltd
3 Fitzroy Square, London W1

An imprint of the Hutchinson Group

London Melbourne Sydney Auckland
Wellington Johannesburg and agencies
throughout the world

First published 1976
© Standard Chartered Bank Ltd

Set in Monotype Bembo
Printed in Great Britain by The Anchor Press Ltd
and bound by Wm Brendon & Son Ltd
both of Tiptree, Essex

ISBN 0 09 126910 5

CONTENTS

ILLUSTRATIONS

Also illustrated on the jacket is a medal issued by the Bank in 1924 in connection with the British Empire Exhibition.

FOREWORD

By Sir Cyril Hawker

THE merger of the Bank of West Africa with the Standard Bank, followed inevitably by its close involvement in the general policy of the Standard and Chartered Banking Group (now Standard Chartered Bank Limited), virtually brought to an end its life as an independent institution. It had played an outstanding part in the economic and financial development of West Africa, first under colonial rule and afterwards when the area was divided into four self-governing territories. And it was felt that its story should be told while a number of its leading personalities were still alive and available to pass on their recollections.

With the agreement of the board, therefore, Richard Fry, for many years Financial Editor of *The Guardian* and an acknowledged student of economic and financial matters, was asked to undertake the task, and he readily agreed. In the event he has written a fascinating and objective history of the Bank of West Africa, lighting up the background of changing political conditions against which the Bank was called upon to operate. It cannot have been an easy task, since the records of the Bank were far from complete, and he had to seek other sources from which to obtain the information needed. I should like to congratulate him on the outcome of his research and offer him the sincere thanks of the board and myself.

The history of the Bank covers almost the entire period of British colonial administration in the area now represented by Nigeria, Ghana, Sierra Leone and The Gambia. Founded in the early 1890's by Sir Alfred Jones, head of the Elder Dempster shipping lines, who wished to help in the development of West African production and trade, the Bank took a leading part in introducing a modern system of cash payments into these territories. It was made responsible for handling the silver currency, first by itself and later as the agent of the West African Currency Board. For many years it was also the banker to the colonial governments.

Although other banks, European and African, played a part in the growth of financial services, the BBWA – renamed Bank of West Africa in 1957 – always held a unique place. In the earlier period it was largely concerned with the financing of overseas trade, which included loans against produce on its way from the villages to the ports and across the ocean. It helped to introduce and develop some of West Africa's main export products such as cocoa, groundnuts, cotton, rubber, gold, diamonds and others.

From trade financing the Bank spread into loans for economic development. In the 1950s, when African independence was obviously approaching, and the European trading companies retreated from their traditional activities of produce buying and general retailing, the BBWA launched a determined drive to expand its branch network. From the ports and the main centres of administration the branches quickly spread out into the inland market towns and smaller trading places. This expansion filled a banking vacuum left by the withdrawal of the trading firms, and it laid the foundations for the active role the Bank was to play in the development of the independent nations.

In 1965 the Bank of West Africa was merged into the Standard Bank. Since then, separate Standard Banks have been formed in Nigeria, Ghana and Sierra Leone. The national governments and the African public have taken substantial stakes in the capital of these banks. Many of their directors and managers are Africans. Back in Britain the Standard Bank has further expanded to form the Standard Chartered Bank Limited, which now spreads its activities over many parts of the world.

West Africa remains a vital field of operations for the Standard Banks. As they emerged from the past efforts of the Bank of West Africa, they took over many of the proved qualities of the old

Bank. This History should make sure that these qualities are not forgotten. It will tell a younger generation that the BBWA made a highly important contribution to the progress of the West African peoples and their economies. There was much good in the past; there is great hope and promise in the future.

AUTHOR'S NOTE

THIS book owes its existence to Sir Cyril Hawker, the former chairman of the Standard Bank which took over the Bank of West Africa in 1965. He thought that a history of the BWA ought to be written while many of the men who had worked for it were still alive. He must also bear the responsibility for entrusting the work to a journalist rather than an academic historian. That choice explains the almost complete absence of footnotes. Any historian who may feel uneasy about this can rest assured that the techniques of an experienced reporter in looking for information and making sure of accuracy are only different from, not inferior to, those taught at universities. But that is not all.

The raw material of this book was largely discovered and sorted out by Mr. J. R. Wilkinson, a former chief inspector of the Bank of British West Africa who returned from retirement in 1973 to devote more than two years to the task. It was due to him that we found many records and files which were believed lost. He coaxed many retired bank officers into writing or talking on what they remembered. Most of the research in the Public Record Office and other libraries was done by him. Above all, his sharp inspector's eye checked every fact and figure of my story. I cannot thank him adequately for his unselfish help.

My gratitude is due also to Mr. John C. Read, for many years general manager of the BBWA/BWA, who gave me both invaluable advice and some written notes on certain periods, which have been incorporated. He read through the draft and suggested essential amendments, though the final text is, of course, my sole responsibility.

In West Africa the chairmen of the Standard Banks of Nigeria, Ghana and Sierra Leone gave me most generous help in meeting bank officials, customers, and pensioners over a very large area. I express my sincere thanks to all of them, and to the many people inside and outside the banks who took such a constructive interest in this history.

I should like to thank the United Africa Company for being more than helpful. I had much good advice from Lord Cole, a former chairman, and from officials both in London and in West Africa. In Lagos, Accra and Freetown senior UAC men talked to me very freely on the past and arranged meetings with present and former African employees to tap their memories. I was given access to the UAC library in London and read an unpublished history of the UAC as well as its Statistical and Economic Review.

Barclays Bank International have kindly given permission to make use of a record of secret talks between their directors and Sir Roy Wilson of the BBWA in the 1930s. I have also been permitted to quote several lively passages from articles published in the staff magazine of Barclays Bank (DCO) and other material collected by Mr. L. A. Borer for a projected history of that bank.

Special thanks are due to the West African Currency Board. Its last secretary, Mr. C. E. Perrin, let me consult the bound volumes of the board's annual reports from beginning to end, as well as a file of correspondence with the BBWA.

Among many others who helped me I can mention only a few. Professor Davies of Liverpool University, whose book *The Trade Makers* records the history of Elder Dempster & Co. and covers the early years of the BBWA, has been lavish with help and advice. Sir Rex Niven, whose *Short History of Nigeria* has gone into many editions, straightened out some of my early ideas on the political background from his vast store of experience as a former Nigerian civil servant. Sir Patrick Reilly, chairman of the United Bank for Africa (and of its parent company, Banque Nationale de Paris Limited, London) arranged some extremely helpful interviews for me.

Sir Michael Wilson, director of Lloyds Bank and son of Sir Roy Wilson, kindly unearthed the correspondence on the original 'treaty of alliance' between Lloyds and the BBWA in 1919. Officials of the Bank of England, efficient and helpful as always, led me to the long series of official reports on West African banking and currency matters, from the Paton Report in 1948 to the two reports by de Loynes on Nigeria in 1957 and on Sierra Leone and The Gambia in 1961.

As for libraries, we (Mr. Wilkinson or myself) found much background material for this history at the Public Record Office, the Foreign and Commonwealth Office Library, the House of Lords Record Office, the library of medical history of the Wellcome Foundation Ltd., and the excellent library of the Institute of Bankers. Much material was also extracted from the library of the Standard Chartered Bank Limited, and some from the archives of the Liverpool City Library. Finally I discovered the astonishing mass of African records and documents at Rhodes House, Oxford.

Apart from the large number of employees of the Bank, past and present, who took much trouble to help this history along, I wish to thank the son and daughter of Mr. Leslie Couper (Mr. W. M. Couper and Mrs. Barbara Rose) and the son and daughter of Mr. D. W. Paterson (Mr. R. S. Paterson and Miss M. W. Paterson) for sending recollections of their respective fathers.

Lawrence Jones & Co., solicitors, kindly read the manuscript of the book.

Throughout this history I have used the present-day spelling of place names in West Africa.

Following is a list of books which I have found helpful in building up a picture of the general conditions in which the Bank had to operate throughout its 75 years.

P. T. Bauer, *West African Trade*, Cambridge University Press, 1954.

E. W. Bovill, *The Golden Trade of the Moors*, Oxford University Press, 1970.

B

Charles V. Brown, *The Nigerian Banking System*, George Allen & Unwin, London, 1966.

Commonwealth Banking Systems, edited by W. F. Crick, Clarendon Press, Oxford, 1965.

P. N. Davies, *The Trade Makers, Elder Dempster in West Africa 1852–1972*, George Allen & Unwin 1973.

J. D. Fage, *An Introduction to the History of West Africa* (3rd edition), Cambridge University Press, 1962.

C. Fyfe, *A History of Sierra Leone*, Oxford University Press.

A. G. Hopkins, *An Economic History of West Africa*, Longman, 1973.

Elspeth Huxley, *Four Guineas*, Chatto & Windus, 1954.

J. B. de Loynes, *A History of the West African Currency Board*, first published 1962, revised 1974 (published by the WACB).

Newlyn and Rowan, *Money and Banking in British Colonial Africa*, Clarendon Press, Oxford, 1954.

C. R. Niven, *A Short History of Nigeria*, Longmans of Nigeria (many editions).

Frederick Pedler, *The Lion and the Unicorn in Africa*, Heinemann, 1975.

H. L. Van der Laan, *The Sierra Leone Diamonds*, Oxford University Press, 1965.

The Nigeria Handbook, Lagos, 1925, 'published by Authority'.

The BBWA Staff Magazine, 1912–1921.

Colonel A. Haywood & Brigadier F. A. S. Clarke, *History of the Royal West African Frontier Force*, Gale & Polden Ltd., 1964.

London 1976   RICHARD FRY

Chapter One

FROM BARTER TO CASH

COLONIES TAKE SHAPE

IN the year 1890, when the idea of opening a British bank in West Africa was first thought of, the political and commercial pattern of the territory had just begun to fall into the new shape which was to endure for nearly seventy years. A brief sketch may help to explain the conditions in which that decision had to be made.

Five years earlier the principal European Powers had agreed at a Conference in Berlin to recognise British, French, German and Portuguese spheres of influence in West Africa. The boundaries were only roughly defined. The territories claimed by Britain were separated and surrounded by those under French and German domination. Border disputes continued for another ten years. France was by far the most active power in the colonisation of West Africa; French efforts to stretch the boundaries of the Berlin Treaty led to a series of clashes.

A definite border line between British and French zones defining the areas of Sierra Leone and The Gambia was agreed in 1895. The boundary between the Gold Coast and the (French) Upper Volta was fixed in 1898. Agreement with Germany on the boundary between the Gold Coast and Togoland was reached in 1899. The most serious Anglo-French friction occurred in Northern Nigeria. In 1894 both the British and the French sent missions to the King of Nikki who claimed to be the overlord of the powerful Sultan of Sokoto and the Chief of Bussa. The British mission, led by Captain

F. D. Lugard, arrived five days before the French and concluded a treaty with the King. The French withdrew but reappeared on the Benue River to make a treaty with the Emir of Muri, which did not suit British interests at all. So it went on. In the end an Anglo-French settlement was reached in 1898.

It was much later, in 1902–3, that a British military force went into Northern Nigeria to assert colonial rule. The immediate object was to suppress the extensive slave trade in which some of the most prominent Emirs were involved. This campaign developed into a large-scale conquest. A garrison was installed at Zaria. The fortified City of Kano was stormed and the Emir fled. Next Sokoto was captured; the Sultan was pursued and killed. One by one the Fulani Emirs on whose power the political structure of a vast area had been built were subdued.

These were not small skirmishes. Lugard's despatch on the storming of Kano is impressive: 'I have never seen, or imagined, anything like the fortifications of Kano in Africa. The wall was eleven miles in perimeter, with thirteen gates, all newly built. The walls were from thirty to fifty feet high and about forty feet thick at the base, with a double ditch in front.'

Between 1900 and 1903 many separate expeditions were sent out to suppress slave raiding and to bring more Chiefs under British control. One of Lord Lugard's biographers observed that 'Lugard and his envoys seem to dash about the country like Knights errant, punishing wicked people, liberating the oppressed, overthrowing cruel kings and elevating new ones.' British civilian administration was only gradually extended throughout Nigeria. Tribal risings and local resistance continued for many years.

The British Government and public were reluctant to become involved in West Africa, and this mood persisted at least until 1895 when Mr. Joseph Chamberlain became Secretary of State for the Colonies. It is true that Sierra Leone, a refuge for freed slaves, was regarded as a British responsibility quite early, though the Protectorate was proclaimed only in 1896.

Farther west the narrow strip along the river Gambia which had been retained by British traders from the advance of the French was based on Bathurst, a fine town built by the traders in 1816 on the

Island of Banjole after two centuries of Anglo-French warfare (not to mention Germans and Dutch) had made earlier settlements up-river too uncomfortable. In 1821 Bathurst was made part of the Sierra Leone Colony. In 1830 this area was the first to export ground-nuts, which became its mainstay; shipments went mainly to France and were paid for in five-franc pieces, and these remained popular even after English money was declared the official currency in 1844. In 1888 Bathurst and the rest of the small British zone along the Gambia was proclaimed a separate colony. (In 1973 Bathurst was renamed Banjul.)

In the Gold Coast, where trading links had the longest history, Britain became involved for a particular reason: the coastal tribes, especially the Fanti with whom the bulk of the European trade was done, were subjected to regular attacks by the land-locked Ashanti. British forces were employed to keep the roads open and to defend the coastal settlements. This led to a long series of wars with the Ashanti, the last two of which took place in 1896 and in 1900-1.

Farther east, the powerful King of Benin was deposed in 1897 after the killing of an ill-timed British mission and a punitive expedition to avenge it. Along the rivers, as British trade spread inland, a number of important Chiefs were ousted before colonial rule was complete.

Lagos itself had been an outpost of the Gold Coast Colony until the island and its neighbourhood were made into a separate colony in 1886. Parts of the country farther east were declared an Oil Rivers Protectorate in 1885 after treaties had been made with the many Chiefs of the area. In 1891 the Protectorate was extended to a larger region with Calabar as the capital. It was only on January 1, 1900 that the two Administrations for Southern and Northern Nigeria were formally established.

CHANGING METHODS OF TRADE

These brief reminders of the political background may show how insecure the foundations for a bank were in 1890. In the field of commerce, three vital changes had occurred since the middle of the nineteenth century. One was the start of regular steamship sailings from Liverpool to West Africa in 1852. The coming and going of the ocean vessels became an incentive to both European and African traders to find more products for shipment abroad, and to broaden the range of imports. Besides the old export products of gold and ivory, hides and skins, pepper, ginger and ambergris, cotton and timber, shipments of palm oil and palm kernels grew rapidly. The oil was in great demand in Europe for lubrication of machinery and for soap-making. The kernels proved to be an excellent raw material for edible oil, later developed into margarine. The total overseas trade of British West Africa increased from £1·3 million a year in 1866–70 to over £4 million a year in 1891–5; ten years later it had more than doubled again.

African traders had been prominent in overseas trade for a time. Some of them did business on a large scale, and were on terms of equality with the leading British merchants. A few lived in the style of merchant princes. As trade expanded more traders were drawn into the business. Competition sharpened and profit margins were squeezed. By 1880 or so the conditions of foreign trade turned against the small independent trader, both African and European. Volume and prices fluctuated abruptly from season to season. More capital was needed to survive; small traders fell by the wayside and larger firms emerged by way of amalgamations. It was in 1889 that the African Association was incorporated, a merger of nine old-established European merchant firms active in the area of the Oil Rivers.

With the growing importance of palm products which were easily harvested and collected from small farmers, the large traders gained a further advantage. In the process many of the independent African merchants became agents of the larger European concerns. This, then, was the second great change: the concentration of external trade in the hands of sizable European companies.

The third change, and the one which most directly led to the plan for a bank, was the growth of cash payments in the place of barter. By the 1880s straight barter was not as universal in West Africa as was later believed. This idea is part of the more general illusion that West Africa was inhabited by exceedingly primitive people who had to be taught the rudiments of commercial production and trade by the Europeans. In fact, trade between West Africa and the Arab world, and even southern Europe, had been flourishing before the first Portuguese ship accidentally made a landfall on the Guinea coast in the fifteenth century.

Various forms of money had been in use, often in combination with a form of barter trading, long before the colonial era. At the time we are looking at, gold coins in use included the Spanish doubloon; the American double-eagle, eagle and half-eagle; the Mexican dollar; the French Napoleon, and the British sovereign. But gold coins never achieved a wide circulation in West Africa. The silver Maria Theresa dollar had also got a hold. For the purpose of small-scale trade, cowrie shells were the most widespread currency, and they were quite practical. Custom had attached set values to various lengths of cowrie strings. In 1893 forty strings of one hundred shells were worth one shilling in certain markets.

Among other accepted forms of money were brass and copper rods and wires, small brass bracelets called manillas,* measured strips of certain cloths, and in some areas small measures of gold dust – the tackie and the larger ackie (equal to one ounce). Many other things were used at times for payment or at least as measures of value: a flask of rum, a bottle or a case of gin, and in the north a sheep, all had a widely recognised worth. Even a slave had a fixed exchange rate at some times in some places as late as the 1880s and perhaps later.

Barter trading was still widely used side by side with cash in many areas, and well into the twentieth century. It was taking more and more complex forms and was increasingly based on prices expressed in money. The time was long past when Moorish merchants arriving with camel trains set out their merchandise on the banks of the Upper Senegal River, beat their drums and retired out of sight, while the locals emerged nervously from the forest, took what they wanted and left behind what they thought were fair measures of gold and

---

*Manillas were introduced by the Portuguese, the word apparently stemming from *manellio*, a bracelet. The exchange of manillas into sterling was fixed later for Southern Nigeria by the Native Currency Proclamation 1902 as follows: Prince Manillas (Abbie), 12 = 1 shillling; Town Manillas (Ama-ogono), 24 = 1 shilling; Awirawu Manillas, 6 = 1 shilling; Atorni Manillas, 12 = 1 shilling. In the nineteenth century bronze manillas were extensively made in Bristol.

ivory. The Moors would then come back and put down more goods if they were satisfied with the prices, or not if they were dissatisfied. This 'silent trade' might go on for days.

Nothing quite so awkward existed in the 1880s, but as a rule the African traders who went into the villages to buy produce from the growers or Chiefs were still bargaining directly in terms of the goods they had to offer in return, such as salt, cloth, metal tools, gunpowder, and drink. That was still the prevailing custom in some parts of Southern and Eastern Nigeria twenty-five years later.

The European trading firms, as they spread their 'factories' up-country, might pay for the produce they bought either in cash – rightly expecting that most of it would be promptly spent in their own store – or in paper receipts to be used in the same way. Or they would advance goods up to an agreed limit to trusted traders who took the stuff into the villages and repaid with produce on their return. Women traders, who were always prominent in West Africa, even in Muslim areas, were normally granted 'buying limits' at the European store, to be paid off or renewed within a month. Sometimes they had to obtain a guarantee from their Chief.

The payment practices of the European traders varied greatly between companies and regions. In some parts of Nigeria European firms – including the big Niger Company – held on to barter methods for a very long time. Even when cash was accepted it was not always used as a measure of value. In 1889 John Holt and Company issued instructions to all their agents in West Africa forbidding the practice of making 'prices based on pieces' (of cotton cloth), and requesting that in future all prices paid for produce should be 'fixed in sterling'. As time went on African customers often pressed hard for cash payment, as they realised that cash in hand gave them more choice and a better bargaining position in buying what they needed. The accusation that some European traders made use of barter to cheat their African suppliers and customers was widely repeated for many years.

In the northern regions of Nigeria and the Gold Coast international commerce had been developed for many centuries, long before contact was made with Europe across the Atlantic Ocean. Some complex forms of barter were widely practised by the Hausa,

Fulani, Tuareg and other caravan traders who had always travelled across the Sahara taking gold, ivory, hides and skins, cola nuts, Kano cloth, Ashanti silk and other local manufactures, as well as large numbers of slaves, to North Africa or eastward to the Nile Valley. Some of these goods became well known in southern Europe.

In the savannah country bordering on the Sahara great cities had grown up almost wholly as trading centres: Kano, Katsina and Sokoto were leading terminals of trans-Saharan routes. There the goods brought in from North Africa or the Central Sudan were on-traded southwards, usually by different sets of merchants. Conversely the cargoes for the desert caravans were assembled here.

In these entrepôt cities the traders would rest themselves and their beasts in large inns whose owners were also brokers and bankers. They would make prices and pay in various forms of money, take deposits from the traders and invest them by granting credit to smaller traders or farmers. Interest was often charged at 10% a month or more. The Koran's ban on usury carried little force in these outlying marches of Islam. From these centres Hausa traders would take cattle, sheep, and leather goods to the coastal towns, especially in the Gold Coast. Returning after many months they would bring back gold, salt, and above all the cola nuts which were the favourite stimulant of all devout Muslims throughout North Africa and the Middle East.

COINS FOR CASH

Clearly a system so highly developed long before the arrival of any European influence cannot truly be described as barter, even though much direct exchange of goods for goods took place along the line. The change-over to straight cash transactions was a gradual process in these parts as much as elsewhere. By 1890, however, the use of cash had grown sufficiently throughout West Africa to present a serious physical problem.

British silver coins had been introduced as the principal currency into most British colonies by a Treasury Minute of 1825. This explained that the value of the Spanish dollar, which had been used either as the main currency for paying the troops and civilian employees or as the basis of exchange for other currencies, had become too unstable. The Treasury suggested that the silver and copper coinage of England was the fittest medium for payments in the British colonies and possessions, and should in future be generally used.

In West Africa British silver coins – the two-shilling florin, the shilling, the sixpence and threepenny piece – were generally imported by the colonial administrations and used to pay troops, public servants and (where suitable) labour. New coins were supplied on demand by the Royal Mint in London, which was ready to deliver them at West African ports at the nominal value free of all charges for packing, shipping and insurance. That was not an act of generosity: since 1870 the price of silver bullion had fallen heavily while the price of a silver coin had remained unchanged. The Mint made a large and growing profit on the coining of silver. The Imperial Treasury, which took the profit, called it by the more refined word seignorage, while the colonial governments which wanted a share of it used the plainer word.

The cost of coining, packing, shipping and insurance, as well as the need to take back used coin of reduced silver weight at the full price, made only a small dent in the gross surplus. However, the traders in West Africa were charged a premium of 1% for new silver coin obtained from the colonial treasuries. Traders could avoid this charge by obtaining 'Mint orders' themselves, but as they had to pay the Royal Mint in London in advance their money was tied up for several weeks, and in 1894 the Crown Agents calculated that the true cost of importing coin 'free' from the Mint was, to the trader on the Coast, well over $1\frac{1}{2}$%. Even so, many used the direct approach, but in the odd trading conditions of West Africa the need for cash could arise suddenly, and then it was useful that money could be got from the nearest Treasurer.

At first the absorption of British silver was slow. In the period 1886–90 an average of £24,000 a year of new coin was imported from England. In the next five years, 1891–5, imports shot up to £116,000 a year and in 1896–1900 the Mint shipped £257,000 worth of new coin each year.

Receiving the coin at Lagos or any other specified landing post was not the end of the expense. It had to be counted – Elder Demp-ster once refused to make good a shortage because they had received a certificate of delivery in good condition – put into a safe, and then packed into the customary green jute bags of 2,000 shillings, or 1,000 florins (two-shilling pieces), or 4,000 sixpenny pieces each.

These bags became the dominant trading currency in British West Africa. Whatever the size of coin inside, each bag was worth £100. It weighed 28 lbs. For many years the most common way to send the money bags from place to place, often over long distances, was on the heads of carriers. A man, or woman, would normally carry two to three bags. At a later date metal boxes were designed to contain four or five bags: some had a flat hollow in the bottom to fit on to a head. Fully laden, each box would weigh nearly 150 lbs, and yet a carrier would be able to support it on the head for some distance. Money carriers were usually accompanied by guards or escorts supplied either by the trading firms or by the police.

A good description of this task comes from the lively pen of Mr. Harry Martin, who later became Agent General of the United Africa Company. He was a lad of nineteen when he arrived in 1902 at Addah on the Gold Coast after a terrifying landing by surfboat. Next morning the firm's African agent sent him by canoe up the Volta River to take three money bags of £100 each in shillings, florins and sixpences to Kpong. A few days later more cash was needed to buy produce and four carriers were sent off to Accra, sixty-two miles away, to get four more money bags. No escort was sent with them and the £400 arrived safely within a few days.

Before the railways were built, and long afterwards where they did not run, money bags or boxes were often sent over hundreds of miles by head-load, canoe, and later by lorry. Only in the north were donkeys or camels used. The task of transporting cash in these cumbersome forms continued to grow with the expansion of trade. As the range of products widened and trade advanced inland the seasonal pressure to have cash available in different places at different times became a major problem. Although the peak buying seasons happily varied from product to product it was always hard to fore-cast precisely how much cash would be needed for each. And there were slack periods when surplus cash would flow back into the bulging safes of the traders and lie there, eating up interest in London, until the next buying season. Yet another complication was that the Africans always valued new coins more highly than worn ones, so that the money stock had to be constantly renewed.

RELUCTANT BANKERS

Any sensible trader must have hoped for the arrival of some institution like a bank which would reduce the cost of importing and distributing cash and take it off his hands in the slack periods. The traders did not express this thought openly. Indeed as soon as they were offered silver coin at a number of West African places at the cost of 1%, $\frac{3}{4}$% or $\frac{1}{2}$% they cried out loudly against 'monopoly'. But the Colonial Officers and Crown Agents in London knew that it would be cheaper and more efficient to have a single channel of money supply which would also take care of the repatriation of worn or redundant coins.

All these were good reasons why a bank seemed to be desirable, but West Africa was not then an area to which the thoughts of the City turned with any enthusiasm. While London bankers had been busy for decades setting up banks in India, China, the West Indies, Egypt, Turkey, South Africa and many other parts of the world no one had been attracted to the Guinea Coast. Perhaps it was considered too primitive, turbulent and unhealthy. Possibly the fact that the trade was centred in Liverpool and Manchester rather than in London had some effect.

Health was certainly a dominating problem for Europeans living in West Africa. There was a good deal of truth in the old byword 'the white man's grave'. Mortality among Europeans was extremely high, especially if they ventured inland. There were malaria, blackwater fever, yellow fever, bubonic plague, typhus and several other deadly diseases. In the central forest belt the tsetse fly caused sleeping sickness in man as well as in animals – this prevented animal husbandry, so there was no milk or fresh meat. Many commercial or military expeditions had failed through sickness and death. In 1896 the annual report on the Lagos Colony stated that out of 150 Europeans, 28 died within a few months of arrival. Not long before,

Government House at Lagos had been described as 'a corrugated iron coffin that contained a dead Governor once a year'.

It was not until 1899 that Major Ronald Ross, sent to West Africa by the newly established Liverpool School of Tropical Medicine, cabled home that his expedition had discovered 'the malarial mosquito'; and many years of research and experiment were still needed to make life safe from malaria alone. Yet some Europeans prospered. Mr. Harry Martin, whose arrival on the Coast in 1902 has already been mentioned, wrote some sixty years later: 'I lived on the produce of the country, yams, cassava, plantain, sweet potato, bananas, avocado pears and groundnuts. The food was often cooked in palm oil in many different ways. I thrived on it.' For over thirty years he took five grains of quinine every day, and though he contracted blackwater fever he recovered and lived to retire to the Sussex coast. Many other British residents of that generation have told similar stories of untroubled survival.

Lagos itself, where the first bank was eventually set up, had become a relatively important trading centre but in 1890 it was still no more than a small town with less than 100,000 inhabitants. The dangerous bar prevented ships from entering the sheltered lagoon; they had to anchor four miles out and trans-ship passengers and cargo into bar boats or surfboats. Passengers were placed in a 'mammy chair', a bucket-shaped structure for two or four persons. This was hoisted overboard by winch and derrick into a boat paddled by six or more men. The last hundred-yard dash through the surf and up the beach often drenched people and cargo, and could be perilous.

Dredging did not begin until 1907, though small steamboats were able to pass into the lagoon earlier. Construction of the western railway, which eventually ran northwards for over seven hundred miles by way of Abeokuta, Ibadan, Kaduna and Zaria to Kano and beyond, was begun in 1893. This must have stimulated trade enormously. But in 1891, when Ralph Moore (later High Commissioner of Southern Nigeria) first arrived in Lagos, he still saw the latter end of the old system of 'floating trade': ships laden with goods from England would lie in the rivers and creeks 'and there sell and barter with the natives and come back laden with produce. The owners, I think, shipped a little on their own account, the captains shipped a little on their own account, and the stewards and the hands in the forecastle head maintained a shop where you could get pretty nearly all your requirements.'

The initiative for the foundation of a bank was taken in the Lagos office of Elder Dempster & Co., the shipping firm which ran the regular steamship sailings between Liverpool and the Guinea Coast. The agent of Elder Dempster was Mr. George William Neville, and it seems certain that he first proposed the setting up of a bank to his employer in Liverpool. This might be seen as a sign of uncommon vision; but perhaps one should also imagine what a confounded nuisance the growing number of silver boxes had come to be in the Lagos shipping office. This traffic needed much more care, more attention to security, larger strong-rooms, and more personal dealings with the people to whom the consignments were addressed, than any other kind of trade. Mr. Neville would not have been human if he had not wished that the whole thing were taken over by somebody trained to look after money.

The French, after all, had been through all this nearly forty years earlier. They set up the Banque du Sénégal in 1853, and this was taken over in 1901 by the government-backed Banque de l'Afrique Occidentale, which was given the task of regulating the supply of money, including notes, throughout French West Africa.

Mr. Neville went home to England in 1891, and, among other things, suggested the establishment of a bank to the chairman of Elder Dempster & Co., Mr. Alfred Lewis Jones. Both these men were accustomed to making decisions, and action followed promptly.

Chapter Two

FIRST BANK IN
LAGOS

ALFRED JONES, SHIPOWNER

THE two men who were responsible for setting up the first British bank in West Africa, Alfred Lewis Jones and George William Neville, were remarkable enough to be described in some detail. Both had the imagination and thrust that made the British business-man of the later nineteenth century so successful throughout the world. In line with the secular trend, they were concerned with shipping and trade rather than with manufacture, on which the earlier rise of Britain's power and prosperity had been mainly based. Neither of them had any special knowledge of banking, but that was not likely to worry any large-minded trader in 1891. There was plenty of expertise to be hired; what mattered was the plan and the leadership.

Alfred Lewis Jones was born in Carmarthen, Wales, in 1845, and taken to Liverpool as a child; at the age of fourteen he joined a sailing ship as a cabin boy for a trip to West Africa. Ships and West Africa dominated his life from that time onwards. Returned home, he was employed by Fletcher and Parr, the Liverpool agents of the African Steamship Company. That line had been founded in 1850 by Mr. Macgregor Laird, a name writ large in the history of British West Africa: he had taken a leading part in the early explora-tion of the River Niger. In 1852 Laird made a contract with the British Government undertaking to run a regular monthly steam-ship service to the West Coast, and his line was awarded a Royal

Charter. Macgregor's brother, William Laird, ran a firm of coal merchants and shippers, housed in the same building as Messrs. Fletcher and Parr. In 1857 William Laird, who had many other business interests, took on a sixteen-year-old apprentice called John Holt for the usual fixed period of five years. John Holt naturally became a friend of the younger Alfred Jones, and the two shared their interest in West Africa. They also got to know Alexander Elder and John Dempster, who had founded a rival shipping line, the British and African Steam Navigation Company.

John Holt was an impatient young man – in fact he never lost his impulsiveness, which led to many quarrels and reconciliations with good friends, including Alfred Jones. As his apprenticeship drew to its close he wrote to his father: 'If I stay I have the prospect of a £60 salary which to my ambitious nature is beggary. No! it is money I want and money I must have if I have to go through fire and water for it.' He begged Mr. Laird to let him go, and took a job as secretary to the British Consul at Fernando Po, which was the consular centre for the Niger Delta and Calabar, on account of its healthier climate. And so the great trading firm of John Holt and Company made its start.

Alfred Jones, too, was a man who would not stay long in anyone's employ. In 1875 he left Fletcher and Parr to set up on his own as shipbroker and insurance broker. Within four years Elder and Dempster took him into their firm as a partner, and the very next year he was the senior partner and the firm had become the Liverpool agents of the African Steamship Company as well as of Elder Dempster's own British and African Steam Navigation Company. He promptly merged the two lines and soon became the principal owner as well as the executive head of the combined business.

By 1902 Elder Dempster described itself in a souvenir brochure as 'the largest shipowners in Britain' and 'one of the largest commercial houses in the world'. Apart from the near-monopoly of shipping services to West Africa, the firm owned oil mills in Africa, coaling stations in the Canary Islands and elsewhere, a hotel in Sekondi (Gold Coast) and others in Jamaica, the first British firm of banana importers and distributors, gold mines, and a number of companies engaged in stevedoring, carting, engineering, lightering and similar adjuncts to ocean shipping. All these activities were largely created by Alfred Jones himself; 'they all seemed to come quite as a matter of course under his personal supervision'.

Seated in his unpretentious little office in Castle Street, Liverpool, Mr. Jones always kept his door open and anyone could see him. He was by turns courteous and curt, pursuing large visions or pushing hard for a petty advantage – testimonies can be quoted for all these moods, and his handwriting reveals an unusual versatility of mind and character. What is certain is that he grasped any new proposition with lightning speed and once he was satisfied that he had got the full facts he made up his mind at once. Grass never grew under his feet.

Some of the tributes paid to him at times are a little bombastic – 'Imperialist, Trader and Philanthropist', says one partisan, who praises 'his marvellous magnetism' and asserts that 'but for his influence West Africa might still be commercially non-existent'. However that may be, Alfred Jones was already one of the leading traders in Liverpool and indeed in England when his agent in Lagos, George Neville, came home early in 1891 and proposed that Elder Dempster should start one more West African enterprise – a bank.

MR. NEVILLE'S AFRICAN FRIENDS

George William Neville was born at Richmond near London in 1852. He joined the African Steamship Company in 1874 and was sent out to Lagos, where he was soon appointed the Company's agent. Recalling his early days later, he wrote that despite the forbidding health conditions, 'we were a united and friendly band of some 70 Europeans on the best of terms with the surrounding Natives, some of whom were men of considerable culture and welcome guests at our tables'.

Fifty years later, when he was a director of the bank, Neville returned to this theme:

After my long association with Africa and the Africans I should like to record my admiration and, I may add, my affection for this remarkable people. The rank and file – merry, joyous – are easily satisfied, and

c

willing workers if properly handled. The cultured class are able, broad-minded and gentlemen in the true sense of the word. Amongst the latter I am proud to own some valued friends.

Let us beware how we deal with the great trust reposed in us. The discoveries of science – railways, mechanical transport, and other inno-vations – immense aids as they are in developing the resources of the country, count for nothing without the goodwill of the people. The greatest care should be exercised in selecting our men for this service, both official and commercial, and no one lacking in sympathy and respect for the Native should knowingly be allowed to set foot in the country.

Among Neville's many African friends was the unfortunate Chief Nanna Oloma of the Jekiri tribe on the Benin River. 'A remarkable man; my friend for over thirty years', wrote Neville in 1914. 'I have seen him at the height of his prosperity, surrounded by his family, in the possession of great wealth and authority; and I have also known him in the hour of dire distress, when, destitute and an outlaw, he at last surrendered to the British authorities.' Chief Nanna, like his father before him, was a powerful ruler who kept law and order along a lengthy stretch of the Benin River, subdued river pirates and robbers, and kept the fast-growing trade under his own control.

But he was charged by the British firms with monopolising trade, and summoned by the acting British Consul-General at Calabar to answer the charge. He refused to appear, fearing that he might be arrested and deported like King Jaja of Opobo (who was indeed treated in that way in 1887). Consular forces with gunboats attacked his capital. He fled and, with twelve followers, arrived one night in Lagos, where he went to the house of his old friend George Neville. There was no escape: Neville had to advise him to give himself up. He was tried at Old Calabar, detained for twelve years and then released and given a piece of land where he built a model farm.

'He was an enlightened and humane ruler', wrote Neville. 'Had he been properly handled he could have done the work of the punitive expedition under Admiral Rawson against Benin City, which resulted in the loss of many British lives and a huge expendi-ture of money.'

About the 'Benin massacre' too, Neville had his own ideas. He agreed with the contemporary view that Benin was a fetish stronghold where slavery and human sacrifice were practised on a large scale, but he did not draw the usual English conclusion from that view. Benin City and its King were 'in no way truly representative of the people'. When in 1897 a Mr. Phillips, Commissioner of the Colonial Government, was sent to Benin with seven other Europeans and some three hundred Africans, and all of them had their heads cut off, the outcry for a punitive expedition left Neville unmoved.

He alone (it appears) pointed out that the Phillips mission had gone despite a strong plea from the King of Benin to postpone it, as he was engaged in a memorial ceremony in honour of his ancestors. Envoys met Phillips half-way and begged him to return but he would not listen. 'I contend', wrote Neville, 'that we have no more right to ride roughshod over the susceptibilities of subject races than we have to storm the tabernacles and tear down the banners of the Salvation Army.'

Yet as soon as he heard that a Royal Navy force had left for Benin he hastened to join it; and after being turned back on the grounds that it was not safe for non-combatants, he got hold of a boat and reached Benin by himself almost together with the naval party. He describes the scene of the massacre, the hundreds of headless bodies, and the continuing slaughter of slaves as the ju-ju men cried out that the gods were not yet sated. Most reports of the occasion record horror, disgust, shock – but Neville has a different comment: 'The motive [of wholesale human sacrifice] is not blood lust but a deep-seated belief in the principle of propitiation, for which authority is not wanting in the Old Testament.'

'In judging the African [he wrote later] let us not forget that, almost within living memory, we Englishmen hanged men for sheep-stealing and exhibited heads on Temple Bar; and I question whether any atrocities in Africa – now things of the past – have ever approached in magnitude the massacres under Cross and Crescent in modern times.'

It might be thought that such a sharp divergence from the common white – and Christian – attitude would have made Neville unpopular in his own small British community. Not at all. In December 1894 the Governor of Lagos, Sir Gilbert Carter, wrote to the Secretary of State recommending Neville for the vacant seat in the local legislature. 'I know of no gentleman in the Colony who is better fitted for the position.' He added that Neville would have been nominated long before if he had not been the Honorary Consul for the Belgian Congo.

Yet this man who could brush aside the strong beliefs of his own community, and who thought nothing of disregarding a British Admiral's order to go home, was a patriot and imperialist when it came to looking after real British interests. He was in Lagos handling Elder Dempster's shipping business when he heard that a German explorer, Dr. N. G. Nachtigal, Imperial German Consul and Commissioner for the West Coast of Africa, was making a long stay at a German trading factory near Mahin Beach, a fifteen-mile stretch of coast half-way between Lagos and the mouth of the Benin River. Neville became curious, especially when he was told that the Consul was making frequent canoe trips in the direction of Benin.

'So I obtained the services of a friendly Native in order to try and find out the object of these movements. He reported that the German flag had been hoisted on the Mahin Beach and that a stretch of coast had been annexed by Germany.' Neville at once went to see the acting Governor of Lagos, who was not interested. 'He understood that no landing from the sea was feasible at this spot; moreover he had no steamer in which he could go to investigate personally; and should he hire one he would in all probability be debited with the cost. I replied that such was my view of the seriousness of the situation that I was prepared to run him down to the spot at no cost to himself or his Government.'

They left the next day and anchored off Mahin Beach. 'His Acting Excellency, a military man, was somewhat disturbed at the prospect of landing on an open beach in a small boat.' But the sea was kept smooth by a cover of bitumen all around, and they landed without discomfort. The Germans were told that all that coast was an integral part of the British zone as defined in the Berlin Treaty; the Foreign Office made representation in Berlin, and the Germans withdrew.

George Neville was clearly not a man to fit a simple formula. A vigorous defender of British colonial interests; a humane and understanding friend of the Africans; a cultured man of independent opinions, yet quite unimpressed by the usual worries about climate, health, discomfort or physical danger. In his work for Elder Dempster, and later for the Bank of British West Africa, he was obviously trusted to advance his employers' business interests. But he wanted always to be fair.

Only a few scant records now remain of George Neville's visit to England in 1891. Sir Roy Wilson, who joined the Bank in 1895 and knew both Jones and Neville very well, is the accepted witness for the statement that Neville 'represented to Mr. Alfred Jones that banking facilities were urgently required in West Africa and especially in Lagos'. Jones, he went on, asked Neville 'to approach some existing bank and try to induce them to establish a branch in the Colony'. That is just what happened.

A TENTATIVE VENTURE

The African Banking Corporation which Neville approached was only barely an 'existing' bank. It had opened for business in South Africa in 1891. The way its directors dealt with the Lagos proposition showed them to be serious and competent people – though later events made it plain that their principal interest was in South Africa and they were not willing to risk any deep involvement on the West Coast. The Lagos branch, started with admirable efficiency, was abandoned on the first encounter with adverse events.

The London board of the African Banking Corporation accepted Neville's plan at once. The board minutes show that at a meeting on June 4, 1891, 'letters were read from Elder Dempster & Co. and from Mr. George Neville relating to the opening of a branch at Lagos'. It was decided to act on the proposal, and to appoint Neville the Bank's agent at Lagos. The approval of the Colonial Office and the Crown Agents for the Colonies was, of course, vital. Jones had kept both informed. As the first task of the Lagos branch would be to import and distribute new silver coin, the Bank wanted to be sure that it would in future be the only channel for silver imports, so that it could regulate the supply of coin and avoid being landed with large seasonal surpluses.

The Crown Agents saw the point but wanted to make certain that the new bank could be trusted to carry out its function efficiently and also to collect and ship home redundant silver. It was only on January 28, 1892, that the Crown Agents finally put on paper the agreement by which the African Banking Corporation was given the right to import new silver coin from the Royal Mint into Lagos Colony free of charges for packing, freight and insurance. Others would still be free to order new coin from the Mint with the Crown Agents' approval, but they would have to pay a premium of 1%. The Lagos Bank was allowed to make a maximum charge of 1% on new silver coins paid out. (This was a good deal less than the £1 11s. 9d. per £100 which the Crown Agents reckoned it cost a trader to import the coin himself, allowing for the interest on his money between prepayment in London and arrival of the coin in Lagos.)

The second basic condition for the success of the Lagos bank was that it should become the banker to the Colonial Government. In principle, the Colonial Office seems to have welcomed the idea of having the handling of payments to public servants, troops, labourers and suppliers as well as the inflow of customs revenue taken off the hands of local finance officials. But there was much detail to be discussed, such as a deposit of £10,000 worth of British Government stock as security, and the charges to be made by the bank.

On July 23, 1891, a board minute of the ABC states: 'Mr. Neville, about to proceed to Lagos, would call on the Colonial Office to discuss terms on which the bank would conduct the business of the Government of Lagos.' It took more than Neville's visit to settle this matter; in December the Chief Manager discussed the terms further with Sir Montague Ommanney, one of the Crown Agents, and it was not until the following May that the Government opened an account.

A letter of instructions to Mr. Neville was approved by the board on August 13, 1891, and the Lagos branch was opened soon afterwards. On October 8 the board decided to send an inspector, Mr. McKenzie, to Lagos 'to see that the machinery of the branch is in proper working order, and if possible to visit other posts and send full reports to the directors on the banking possibilities of the West Coast'.

Almost at once things began to go wrong. In October 1891 the London manager, at the request of the Lagos branch, asked the Crown Agents to issue an order on the Mint to ship £50,000 worth of florins to Lagos. The Crown Agents refused (on Colonial Office instructions), saying that there was plenty of coin 'in the treasuries of the various colonial governments on the West Coast'. That was a new argument. It was decided that a director (Sir Francis Knollys) and the Chief Manager should call on the Colonial Secretary to see what the real objection was. Lord Knutsford received them but refused to sanction the shipment until he had got a full report from the Lagos Government. Meanwhile Neville was asking urgently for the florins. He got two shipments of £5,000 each but needed more.

On December 1, 1891, Mr. Alfred Jones took a hand in the tussle. In a letter to Sir Augustus Hemming, a senior official at the Colonial Office, he said the Lagos manager of the bank had written 'imploring us to send more money in silver florins, and we are prepared to supply it, but this restriction at the Mint prevents it. Governor Carter at Lagos tells our agent that all restrictions are removed. I have sent out two shipments but must get more. . . . I am sure you will help me in every way you can to get matters put on a proper footing as regards this Bank. We have put our names to it and we must not allow it to be weak in any point. A good sound bank in Lagos, and in other Colonies in Africa, is an absolute necessity for the development of the country. Don't let us fail now in any little point. . . . I shall be glad to hear also that the Government has given our Bank in Lagos their account.'

On December 10 the Crown Agents finally gave permission to the bank to ship silver 'without restraint'.

Three months later a serious outbreak of unrest among the Jebus and Egbas made the roads between Lagos and Abeokuta impassable and virtually halted the trade of the colony. A letter received by Elder Dempster in March 1892 confirmed the 'serious consequence' of the rising, though Lagos was described as in no immediate danger. Peace was restored by midsummer, but trade did not recover at once. In July, a trade depression was reported from Lagos, and on September 8 Elder Dempster wrote advising that the bank's funds in Lagos might be transferred to London for better use.

Around that time the board of the African Banking Corporation had suffered yet another unpleasant surprise. In October 1892 they were told that some prominent traders in Lagos had complained to the Colonial Secretary about the bank: 'They allege that the management of our branch at Lagos is in the hands of a gentleman who is himself interested in the trade of the place.' The charge, it seems, was that Mr. Neville had too many irons in the fire, and that Elder Dempster, his principal masters, were competing with the Lagos traders by allowing their captains and pursers to carry on some trading on board their steamers on their own account. This was the first of many such complaints which were repeated in various forms over the next fifteen years.

The chairman of the ABC wrote to Mr. Jones (September 19, 1892) expressing dissatisfaction with the progress of the Lagos branch and asking if Elder Dempster would be prepared to take it over. The African Banking Corporation certainly had its hands full in South Africa. It had established itself there in 1891 by taking over the Cape of Good Hope Bank which had run into trouble. In the following year or so it absorbed three other small South African banks with much of their staff and premises. It was competing hotly with the Standard Bank, which had many advantages – among them a customer called Cecil Rhodes. It is not surprising that the directors of the ABC felt that they had made a mistake in diverting some of their attention to the forbidding West African outpost. The chairman had a private meeting with Mr. Jones about the matter. It was decided that ABC should carry on for three months, and if it then wished to withdraw, Elder Dempster would take over the branch and refund the money lost by ABC. In October the Bank's chief inspector, Mr. Herbert, was sent to Lagos to report. On November 24 he cabled advising a sale to Elder Dempster. In December the board decided to act on this advice; in January Mr. Alfred Jones attended a board meeting of the ABC to discuss terms. He agreed to pay £1,000 and to take over the branch on March 31, 1893.

BANK OF BRITISH WEST AFRICA

It was not to be plain sailing. The Crown Agents said they could not transfer the right to import Mint silver free of charge to a private firm like Elder Dempster, even though a new name was to be given to its Lagos bank. Until that bank had been properly constituted and £10,000 of securities had been deposited, to replace those to be withdrawn by the African Banking Corporation, 'all silver shipments required by the trading community at Lagos shall be supplied by the Crown Agents direct to the Governor'.

The securities were handed over in May 1893, and the formation of the *Bank of British West Africa* was announced. But the authorities were not satisfied. The Crown Agents refused to restore the silver monopoly, and the Colonial Secretary instructed the Governor of Lagos to close the official account with the Bank and to withdraw all Government funds by March 30, 1893. Considering the hostility of some leading local traders, that might well have been the end of the venture.

But George Neville was not so easily put off. He called on the acting Governor, Captain G. C. Denton, and told him that the withdrawal of Government funds at the same time as the Bank was changing owners was likely to cause a run. He offered to deposit in the Treasury Chest £5,000 sterling in specie as security for the account if it was allowed to continue. Denton reported the offer, and Lord Ripon replied by cable: 'If there is reason to fear run on the Bank better leave public money for the present in their hands, taking security as proposed.'

So the acting Governor held his hand; and on reporting back to London that the five thousand pounds had been duly deposited, he added that 'as far as I have the means of ascertaining the Lagos branch of the African Banking Corporation has conducted its business on very fair lines and has given general satisfaction. . . . It has undoubtedly very materially assisted the smaller traders by the system of making advances to the extent of 75% of the value of produce as soon as it is shipped, and generally I believe to break down the extortionate interest hitherto obtained for small loans. From a Government point of view a bank is a decided convenience.'

On July 8, 1893, a further £5,000 was deposited by the bank in gold in the Lagos Treasury Vault.

The Bank of British West Africa, though little more than a department of Elder Dempster & Co. – housed in its offices and managed by its agent – had got under way. It retained the Government account but did not regain the exclusive right to import silver direct from the Mint. It seems that one of the Crown Agents, Sir Montague Ommanney, who later became Permanent Secretary of the Colonial Office, had taken a dislike to Alfred Jones.

Sir Montague, asked by the Colonial Office to give the Crown Agents' view on 'whether the new Bank is a sound and genuine concern', replied that 'the so-called British West African Bank' had at present no existence; 'leaving public funds with it meant in effect leaving them in the hands of Elder Dempster & Co.' (March 29, 1893). In June, when the Governor cabled that he had remitted £10,000 to the Crown Agents by cable transfer through the Bank of British West Africa, Sir Montague complained of delays in transfers 'through this so-called Bank'. The Governor replied that the manager of the new bank, Mr. T. Denny, had told him the cables were sometimes held back until the news could be sent at the same time, as the Bank paid for the cables. 'Curious banking,' commented Sir Montague.

In October Sir Montague had a new complaint: Elder Dempster had asked for shipment of £20,000 in silver 'and said they were under contract to supply this sum to firms in Lagos'; information showed that they were committed to supply £500 to one firm only. 'It is impossible to feel any confidence in this firm and I think the greatest caution should be exercised in all dealings with them' (minute to Colonial Office, October 6, 1893).

Alfred Jones, whose relations with the Colonial Office were very friendly, must have been aware of these views and their source. He had always considered the Lagos bank 'his', even when it belonged to the African Banking Corporation. On April 20, 1893, he had written to the Secretary of State for the Colonies explaining the change of ownership: 'The African Banking Corporation are withdrawing to concentrate on the Cape. We have identified ourselves with the Bank and desire it to carry on. We do not wish to set up a public company at present, as we hope first of all to arrange for some other established bank to open an agency . . . or to create a good bank of our own. One thing necessary is for the Bank to have control of silver imports.'

The reply, dated May 1, from the Colonial Office was that the Government account was to remain with the new (Elder Dempster) bank until October 1, 1893; but Lord Ripon regretted that he was unable to sanction the continuance of the silver import privilege 'to a private bank or individual firm'. In the meantime the importation of silver would remain in Government hands.

That correspondence fully explained the Crown Agents' attitude, but Jones was not accustomed to having his plans upset. Soon Sir Montague Ommanney was complaining to the Colonial Office of 'imperative demands'; of an 'unsatisfactory mode of conducting business'; of 'want of courtesy', and even of 'an attempt to force our hand'.

As soon as Elder Dempster took over the Lagos bank their London representative, Mr. Leslie Couper, was put in charge of the Bank's affairs in London. It was not unreasonable, therefore, for the Colonial Office to point out that everyone concerned with the Bank was an Elder Dempster man – and Sir Montague Ommanney, who clearly disliked the whole arrangement, was quick to add that Elder Dempster & Co. did not publish its accounts.

In December 1893, Alfred Jones gave in. A letter dated December 13 from 'Bank of British West Africa – Elder Dempster Company, agents' was sent to the Under Secretary of State for the Colonies, asking for the Government account to be left with the Bank for two or three months more 'pending the formation of a Bank with a capital of £100,000, paid up £30,000'. The writer 'presumed' this bank would be granted the same facilities as the African Banking Corporation as regards silver import and the Government account. Security of £10,000 would be transferred, and the writer 'will also give his own personal guarantee'.

After some further argument on details an agreement was reached granting the new BBWA the sole right to import silver coin free of charge from the Mint, with permission to charge a commission of 1% for supplying coin in the colony; it would continue to act as

Government banker (draft letter from Secretary of State to Mr. Alfred Jones dated March 14, 1894; formal agreement with BBWA, May 4, 1894).

The Bank of British West Africa was registered in London as a Limited Liability Company on March 31, 1894. The nominal capital was £100,000 in shares of £10 each, £4 paid. As 3,000 shares were issued the paid-up capital was £12,000. The head office of the Bank was in Liverpool (with a staff of two) and it had one branch at Lagos with a staff of three Europeans and three Africans. A modest beginning, but sufficient to satisfy the Colonial Office and Crown Agents.

Four gentlemen were nominated directors: A. L. Jones; F. W. Bond, who was chairman of the African Steamship Company; Henry Coke, the Liverpool agent of David Sassoon and Company, East India merchants and bankers; Edward Lawrence, head of his own Liverpool merchant firm. Of the 3,000 shares issued in the first place Alfred Jones took up 1,733. His partners in Elder Dempster, Alexander Sinclair and W. J. Davy, took 433 each. The rest went to the other directors.

They held a number of preliminary meetings with the Crown Agents and Elder Dempster & Co., which led to the drafting of the Articles of Association and the formal taking over of the Lagos banking business from the Shipping Company. The first recorded board meeting was in London on May 4, 1894, when William (Sandy) Ross was appointed Secretary. It was not until the fourth meeting on June 1 that A. L. Jones was elected chairman.

With the exception of Henry Coke, who had gained knowledge of finance and currency matters, first in India and then in Liverpool, none of the directors had any banking experience. They were cautious men and wanted safe and sound progress rather than brilliant successes. In the first six years the Bank was, in effect, managed by the directors, and the directors were dominated by the chairman, Alfred Jones. At first board meetings were held monthly – though between meetings Henry Coke would call to read the monthly returns from branches – but by 1901 they had almost one meeting a week and that became the custom. Meetings took place mainly in Liverpool, either at 14, Castle Street or at the chairman's house, 'Oaklands', at Aigburth, Liverpool.

The board spent much time on establishing safe and efficient routines. Much of this had actually been done very well by the African Banking Corporation which had set up book-keeping and other systems that served as a model for BBWA staff during the early years. Among innovations in 1894, a rule was introduced under which customers were to be notified quarterly or half-yearly of the balance on their current accounts and required to sign a certificate that it was correct. This was to continue for many years afterwards, at least in West Africa.

Business in Lagos looked up at once. To help George Neville with the new bank, D. W. Paterson was sent out to be his right-hand man. David Paterson spent many years in West Africa and became Inspector of Branches and finally General Manager of the Bank. After ten months, the first balance sheet showed deposits of £87,665 – more than seven times the amount of the Bank's paid-up capital. Almost the whole of this sum was deposited by Africans. There was a net profit of £318 5s. 3d. and no dividend was paid.

At the first Annual Meeting of shareholders Mr. Jones, as chairman, said the results of the first year had exceeded expectations. 'The Bank has as much business as it cares to do at present, and the Directors do not intend to expand too rapidly, although there is, in their opinion, an unlimited demand on the Coast for money with good security. I am quite convinced that there is a very great future for the Bank.'

A year later, the second report showed that in addition to the paid-up capital of £12,000 there was now a reserve fund of £2,000, and money held on current or deposit accounts had risen to £108,262. A dividend of 8% was paid, and this rate was repeated for many years afterwards. At the Annual Meeting in July 1896 the chairman invited shareholders to subscribe for a further 7,000 shares at a premium of £1. In fact only 2,485 shares were taken up during the following year, and the Report issued in June 1897 showed the paid-up capital at £21,940, but the reserve fund up to £4,285. Deposits had risen further to £148,000.

Two new branches were opened soon: one in Accra, Gold Coast, in 1896, and another in Freetown, Sierra Leone, in 1898. Further agreements were made with the Crown Agents for the Bank to carry the Government account and the sole responsibility for importing and repatriating silver coin – for the Gold Coast on June 16, 1896, and for Sierra Leone on April 15, 1898. Similar agreements were to follow for Old Calabar (July 18, 1900) and Bathurst (September 8, 1902). In 1902 a revised agreement was extended to Northern and Southern Nigeria, the two separate administrations set up on January 1, 1900.

There is no doubt that the facilities offered by the new Bank were widely appreciated – though they also provoked opposition, as will be seen. It had been both costly and cumbersome for the merchants, before any bank existed, to make sure that they always had enough cash in the right places for the various buying seasons; and when the cash flowed back during slack trading, it was useless for several months. At the height of the produce season, before 1891, spot cash sometimes commanded a premium of up to 7%. The African Banking Corporation had charged 3% in the season. The new Bank of British West Africa offered to supply cash throughout the year at $\frac{1}{2}$% commission to any firm that would undertake to do all its cash business with the Bank for twelve months.

In any case the Bank was not allowed to charge more than 1% commission for paying out new silver – but that was 'irrespective of any banking charges', and if a trader came along at the last moment when money was short, he might have to pay $1\frac{1}{4}$% or $1\frac{1}{2}$%. On the other hand everyone was able to turn unwanted money into the Bank at face value. As the Bank had accepted responsibility for returning to England, at its own expense, worn or redundant silver coins, the whole 'monopoly' might have operated at a loss – except for one advantage of the Bank which was never mentioned in the lengthy correspondence with the authorities: while it cost the Bank 13s. 8d. for £100 (interest on its prepayment for about 50 days) to get the money to Lagos, it did not have to import every bag of coin but could re-issue a great deal of silver returning from circulation. Thus, while the Crown Agent was not correct when he predicted that the 1% commission would be 'nearly all clear profit' for the Bank, nor was Mr. Leslie Couper when, speaking for the Bank before the 1907 Royal Commission, he described the monopoly as 'not very profitable'.

The colonial governments were pleased to have this business off their hands. The Lagos Government Report for 1896 says: 'This Bank has benefited the Colony in many ways and supplies a want which was much felt in the past.' And the Report for 1897 adds: 'The Bank of British West Africa is of the greatest assistance to the Government'.

The use of cheques was rapidly spreading. They were soon almost universally used for payment of customs duties and other revenue, and for the regular remittance of Government funds. Most (but not all) of the trading firms took full advantage of the Bank to open accounts, to obtain cash when needed, and to dispose of surplus coin. By the close of the century the Bank was safely established in West Africa and its home base was strong and stable.

Chapter Three

INTO THE TWENTIETH CENTURY

THE BANK PROSPERS

EVENTS favoured the expansion of the Bank. The British public had at last become interested in Africa. After the start of organised diamond digging in South Africa in 1870 and the gold discoveries of 1886, large sums of British capital were invested in that area and large-scale emigration followed. When in 1895 Mr. Joseph Chamberlain, who was enthusiastic in support of colonial development, was appointed Secretary of State for the Colonies, West Africa gained its share of official attention.

British rule was being steadily extended by military action throughout the lands claimed in the Treaty of Berlin. Railway construction starting in 1893 helped to spread trade into the hinterland. Road and river transport was gradually made safe. Attempts by powerful Chiefs to retain their grip on trade in certain areas against the growing competition of the European merchants were overcome. *Pax Britannica* descended on the territories under British administration.

Production of crops and materials for export overseas was stimulated by these conditions. Output of palm oil and kernels, which held first place in the export trade, was increasing and spreading to larger areas; in 1903 three-quarters of all exports from Lagos consisted of palm products. In the Gold Coast an entirely new product, the cocoa bean, made its appearance, and its early history is typical of the period.

Efforts to grow the cocoa tree (*Theobroma*, Greek for 'food for the Gods') in the Gold Coast had been made even before in 1879

G. W. Neville, 1912

G. W. Neville, first Lagos
Manager 1894, and a Director
1900–1929.

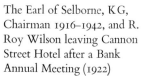

The Earl of Selborne, KG,
Chairman 1916–1942, and R.
Roy Wilson leaving Cannon
Street Hotel after a Bank
Annual Meeting (1922)

Viscount Milner, GCB,
GCMG, Chairman 1910-1916

(*Left*) Sylvester Gates, Chairman 1959–1965, opening the new building at Freetown 1961

(*Below Left*) Sir Cyril Hawker, Chairman Standard Bank of West Africa Ltd., 1965–1973

(*Below*) Leslie Couper, CMG, Chief Manager 1910–1918, General Manager 1918–1929

(*Right*) R. Roy Wilson in
April 1912 when Manager of
the Liverpool Office.

(*Below*) D. W. Paterson,
about 1936–1937 when he was
General Manager

a labourer called Tetteh Quarshie smuggled some seed from Fernando Po into the mainland. The seeds he brought prospered, and the Governor of the Colony was so impressed with the results that he obtained some further seeds from San Thomé, a Portuguese island off the Guinea Coast. He asked the Basel Mission to supervise their growth, and in 1887 distributed some of the plants bred from them.

The news must have spread fast, as commercial news usually did in West Africa. Both labour and enterprise have always been highly mobile, if only in constant attempts to escape oppression or the risks of slavery. A group of migrant farmers in the south-eastern Gold Coast moved to virgin land expressly to grow cocoa for export. It seems that the same group or a similar one had previously moved into cash production of palm oil and kernels, and had accumulated savings for a further venture; or they may have raised capital from families and tribes.

The first shipment of cocoa was made in 1891 when 80 lbs, worth £4, were exported to Hamburg. By 1906, when cocoa tree cultivation had spread to other areas, exports from the Gold Coast had risen to 9,000 tons and those from Nigeria were 1,000 tons. It was not many years before the Gold Coast became the world's leading supplier of cocoa.

BBWA was drawn into the financing of cocoa quite early. As the cocoa tree takes several years to yield fruit, its planting requires capital. Since in British West Africa it was grown by African farmers in relatively small plots, rather than in large plantations, the seasonal purchase, transport and shipment of the beans absorbed a great deal of cash all along the line, and this was for many years provided by bank advances. In later years the Bank was so heavily involved in this business that it was often spoken of as 'the cocoa bank'.

Rubber was another product in which BBWA took an early interest. Indeed in Nigeria it was in at the beginning. In 1894 the Governor of Lagos, Sir Gilbert Carter, brought in a group of native rubber experts from the Gold Coast, who reported that some districts they inspected were rich in rubber-producing plants. But (as Sir W. M. N. Geary wrote in the magazine *West Africa* in 1924) the samples brought to Lagos did not interest the local merchants, who said they knew nothing about rubber. So Sir Gilbert Carter

D

went to Mr. Neville, the manager of the BBWA, who said: 'I am not a merchant or an expert in such matters, but if you say this strange-looking object is rubber, and in order to help the Colony with a new industry, I will advance you the cost of obtaining this rubber.'

In the following year the Report for Lagos Colony stated: 'This confidence was quickly justified. Merchants took up the idea with enthusiasm. With startling suddenness the easy-going native awoke to the fact that wealth, easily acquired, abounded in the forests around him.' (How little the early colonial officials knew of the ancient West African business sense!) Rubber exports grew from 56 lbs, worth £3, in 1893 to 927,627 lbs, worth £91,260, in 1906. This progress was not, in fact, maintained. Owing to over-tapping and cutting down of rubber trees it was estimated in 1899 that three-quarters of the trees in the planted area had died. The forests of 'wild' rubber never recovered.

The external trade of the British territories in West Africa had remained fairly stagnant between 1840 and 1890. In 1891 it began to grow fast: aggregate import and export trade was valued at £2,707,000 a year in the period 1886–90; £4,166,000 in 1891–5; £6,266,000 in 1896–1900; £9,708,000 in 1901–5; and £16,314,000 in 1906–10.

Commercial expansion, and the rapid spread of cash payments, led to an extraordinary growth in the demand for British silver coin. The average annual amounts of sterling silver issued for West Africa in successive periods increased as follows (as recorded by the Emmott Commission in 1911):

1886–1890	£ 24,426
1891–1895	£116,000
1896–1900	£257,000
1901–1905	£263,000

Silver imports into West Africa more than trebled again in the subsequent six years, and this provoked the problems for the British Treasury which led to the currency reform of 1912. These events will be described later. What mattered for the BBWA in the early years was that from 1894 onwards it was the sole supplier of new silver coin, the distribution of which was its main function at this time.

Once the Bank of British West Africa was firmly established in its new independent form, relations with the Crown Agents and the Colonial Office settled down fairly well, despite occasional argument. Serious trouble came early from the British traders. John Holt had been a good friend of Alfred Jones in Liverpool, and in 1895, when he sent his son to Elder Dempster's office in Hamburg to learn the trade, Jones wrote a glowing introduction: 'Mr. John Holt is a very great friend of ours; he never misses a chance of doing us a good turn.'

However, a year earlier, John Holt had become chairman of the African Association, the group of West Africa merchants in Liverpool and Manchester which had been formed in 1889. He promptly advertised for tenders to carry the Association's goods to and from West Africa – a service which was then almost entirely in the hands of Elder Dempster. Jones wrote him a curt note to say he was 'surprised'. They met, and Jones hinted that if Holt and his associates were to take the carrying trade away from Elder Dempster, he might enter the trading field. Holt first said he did not care. Then he disclosed what he really wanted: preferential treatment for the African Association – for instance, an annual bonus equal to 5% of the Association's capital, as well as freight rates no higher than anyone else paid.

Elder Dempster's board refused to consider such terms. In a quick defensive move Jones in 1895 formed a 'West African Shipping Conference' which fixed tariffs for Elder Dempster's two lines and the German Woermann Line. In reply the African Association chartered some outside steamers, and in 1896 John Holt & Co. ordered its own steamer to be built. That turned the tables on Elder Dempster. They agreed to a rebate on freight rates, and later that year Jones offered to buy John Holt's vessels, built and building, for £70,000. Next day the fight took a new turn: when Jones sent a formal agreement along for signing, it contained an annual minimum freight and a penalty clause – and according to Holt, that had not been agreed in their talk.

'My dear Jones', he dashed on to a small piece of paper, 'If you want to keep faith with me carry out the terms of the agreement you made with me.' Peace was soon restored, but the skirmish was typical of the contemporary style of competition.

One regular complaint of the traders was that the shipping lines, including Woermann, carried on some trading on their own account which gave them an unfair advantage over the traders who had to pay full freight rates for their goods. A protest meeting of West Africa merchants was held at Liverpool on January 27, 1897, to decide how to put a stop to this practice. Mr. George Miller, chairman of Alexander Miller Brother & Co., was asked to organise action. Among those present were many of the leading names in the West African trade: John Holt, John Walkden, Charles McIver, Fr. Burman of Pickering & Berthoud, and partners of F. & A. Swanzy and Paterson Zochonis.

The charge, George Miller explained, was that the shipping companies had been selling coal, kerosene, rice, cement, provisions, salt and other articles directly to buyers, 'using the ships as warehouses and the officers as agents'. He suggested that traders should boycott vessels which did these things. Elder Dempster replied that they had tried hard to stop any trading by the company's servants but that it was not possible to stop all of it. So the firms formed a West African Trade Association 'to protect the interests of the Trade'.

Little came of the proposed action at the time; but the leaders soon thought of a new way of making life harder for Alfred Jones and this time they decided to start a bank of their own – not in Lagos but in Old Calabar, where their members dominated the trade.

In 1899 the Anglo-African Bank was established with a nominal capital of £150,000, subscribed shares £32,000, and £24,000 'called up', of which only £18,400 had been paid four years later. The backers of the new bank were the Royal Niger Company, The African Association, and Alexander Miller Brother & Co. – a powerful group of trading firms.

So began an intense rivalry between two banks which lasted for thirteen years and had much influence on the British Government's monetary policy in West Africa.

At first the Bank of British West Africa did not worry much about the new competition. Things were going well. At the fourth Annual

Meeting the chairman 'congratulated the shareholders upon steadily increasing business and enhanced profits'. At the start in 1894 the paid-up capital had been so small that additional working funds were needed, and in 1895 a loan of £30,000 was obtained from Elder Dempster & Co., Parr's Banking Co., and the Alliance Bank Ltd. In 1899 the paid-up capital had risen to £27,240 and the Reserve to £7,500, while deposits had grown to £252,000. In 1900 the author-ised capital was raised to £250,000, and in the following four years several share issues were made at rising premiums.

Although the balance sheet grew healthier year by year the directors remained cautious. Expansion plans came almost invariably from the men on the spot and were nearly always damped down by the board. During the first ten years the board minutes are full of negative decisions. It took the directors a year before they approved the installation of a telephone at the Liverpool office. After the Accra branch was opened in 1896 the board discouraged proposals to open at other places except Freetown: and a renewal of the lease to the Freetown premises was only agreed in 1898 after a study of the branch accounts. In 1903 Mr. Henry Coke submitted to the board that 'no more money should be spent on buildings or sites at Tarkwa or Kumasi until it is seen how the gold industry develops'. A bank building at Kumasi was only completed in 1908. In Accra the first bank premises were occupied in 1906.

In Lagos, the erection of a new bank building was first considered in 1900, but it took three years before the old premises were pur-chased for £2,000 from the Government, and it was 1905 before the Bank moved into its new home, in which Elder Dempster & Co. took offices at a rent of £425 a year.

Unnecessary expense was not approved. In 1902 'the directors see no necessity' for a house warming party for which the Sekondi manager had asked permission on the occasion of opening new premises.

In 1899 George Neville retired from the Coast to London, where he was elected to a seat on the board. David Paterson, who had been his second-in-command since 1894, took over as senior manager.

There were occasional disputes with the authorities. In 1898 the Governor of the Gold Coast complained that the Bank had paid out

£4,000 in gold which the Government wished to withhold from circulation. Soon afterwards the Colonial Office warned the Bank 'not to jeopardise its privileges' by refusing to repatriate surplus coin. On the other hand the Crown Agents complained of 'frequent pressing demands for silver coin for shipment to the Coast which they considered unnecessary'. The truth was that it was impossible for the Bank to forecast the demand for money accurately in advance of each season, and it caused more trouble to be caught short of cash than to have a little too much – despite incessant reminders from Head Office that cash stocks must be kept low. The Crown Agents also discovered that the Lagos branch was shipping coin to the Gold Coast, and protested.

In any case the staff on the Coast was still small and largely inexperienced. Some slow reactions may have been caused by the fact that the staff of the Bank of British West Africa, dealing so largely with the movement of currency and other Government business, were encouraged to think of themselves as engaged on an Imperial mission rather than in ordinary business. Something of this attitude survived for many years.

All matters concerning the staff were in the hands of the directors. Such items as apprenticeships, appointments, fidelity insurance, leave, promotions and salaries arose frequently at board meetings. After six months of operation the board heard that there were four employees at Head Office, five in Lagos and one on leave, with a total salary bill of £1,685 per annum. Six years later, in 1901, the staff in London numbered six, plus a commissionaire.

In view of the health reputation of West Africa, as well as the small salaries offered, it was not easy to recruit staff. In 1901 it was decided to advertise in English and Scottish newspapers. Shortage of staff was sometimes the main reason for delay in opening new branches. Some of those engaged were not of the required standard. In June 1900 David Paterson, whose letters were often peppery, wrote from Accra: 'We have not got a single assistant of intelligence and average competence.' In some cases men broke down in health and were invalided home; the board soon decided to have each new recruit examined by the Bank's doctor, the famous Major Ronald Ross.

European staff for service on the Coast were taken on for one year only – soon extended to eighteen months. The first salary was usually £200 per annum, sometimes only £160, with free passage out, a small 'Kit allowance', free lodging (usually above the Bank's offices, with one bedroom each and a joint mess room) and medical care.

First contracts were normally renewed on expiry but they might not be. Regular leave with half-pay was introduced in 1900. Only in 1905 was a uniform salary scale laid down for Coast staff; £250 for the first year, £300 for the second and £325 for the third. In 1906 the Lagos manager's salary was fixed at £550 p.a., plus £3 a month for a cook. On appointment as Branch Manager the salary went up by about £50–£100 a year. The pay scales for African staff are not recorded for the early period, but in 1899 the directors were told that Mr. E. A. T. A. Johnson, who later became well known as the senior African clerk, had asked for three months' leave as he had had no holiday for five years since serving in the Liverpool office in 1894. The matter was 'left to the Lagos manager to decide'.

In 1907 the Chief Manager, Gold Coast, complained that the Bank was 'losing its best men to Government and other appointments'. The board responded not by raising pay but by asking staff to undertake not to offer their services elsewhere while under agreement with the Bank.

Among many suggestions turned down by the board was one from the Freetown manager proposing that one European manager was enough, the rest of the staff should be African. (It must be remembered that Freetown was favoured with a large English-educated Creole community). A scheme for a mobile branch was put up from the Gold Coast: a bank official should travel up and down the railway disbursing cash against railway vouchers at all stations. Rejected. Nor could the directors agree that Coast managers might secure life assurance business.

The impression created by reading through the board minutes is that the Bank was for its first fifteen years directed by a group of exceedingly prudent, almost timid men. This cannot be the whole truth. It contrasts sharply, for one thing, with the record of Alfred Jones – the Bank's very active chairman and largest shareholder – as a daringly enterprising business man. Jones had many irons in the fire, it is true; he never ceased to expand his shipping and trading empire until the very end of his life. In the early years of the century, he was in the best of health and vigour, and every detail of the Bank's business seems to have passed through his hands. He insisted on full information, he dashed off instructions to the managers and proposals to his few fellow-directors (all of whom except Mr. Henry Coke were in fact 'his' men), and he was constantly in touch with the Colonial Office, by letter or visit, to safeguard the Bank's affairs.

Yet the board meetings frequently ended with a decision to put off action till next time, or to give 'further consideration' to some fairly urgent matter. Certainly the board was growing small and elderly. F. W. Bond had died in 1901. Apart from George Neville and O. Harrison Williams (husband of Jones's niece) who became directors in 1900, there were only Henry Coke and Sir Edward Lawrence. The latter died in 1909 aged 83. Incidentally the directors were paid a fee of only £50 a year each from the formation of the company at least until 1909; presumably they were claiming expenses.

The colonial Governors and their staff did not always see eye to eye with the Bank. A serious conflict erupted in 1900. David Paterson wrote from Lagos that his manager in Accra, Mr. Riach, was having a 'most unpleasant time with the Government and seems to despair of coming to any arrangement with regard to [silver] supplies'. The Gold Coast Government had been 'purchasing money in Accra at $\frac{1}{2}$% premium against Bills on England'; and 'the authorities have shown a decidedly hostile attitude to the Bank'. (Under the Agreement the colonial governments were not, in fact, bound to obtain their funds only from the Bank.)

The Colonial Secretary in Accra, a Mr. Low, had told the manager that 'he was dead against the monopoly the Bank held, and when he was Governor he would sell the government bills by auction.' He had also added that there was no monopoly of banking business in London or in the West Indies, and there ought not to be one on this Coast. These were strong English free-trade and anti-monopoly views of the period, passionately held by many. The official in Accra pushed them to the length of keeping his Governor, who disagreed, out of all discussions with the Bank.

In 1899 the Colonial Office set up a high-level enquiry into the currency of the West African Colonies. The chief motive was the urgent desire of the colonial administrations to get some share of the large profits from the issue of silver coin.

A committee under the chairmanship of Sir David Barbour was appointed by the Secretary of State, Mr. Chamberlain, to look into this question. In the previous year Mr. Chamberlain, who had large ideas of economic development for the Colonies, had twice tried to persuade the Treasury to share with the colonial governments the profits from the minting of silver for colonial circulation. The Treasury would not admit that the Colonies had any right to a share in the seignorage profits on British silver that happened to be used in their territories. If the Colonies were to share in the risks of managing the currency it might be another matter.

So the Barbour Committee was asked to say whether a special silver currency for West Africa was feasible. Sir David Barbour was an eminent expert; he had been finance member of the Viceroy's Council in India and had taken part in the Indian currency reform of 1893. The report, which was not published (but can be read) found that a special currency had many attractions – but that it would be best to retain sterling silver and to ask the Treasury to give up its profits, one half to go to the Colonies and the other half towards forming a Colonial Gold Reserve.

The Treasury thought this 'naive'. It took up the idea of a special currency, but after asking all the Governors for their views and finding the majority doubtful, Chamberlain decided in May 1902 to drop the scheme.

The Bank of British West Africa had followed the discussions of the Barbour Committee with some anxiety, as a decision in favour of a special colonial silver currency would have involved the appointment of a supervisory board and, presumably, the end of the Bank's silver import monopoly. Mr. Jones gave evidence in favour of 'no change' and persuaded the Liverpool Chamber of Commerce to tell the Colonial Office that a special colonial currency would 'harm trade'. No change was made.

THREE MANAGERS

This seems a good point to mention three men who joined the Bank before the turn of the century and rose to be among its leading

personalities. *Leslie Couper* joined Elder Dempster's London office
in 1891 when he was twenty years old. In 1895 he was moved over
to the Bank, whose London office was then in the same building
(No. 4 St. Mary Axe), as assistant secretary – the secretary was in
Liverpool. He was born in Glasgow, the son of a West Africa
merchant whose firm, Couper Johnstone & Co., was merged into
the African Association. He was a painstaking, loyal and tenacious
man, with the manners of an old-time country banker. Alfred Jones
quickly took to him and by 1901, when the BBWA moved to
independent London offices in Leadenhall Street, he was made the
first London manager. After Alfred Jones's death he became Chief
Manager of the Bank, a post (later called General Manager) which
he held until his death in 1929.

In 1911 Couper was invited to join the Colonial Office Committee
on the West African Currency under Lord Emmott on whose
recommendations a special currency for West Africa was established,
with a Currency Board to manage it. Couper then became the only
non-official member of the Currency Board, which in turn appointed
the Bank its agent in West Africa. He visited West Africa repeatedly
but never worked on the Coast for any length of time. He also
travelled in Morocco, Egypt and on the continent of Europe; he
was an early user of passenger airlines. He was highly regarded in
the City and in Whitehall, and when he died at his post, only fifty-
eight years old, a Memorial Service was held for him. An obituary
notice in *The Times* described his 'mellow voice, hale appearance,
fine broad brow, kindly eye and firm yet humorous mouth'.

Leslie Couper was on terms of friendship with Sir Alfred Jones,
Lord Kylsant, Lord Lugard, the Earl of Selborne, Lord Milner, and
Marshal Lyautey who was said to have held him in 'affectionate
regard'. He kept in close touch with French North Africa, and in
1920 he was Vice-President of the British Merchants Morocco
Association.

The second of these men who did so much to shape the fortunes
of the Bank was *Roy Wilson*. Born in 1876 in the south of England,
he joined the Bank in Liverpool in 1895 (after working for a Manchester Shipping House) and a few months later sailed for Lagos.
His stay on the Coast was short; in 1897 he returned to Liverpool as

cashier at Head Office. He paid several visits to West Africa but his main work was in England. In 1910 he became Manager of Liverpool office and ten years later Assistant General Manager of the Bank, jointly with D. W. Paterson.

Wilson developed strong political interests and in 1924 he was elected Conservative Member of Parliament for Lichfield. He carried out several official tasks for the government of the day, became a member of the powerful Public Accounts Committee of the House of Commons, but did not seek re-election in 1929. Returning to the Bank he was elected a director; shortly afterwards Leslie Couper died and Wilson took his place on the West African Currency Board. He was knighted in 1929.

In 1937 Sir Roy Wilson was elected Vice-Chairman of the BBWA; in 1942 he resigned on medical grounds and died in the same year.

David Wells Paterson has already been mentioned. He joined Elder Dempster in 1893 at the age of twenty-one, and was sent to Lagos in the same year to assist Mr. Neville with the banking business. Within three years he was appointed manager to open a branch of the BBWA at Accra. In 1899 when Neville left for England to become a director Paterson took over as senior manager on the Coast. In 1904 he was appointed Inspector of Branches. In 1907 he was in London and attended the Royal Commission on Shipping Rings when Leslie Couper, by then the Bank's London manager, gave evidence.

Two years later he reported on a visit to Jebba and a journey down the Niger; in 1911 he made a tour of Northern Nigeria which led to the opening of the Bank's first branch in the north – Zaria on April 16, 1912. In the same year he was again back in London to give extensive evidence on the work of the Bank to the Emmott Committee on the West African currency.

In 1912 he carried through the takeover of the Bank of Nigeria – for which the board voted him a grant of one hundred guineas. He was appointed Assistant Manager at Head Office in 1913 and finally rose to be the Bank's General Manager in 1929. He retired in 1937, being voted a farewell gift of £250, and he lived another twenty-two years to die at the age of eighty-seven.

Chapter Four

RIVALS AND OPPONENTS

THE BANK OF NIGERIA

THE Anglo-African Bank which had been set up in 1899 by a strong group of traders in Nigeria to compete with the Bank of British West Africa soon had to be taken seriously. Its first branches in Calabar, Burutu and Lokoja were followed by one in Jebba on the Niger and another in Grand Bassam, in the French Ivory Coast. More branches and agencies were clearly being prepared. Although the new bank had to obtain all its new silver coin from the BBWA at a premium of 1% it made steady progress. In 1905 it felt substantial enough to change its name to *Bank of Nigeria*, and it began to invade the territory of the BBWA. Above all it redoubled its complaints to the Colonial Office against the silver import privilege of the BBWA. By 1906 these representations, submitted in a steady stream through various channels, had persuaded both the Colonial Office and the Treasury that something ought to be done.

In March 1906 Lord Elgin, the Colonial Secretary, wrote to the BBWA board that he proposed to terminate the silver agreement and substitute another, giving equal silver import facilities to both banks. He added that it would be more acceptable to the Government if the BBWA either severed its connections with the shipping interests or amalgamated with the Bank of Nigeria.

After a long delay the directors wrote a detailed reply, reinforced by personal talks with officials, in which they argued that the Bank of Nigeria was merely 'a syndicate of merchants' and not independent at all (as BBWA claimed to be). By contrast, BBWA was tied by strict rules and was rendering services to the Colony which the Bank of Nigeria was not. The costly obligation to collect and ship home worn or surplus silver coins was emphasised. Nevertheless the directors assured his Lordship that they were anxious to meet his wishes, and soon afterwards Alfred Jones was ready 'to discuss the question of amalgamation with the Bank of Nigeria'.

But now the BN was not prepared to yield an inch. It had to be the joint silver facility or nothing. In addition an equal share of Government business was now claimed. Letters passed between the two boards and managements, interviews took place, even joint board meetings were proposed, though not held. A typical dispute was over the rate at which BN might draw on BBWA in Lagos for transferring Government funds. BBWA proposed 1%, BN demurred, and after some tension ½% was agreed.

By 1907 an open challenge was thrown down: the Bank of Nigeria asked BBWA 'to undertake not to extend their sphere of operations'. BBWA refused to give any such pledge; the Bank must be free to open in any part of Nigeria. BN replied by announcing its intention of opening a branch in Lagos. Very well, said Jones: then we shall open in Calabar. 'Tell them' he instructed the London office 'that we are prepared to receive them with open arms in Lagos and expect they will receive us in the same way in Calabar.'

In fact, the Colonial Office had suggested three years earlier that BBWA should open a branch at Calabar, but the directors, cautious as always, had deferred action. When the matter was again considered in 1907 David Paterson was sent to Calabar to examine the prospects, and he sent a favourable report. A Calabar branch, he wrote, would 'protect us against aggression on the part of the Bank of Nigeria . . . and prevent the introduction of a third bank into a region which seems likely to develop very greatly'. Paterson was instructed by cable to open the branch.

In England, meanwhile, the Bank of Nigeria approached some of the BBWA's customers, offering better terms if they would transfer their business. BBWA was forced to offer the same lower rates. The same process then started in Lagos. Jones wrote to the Bank of Nigeria: 'You are cutting into our rates at Lagos. Are we to defend

ourselves or would your directors care to enter an arrangement as
to rates at Lagos and Calabar?' BN replied in a belligerent strain:
if BBWA were to share the silver import privilege with them, there
might be a fair basis for friendly cooperation; otherwise BN might
'open all along the Coast as soon as BBWA opens at Calabar'.

No reply was sent to this letter. Around this time BN began to
attack the second privilege of its rival, the holding of the Government account. The colonial governments had found it useful to let
BBWA handle all their banking business but they were not bound
to stick to one bank. Some officials were no doubt irritated by the
lack of choice. When the Bank of Nigeria offered to undertake
official transfers at lower rates of commission than the BBWA it
soon obtained a share of the Government business, especially in
Southern Nigeria. Even the Colonial Office recognised that 'the cut-
throat rates for remittances now secured by the Government of
Southern Nigeria owing to the rivalry between the two banks cannot
last'.

Lord Elgin – a former Viceroy of India, not used to being kept
waiting – now showed signs of impatience. In view of the stalemate
between the two banks the Colonial Office wrote on November 19,
1907, proposing to cancel the Bank's silver monopoly on three
months' notice and to substitute an agreement in favour of both banks.
Once more Jones tried to stave off defeat. BBWA, he argued, had
always strictly observed all the agreed conditions. It had never
abused the silver monopoly. The withdrawal of even a part of the
Government's business 'would probably injure the Bank in the eyes
of the native community'.

Trusting to its agreement with the Government the Bank had
erected expensive buildings, raised additional capital and established
new branches while helping to foster trade and open up the country.
Moreover, 'one bank only acting as Agent for the Government can
properly control the importation of silver currency into the West
African colonies and be held responsible for the repatriation of
redundant coins'. If the Secretary of State were to yield to the
'importunity' of the Bank of Nigeria other banks might later claim
the same privileges.

Once more Lord Elgin held his hand. It was an awkward issue to confront, and he had only a few more months to go as Colonial Secretary. In the following months the two banks discussed a scheme to keep out of each other's territory; but when BN demanded all of Nigeria except the town of Lagos – involving the closing down of the new BBWA branches at Calabar and Forcados – the discussions came to nothing. Indeed Lord Scarbrough of the Niger Company told Jones that the BN would not amalgamate with BBWA 'on any terms'. After some further correspondence between the London manager of BBWA, Leslie Couper, and Clifford B. Edgar, chairman of BN, Alfred Jones asserted 'we must stand our ground' even though 'it may be unpleasant'.

The Bank of Nigeria was not content to stand its ground. It went into the attack. On May 26, 1908, the Earl of Crewe, the new Colonial Secretary who had come in with the Liberal Government of Mr. Herbert Asquith in April, received a 'Humble Petition' from the principal firms of merchants operating in West Africa, urging him very strongly to end 'the monopoly of the Bank of British West Africa' in the importation of silver, which they had found 'very onerous'.

The petition was signed by many of the leading names in West African trade. Among them were Lord Scarbrough of the Niger Company, Harry Cotterell of the African Association, Jonathan Holt of John Holt and Company, Alex Cowan of Miller Brothers, Wm. Cleaver of F. & A. Swanzy, and Mazzini Stuart of Pinnock Limited. This stately document ends with an assurance that 'your petitioners will ever pray, etc. . . . .'.

The Petition was sent to the Colonial Office, on behalf of the merchants, by the West African Trade Association of Liverpool. The Colonial Office simply acknowledged receipt. No other reply seems to have been sent, and two internal minutes survive: the first says, 'The array of signatories is imposing, it consists principally of those who control the Bank of Nigeria and those who are hostile to Sir A. Jones on other than banking grounds.' The second minute reads: 'I notice the absence of Paterson Zochonis & Co. and The Lagos Stores. It is rather remarkable that in matters like this . . . the big German firms and also the French West African Company do not join in agitation.' The Petition, in fact, made little or no impression.

To The Right Honourable The Earl of Crewe K.G.
His Majesty's Secretary of State for the Colonies

The humble Petition of the undersigned
Merchants trading in West Africa:

Sheweth as follows:-

Your Petitioners are informed that negotiations are in progress with the object of an Agreement being come to between the Crown Agents for the Colonies and the Bank of British West Africa affecting Northern and Southern Nigeria. Your Petitioners would respectfully but very strongly urge that such Agreement, if it proposes to confine the importation of Silver currency to one institution, is very greatly to be deprecated in the interests of the trade of the Colony and Protectorate, which has found the monopoly of the Bank of British West Africa very onerous in the past.

And your Petitioners will ever pray etc

Dated this twenty six day of May one thousand nine hundred and eight

THE COMPANY OF AFRICAN MERCHANTS, LTD.
C. A. Moore
Chairman

For MILLER BROTHERS (OF LIVERPOOL) LIMITED,
Alex A Cowan Director.

HATTON & COOKSON, LIMITED
E H Cookson
Managing Director

STUART & DOUGLAS, LIMITED.
J Stuart
Director

ESWANGA LIMITED.
Robert Schilling
Director

NIGERIAN COLD STORAGE CO. LTD.
George Watts
Director

M'NEIL, SCOTT & CO., LTD
C R Shepherd Director

THE BENIN RIVER PRODUCE COMPANY, LD
W. S. Porter
Director

For THE NIGER COMPANY, LIMITED.
Scarbrough Chairman.

For AFRICAN ASSOCIATION LIMITED
H J Greer Chairman.

JOHN HOLT & COMPANY,
(LIVERPOOL) LIMITED,
John Holt Director

Thos Welsh & Co
Holt Brothers
Welsh & Macfarlane
J. P. L. Peters Co. Ltd
Joseph Crowdson (over)
Managing Director

PINNOCK, LIMITED.
Mazzini Stuart
Director

For W. B. MAC IVER & CO. LIMITED,
Manager

F. & A. SWANZY, LIMITED,
Director

For THE AFRICAN TRADERS CO., LIMITED.
M J Thompson
Director.

The original petition is in the custody of the Public Record Office and is reproduced with permission. P.R.O. reference CO520-73-3502.

Group at Lagos
Marina Branch, 1952
(centre of front row,
seated l. to r.: E. J.
McQuin, Lord Harlech,
J. K. Agbaje)

Group at opening of
the new Lagos Marina
premises, 1952 (l. to r.:
E. J. McQuin, Sir John
Macpherson, E. Whitley-
Jones, W. E. Sells)

Head Office
evacuated to Seacox
Heath, Hawkhurst, Kent
(centre of front row,
seated, l. to r.: Sir Roy
Wilson, Lady Goschen,
Lord Selborne and Lord
Goschen; about 1940)

City of London War
Bond parade outside
Head Office, 17/18,
Leadenhall Street,
EC3. October 11,
1918

But the Bank of Nigeria for whom the merchants were making their gesture did not rely on prayer alone. Later in 1908 the Lagos manager of the BBWA wrote that 'it was unpleasant to see old clients of the Bank going over to the BN.' On the other hand BN complained that BBWA had tried to induce their staff to transfer to it.

At one stage during these hostilities the board of BBWA had tentatively suggested that it might be prepared to pay out silver coins at Lagos free of commission to the BN. This idea was welcomed by the Governor of Southern Nigeria, Sir Walter Egerton, who had already come out strongly in favour of sharing out both the silver privilege and the Government's business between the two banks. He wrote at length on the whole issue to the Colonial Office and expressed further views. So the Colonial Office decided to do nothing until Sir Walter Egerton's return to England in October 1908.

THE LINK WITH SHIPPING

Quite apart from the attacks on the silver import monopoly some of the trading firms complained year after year to the Government that the Bank of British West Africa was unfair to them because it was too closely linked to the shipping lines. Alfred Jones was the chairman and a large shareholder both of Elder Dempster & Company and of the BBWA. He seems to have regarded both as parts of his growing business empire and as beneficent tools of imperial development. In practice, he managed to keep the two interests apart as well as human nature allowed; but that was not good enough for his opponents. John Holt and George Miller, the two leading 'personal friends but business enemies' of Alfred Jones, saw a fresh chance of airing their grievance when in 1907 a Royal Commission on Shipping Rings was set up in London. While the main subject of the enquiry was freight rates, Holt and Miller saw to it that the BBWA was dragged in.

They alleged that the Bank (1) engaged in trade or used its funds to help certain shipping companies to trade as merchants, (2) used its position to influence freight in favour of these shipping companies,

E

and (3) operated its silver import monopoly to the disadvantage of the traders.

Leslie Couper, London manager of the BBWA, was called before the Commission to give evidence on these charges. With him went David Paterson, then Inspector of Branches. Couper's evidence was detailed, lucid, and convincing. On the first charge he affirmed that it was just not true; the Bank had never made a single advance to any steamship company against any of the commodities in which Holt and Miller alleged the Elder Dempster ships were trading.

On the second charge Couper insisted that the Bank had never tried to influence any customer to use any particular shipping line. The Bank never asked, when a customer required an advance on goods or produce, by which line the shipment was to be made.

As to the cost of new silver coin to the merchants, commission rates for spot cash in Lagos had been much higher before the BBWA was established. Although the Bank was authorised to charge 1%, it had reduced this to $\frac{1}{2}$% for traders who made a contract for a year. Both Holt and Miller had taken advantage of this offer in 1905, but when Holt refused to renew the annual contract for 1906 and suddenly demanded cash at the height of the produce season he was naturally charged $1\frac{1}{4}$%, as the Bank was then having to meet the pressing demands of many produce firms in a short time.

In any case it would cost the traders well over a $\frac{1}{2}$% (13s. 8d. per £100) to buy their silver direct from the Mint, allowing for interest; and they now had the convenience of getting cash on the spot whenever their own forecasts of needs went wrong during the produce season. The Bank had to keep large stocks of silver for the convenience of the merchants at its own expense and risk. It had also to weed out and ship home worn coins, again at its own expense. There was in fact nothing like the large profit in the silver import monopoly that the traders imagined.

Leslie Couper was of course aware that the Bank's silver privilege was being assaulted elsewhere. He seems to have taken the opportunity of the Shipping Rings enquiry to set out the BBWA view of this arrangement in broad terms: 'The necessity for exercising a control in regard to the circulation of silver coinage is recognised in England, where the issue of silver is solely in the hands of the Bank of England; so in West Africa the extension of commerce decided the Government to delegate the supervision of the currency to a responsible bank which would regulate the supply according to the demand and relieve the Government of the loss and trouble of repatriating any redundant stock.'

He went on to list some of the benefits: the introduction of proper banking facilities had led to the use of cheques in place of the cumbersome method of paying revenue and other bills in silver coin. The Colonial Governments had been able to make staff economies; the remittance of Government funds had been made safe and regular.

By the time Couper had finished his evidence the Chairman of the Royal Commission asked his colleagues 'Do we need to carry this any further?' and the subject of the Bank was soon dropped.

ANOTHER SILVER TUSSLE

However, before long the silver controversy was resumed. We left it when in 1908 the Colonial Office adjourned the matter until the arrival in London of Sir Walter Egerton, the Governor of Southern Nigeria. In the following spring, in March 1909, a fateful meeting took place at the Colonial Office. It was attended by one of the Crown Agents, by the Deputy Master of the Mint and by Sir Walter Egerton. The subject was much wider than the silver issue: 'To discuss the position of banking in West Africa.' From the official correspondence of the time one can take it that the Colonial Office and the Mint appreciated the services of the BBWA and did not wish to lose them; the Treasury thought the banking arrangements illogical and resented the idea that a commercial bank should regard itself as having a mandate to control a Colonial currency; and the Governor strongly disliked any monopoly. On one point all parties agreed. Whatever the position in the past, there were now two important banks in West Africa and this had entirely changed the basis of the agreements with BBWA on silver and Government business.

The meeting decided, subject to the final approval of the Secretary of State, that in future the supply of silver coin to West Africa should be controlled by the Royal Mint, which should give equal treatment to all recognised banks. The Government banking business in Southern Nigeria would be divided between the two banks. The silver agreement with the BBWA for Lagos was to be cancelled, and any new agreement would probably be made by the Governor. In July the Bank was informed that the agreement was to be terminated.

After these decisions had been taken Sir Walter Egerton left for Nigeria. Soon after his arrival he heard that the decisions had not been confirmed by the Secretary of State, and everything was to be left as before. It was a dramatic reversal and needs some explanation.

A memorandum containing the proposals of the March meeting for the change in the silver and official business arrangements had been sent to the Secretary of State, now Lord Crewe. Before putting his signature to it he agreed to receive a deputation from the BBWA. Sir Alfred Jones and some of his fellow directors called on August 11 and once again pleaded that the Bank's position should not be changed. An official (C. T. Davis) who was present noted that 'Sir A. Jones was in a chastened mood. He offered to retire if the S. of S. thought his connection with the Bank detrimental.'

The BBWA directors seem to have had little hope left that they could preserve the status quo; Mr. Henry Coke actually suggested to Lord Crewe at this meeting that the control of the silver currency should be taken over by the Treasury and the Mint. That was going more than half way towards the sharing of the silver import privilege with the other bank. Mr. Davis, who records this strange collapse of the Bank's battle front in his report (dated August 25) to Sir Francis Hopwood, the Permanent Under-Secretary, adds 'Lord Crewe told me that he proposed to discuss the matter further with you before coming to a decision.'

We do not know what happened at this conversation between the Minister and his most senior official. What we do know is that on August 28 Lord Crewe wrote the following minute in his small, cold, authoritative handwriting:

I have decided that it is not necessary to hurry this matter on, and the existing arrangement need not be disturbed for the present. The Governor can be so informed.

One can only make a wild guess at the reasons which induced Lord

Crewe to ignore the concerted advice of his officials, the Crown
Agents, the Royal Mint, the Imperial Treasury and the Governor on
the spot. Some historians have assumed that Alfred Jones dazzled
Lord Crewe with his famous personal magnetism, or that he used
irresistible new arguments. The description of the interview by Mr.
Davis – Jones offering to retire and Coke virtually accepting defeat –
suggests that this cannot be the true story. It seems just possible that
the Minister, taking a wider and longer view than the experts, felt
in his bones that the time was not yet ripe for changing a system
which had introduced a great deal of financial stability into West
Africa.

It was the crowning victory in Alfred Jones's long and successful
career. Lord Crewe's verdict kept the Bank's silver monopoly going
for less than two more years, but that gain was vital. In the interval
the Bank of Nigeria seems to have lost its aggressive confidence,
and by 1912 when the silver privilege was finally abolished BN sold
out to BBWA.

DEATH OF SIR ALFRED JONES

Within a few weeks of his triumph over the massed might of
Whitehall Jones fell ill. Late in October he called once more on the
Colonial Office to discuss the future arrangements for the handling
of the Government account. On November 30 he attended another
board meeting where he was informed that an issue of 25,000 shares
of £10 each, £4 paid, which had been offered to shareholders at a
premium of £1, had been such a success that he could have only
4,888 new shares instead of his larger application. Even so he was the
Bank's largest single shareholder, as he had been from the outset.

Sir Alfred Jones died on December 13, 1909. His death marked
the end of an era for the Bank of British West Africa. He had
inspired the Bank's creation and dominated its affairs. 'Until his death
in 1909 it may be said that Sir Alfred Jones dictated the policy of the
Bank' wrote Sir Roy Wilson. The directors he had gathered around
him were his executives rather than equal partners, though they were
able and experienced men of business. After the first few years the
board met at least once a week, and it dealt with a mass of detail

CIRCULAR TO SHAREHOLDERS.

This Circular has been filed with the Registrar of Joint Stock Companies.

The BANK OF BRITISH WEST AFRICA, LIMITED, will receive applications for Shares at their Offices, 14, CASTLE STREET, LIVERPOOL; 17, LEADENHALL STREET, LONDON, E.C.; or at any of their Branches.

Bank of British West Africa,

LIMITED.

(Incorporated under the Companies Acts, whereby the liability of Shareholders is limited to the amount of their Shares.)

AUTHORISED CAPITAL—£1,000,000, in 100,000 Shares of £10 each.

SUBSCRIBED CAPITAL—£250,000 in 25,000 Shares of £10 each, on which £4 per Share has been called up.

PRESENT ISSUE—25,000 Shares of £10 each (of which £4 per Share is to be called up) at a Premium of £1 per Share, payable as follows:—

£1 per Share Premium on application.	£1 per Share on Nov. 30th, 1909.
£1 " on Allotment.	£1 " on Jan. 15th, 1910.
£1 per Share on March 1st, 1910.	

DIRECTORS.

SIR ALFRED L. JONES, K.C.M.G., CHAIRMAN.
HENRY COKE, ESQ.
GEORGE W. NEVILLE, ESQ.
O. HARRISON WILLIAMS, ESQ.

SOLICITORS.

MESSRS. BATESONS, WARR & WIMSHURST, LIVERPOOL.

AUDITORS.

MESSRS. HARMOOD BANNER & SON, LIVERPOOL.

HEAD OFFICE.

14, CASTLE STREET, LIVERPOOL.

LONDON OFFICE.   HAMBURG OFFICE.
17, LEADENHALL ST., E.C.   GLOBUSHOF, TROSTBRÜCKE.

SECRETARY.

WILLIAM ROSS.

BY a Special Resolution of the Shareholders, confirmed at an Extraordinary General Meeting held on the 12th November, 1907, the Authorised Capital of the Bank was increased to One Million Pounds (£1,000,000) by the creation of 75,000 new Shares of £10 each. Of these Shares it has now been decided by the Directors to issue 25,000 of £10 each (£4 to be called up) at a premium of £1 per Share.

Circular to shareholders in 1909, offering 25,000 new shares.

rather than delegating anything substantial to the group of competent young managers who had grown up. In effect virtually all decisions were taken by the chairman, and the minutes of the board meetings during those first fifteen years show that whenever an awkward problem turned up the directors expected Jones to deal with it.

The board had in fact shrunk steadily. The sudden death of the chairman left only three directors, Henry Coke who had been there from the beginning, George Neville who had returned from Lagos and joined the board in 1900, and O. Harrison Williams who had married a niece of Jones and became a director in the same year. Sir Edward Lawrence had died the previous July, aged eighty-three. New blood was obviously needed, though in the meantime the senior officials, especially Leslie Couper in London and Roy Wilson in Liverpool, could be relied on to shoulder the main weight.

A few days after the chairman's death a special meeting of the board recorded the heavy loss which had fallen on the Bank. 'His services to the Bank, both in its foundation and expansion, were invaluable. The Institution remains a Monument, among many others, to his foresight in initiating, and ability in consolidating, large measures for the advancement of the Trade of the British Empire.'

Alfred Jones had made his mark in England and in West Africa by his single-minded drive for business success. As a man he had both generosity and greed, both charm and thrust. All his life he was capable of quick decisions on large matters, and he made full use of any advantage which luck or planning gave him. His untiring efforts to expand his enterprises blended in with a desire to be of service to public causes, whether it was for the good of the British Empire or the advancement of some trade or charitable undertaking. In 1901 his public services were rewarded with a Knighthood (KCMG). In 1906 King Alfonso of Spain appointed him a Knight Commander of the Order of Isabella La Catolica.

His career was summed up in an inscription, placed with a bronze bust by Sir George Frampton on a memorial erected at the Pierhead, Liverpool, by a public subscription:

In memory of Sir Alfred Jones, KCMG. A shipowner. Strenuous in business, he enlarged the commerce of his country in his mercantile enterprise and, as founder of the Liverpool School of Tropical Medicine, made science tributary to civilisation in Western Africa and the Colonies of the British Empire.

The title 'Founder of the Liverpool School of Tropical Medicine' has been questioned. As the Liverpool School was the first of its kind in the world and can claim a place of honour among the benefactors of mankind, it may be of interest to record the story of its foundation as told by Professor B. G. Macgraith in the journal *Medical History*. The episode is typical of Alfred Jones's way of operating.

In 1898 Joseph Chamberlain, then Colonial Secretary, was shocked to hear from Dr. Manson, Medical Adviser to the Colonial Office, that Britain was sending out to her Empire a steady stream of doctors entirely untrained in any of the specific maladies that occur in tropical climates. He wrote a letter to the General Medical Council, to the principal medical schools and finally to the Governors of all colonies pointing out the urgent need for proper research and training facilities in tropical medicine.

The Minister's appeal was mentioned by a speaker at the annual dinner of students of the Royal Southern Hospital in Liverpool. Alfred Jones was one of the guests, and he responded in a flash. After a whispered conversation with the President of the hospital he rose and announced that he had offered £350 a year for three years for the promotion of the study of tropical diseases. An organising committee was at once formed with Jones as chairman. The School started operations in the spring of 1899, six months before the opening of a similar one in London which had the Government's financial support.

One of the first acts of the new institution was to advertise the post of Lecturer in Tropical Disease. In April 1899 Major Ronald Ross, late of the Indian Medical Service, was appointed at a salary of £250 per annum. Ross had completed his great work on malaria before this time, but within three months he led the School's first expedition to West Africa and shortly afterwards isolated the 'malarial mosquito' in Sierra Leone. In 1902 Ronald Ross was awarded the Nobel Prize and in the following year Alfred Jones (who had neatly secured the services of the great man as Medical Adviser to the BBWA) founded a Chair of Tropical Medicine with Ross as the first Professor.

These events show Jones in his characteristic manner. He could immediately recognise the practical implications of an idea, and when he saw a chance of effective action he would without hesitation offer money, advice, and personal involvement. This is how he reacted a number of times to other ideas – for instance the formation of the British Cotton Growing Association which he helped to set up and led for some years.

John Holt, the founder of the trading company bearing his name, was only very slightly behind Alfred Jones in backing the Liverpool School. He was a member of the first committee, but he then shifted his main support to the rival school in London. His concern with the ravages of malaria on the Coast was so serious that in 1908–9 he ordered Cammell Lairds to build the stern-wheel steamer *Axholme* which sailed from Liverpool to the Niger River with full mosquito-proofing of quarters for officers and crew. Next he built the *Jonathan Holt* of 2,350 tons dwt and shallow draught for service on the Niger River. Following a plan recommended by Professor Ronald Ross the ship had mosquito-net windows, doors and covers for all ventilators, made of close mesh copper gauze. It was said at the time that the precautions were bound to be useless because people would forget to close the screens. But in fact deaths from malaria (John Holt noted) were reduced to 'very few' by 1910.

At the centre of Alfred Jones's life work was undoubtedly the development of the Elder Dempster group of shipping services. He had brought them together and led them to success. It has been described in earlier chapters how the regular steamship services contributed to the growth of trade in West Africa. The foundation of the Bank of British West Africa may have seemed a relatively small enterprise at first, but Jones devoted a large part of his time and energy to the Bank, and it was undoubtedly due to his leadership that it achieved a position of such importance in West Africa.

Chapter Five

NEW STATUS FOR
THE BANK

NEW SHAREHOLDERS

WITHIN a few days of Sir Alfred Jones's death the sole surviving
executor of his will, Mr. Owen Harrison Williams, received an offer
for the entire shipping and commercial assets of the estate. It came
from two leading men in the shipping and shipbuilding world: Sir
Owen Philipps (later Lord Kylsant), chairman of the Royal Mail
Steam Packet Company, and Lord Pirrie, chairman of the Belfast
shipbuilders Harland and Wolff. Lord Pirrie had been a close
business associate of Jones for many years. He became a director of
the African Steamship Company in 1891 and its chairman in 1901;
and his yard had built most of the vessels of the Elder Dempster
Group.

No doubt Williams – a director of the BBWA and husband of
Alfred Jones's niece – judged that it was in the best interests of the
estate to dispose of the bulk of the business, including above all the
Elder Dempster fleet of 109 vessels, in a single package. The sum
offered was £500,000. He gave Philipps a firm option. Yet he might
conceivably have done better if he had waited a little. In a few weeks
came a counter-bid from a consortium of the leading West African
trading firms, including the Niger Company, the African Association, Millers and Swanzys.

The traders had carried on some hurried consultations; they were
anxious to seize the chance of acquiring their own shipping lines. But
when they were ready to make an offer Williams had to tell them

that they were too late. Lord Scarbrough, chairman of the Niger Company, saw Lord Pirrie to suggest a combination, and Lord Pirrie promised to offer the trading group some participation. In fact Philipps and Pirrie completed the purchase of the Elder Dempster Group on April 2, 1910, but nothing came of the plan to link up with the Niger Company consortium.

The failure of that particular scheme was crucial for the Bank of British West Africa. If the trading firms who were backing the Bank of Nigeria and had for years harboured a bitter hostility towards the BBWA had got a foot in the Elder Dempster door they might well have gained control of the Bank through the shareholding of the late Sir Alfred Jones. In that case the merger of the two banks would have come about on the Bank of Nigeria's terms, with different personalities and policies.

Sir Owen Philipps had become interested in West Africa in 1907, when he was a member of the Royal Commission on Shipping Rings and had to listen day after day to the controversies between West African traders and shippers. But while he made a lightning grab for the Elder Dempster fleet he does not seem to have been actively interested in the banking business. It is true that the bulk of Sir Alfred Jones's shareholding in BBWA – 12,633 shares with a paid-up value of £50,532 – went to the new Elder Dempster Company formed after the change of ownership. On February 2, 1910 (according to the share register), 7,745 of Sir Alfred's shares were transferred to Sir Percy Bates, a young shipping man who 25 years later became chairman of Cunard, but he was only a temporary custodian. On May 25 he passed on 6,255 shares to Elder Dempster and within two further months he had entirely disposed of all his BBWA shares by numerous transfers to private individuals. Another 4,211 shares out of the Jones estate were transferred to Elder Dempster in May, making their holding 10,466 shares (paid-up £41,864), almost a quarter of the Bank's total capital. It was over a year later that Sir Owen Philipps joined the board of the Bank and acquired some shares for himself.

The purchase price of £500,000 was paid in three parts: £200,000 in cash, £200,000 in 5% Debenture Stock and £100,000 in Cumulative Preference Shares of the new Elder Dempster Company. The assets transferred by this deal included land and offices in Liverpool, hotels, estates and a shipyard in Grand Canary, a hotel and other properties in Tenerife and in Jamaica. In West Africa a number of buildings and parcels of land were included. All this was additional to the Elder Dempster fleet. The new owners also obtained share-holdings in many companies, some of them substantial, and including the BBWA shares already mentioned. By agreement with Mr. Williams all the investments and other assets were to be kept under a single control.

Under the will of Sir Alfred Jones his sister, Mrs. Mary Pinnock, was left the use for her life of Oaklands, Sir Alfred's residence where she had kept house for him; she also received £1,500 and an annuity of £2,500 a year. His niece, Mrs. Florence Williams, was left £20,000 in trust for life, and another niece, Miss Pinnock, £30,000 on the same terms. Apart from several bequests to friends and liberal provisions for clerks and servants the residue of the estate was to be formed into a Trust Fund for the support of charitable causes in England and West Africa.

For the guidance of the trustees Sir Alfred had mentioned as worthy objects the advancement of technical education in West Africa, original research into the causes of disease in West Africa, and the advancement of education or science in general. Particular bequests were made to the Liverpool School of Tropical Medicine, Mission schools in West Africa, and a long list of other beneficiaries including the entire staff of the Bank.

The total value of the estate was sworn at £583,461 but the final settlement was not made until 1928. By then £325,000 had been distributed to charitable and other institutions, and about 800 clerks who had been employed by companies in which Jones was involved received a total sum of £70,000.

LORD MILNER TAKES THE REINS

Three important changes in the Bank's status took place in the three years following the death of Sir Alfred Jones. One was the appointment of a new chairman and the creation of a new board and management structure. The second was the loss of the silver import monopoly and the setting up of a West African Currency Board in 1912, with BBWA as its agent. The third was the purchase and absorption of the Bank of Nigeria.

The Bank not only survived these drastic changes but emerged from them with greatly increased strength and vigour.

On February 16, 1910, the three remaining directors elected Lord Milner to the board as chairman. The Right Honourable Viscount Milner was one of the leading public figures of the day. He had profound experience both in financial affairs – having been at the Treasury, and for five years chairman of the Inland Revenue Board – and in the management of the Empire. He had been High Commissioner and later Governor in South Africa before, during and after the Boer War of 1899–1902. On his return to England in 1905 for health reasons he was impoverished by his South African expenses and refused to ask for a pension. 'I hardly know what to be at' he wrote to a friend in 1906. 'I have a certain amount of City work, which while agreeably supplementing my income, rather interests me.' He became a director of the Rio Tinto Company, the London Joint Stock Bank (later the Midland Bank) and a mortgage company in Egypt. He was also a member of the Port of London Authority. But all this City work, he wrote, 'does not by any means monopolise my time and thought'.

In 1910, when he was persuaded to join the Bank of British West Africa, Lord Milner was in the middle of leading the opposition in the House of Lords against Lloyd George's Reform Budget of 1909 and the subsequent threat to swamp the Peerage. But though he had fallen out with the Liberal Party ever since his South African activities, he enjoyed universal respect. Indeed as soon as Lloyd George became Prime Minister in 1915 he called on Lord Milner to join his War Cabinet.

The new chairman, then, was a man accustomed to exerting leadership. He took his seat on the board for the first time on April 6 and at once called for a general policy review. In June Mr. W. F. Moore, of the merchant firm of George Melly and Co., Liverpool, was added to the board; he later became chairman of the Liverpool committee. A year later, in July 1911, a more powerful newcomer appeared: Sir Owen Philipps, whose purchase of the Elder Dempster business has been recorded above. Philipps was described by Roy Wilson as 'unquestionably the most striking personality in the shipping world'. With a quarter of the Bank's shares under his control – a holding that was greatly increased over the years – Philipps was in a position to exert great influence but he does not seem to have had that ambition. In practice his weight on the board was probably balanced by the prestige of Lord Milner. Yet another new board appointment was made in October 1911 when Mr. D. Q. Henriques, of the old-established Manchester stockbroking house, became a director.

The new board soon decided to move the head office of the Bank to London. The premises at No. 17 Leadenhall Street were enlarged by taking in the offices at No. 18. Leslie Couper, manager of the London office, was made chief manager of the Bank. In Liverpool Roy Wilson was appointed Manager and W. Ross, the Secretary, became local secretary for Liverpool, while J. R. Bingham, who had spent nine years in Freetown, was brought home to London as the Bank's new Secretary.

Within a few weeks of taking office Lord Milner made an end to the practice of the full board running the Bank's day to day affairs. Two board committees were formed in London and Liverpool to deal with 'details', and the number of full board meetings was reduced by half. Incidentally a new scale of directors' fees was fixed: £500 a year for the chairman and £300 each for other directors.

Oddly enough the directors did not revive a scheme to change the name of the Bank to 'Bank of West Africa'. This had been approved on October 13, 1909, mainly because of plans to expand into territories outside the 'British' sphere. A few weeks before his death Alfred Jones had discussed the matter privately with Harrison Williams and they had agreed to adjourn it until the following April. By then Jones was dead and the proposal lapsed. It was briefly considered again in November 1911 but not acted upon – not, that is, until forty-six years later, when the motives were different.

BANKING ON THE COAST

The changes in the ownership and direction of the Bank in England did not immediately affect its operations in West Africa. There the Bank had steadily extended its network of branches, and despite competition from the rival bank and occasional disputes with officials and traders the business was solidly established. It was not vastly profitable. The balance sheet published soon after the death of Sir Alfred Jones, dated March 31, 1910, showed the authorised capital at £1,000,000 and the paid up capital at £200,000 – this had been doubled in the previous two years. The reserve fund had risen to £80,000. Deposits amounted to just over £1 million. Net profits for the year were £22,697, a return of 8% on capital employed, which was hardly brilliant.

Clearly after 20 years the Bank was still living up to Alfred Jones's declaration that it was less important to make large profits than to help the trade and welfare of West Africa. Modern business theory would call this a high-minded excuse for poor management, but the times were different, and the minds of the directors, managers and staff were certainly much concerned with high politics and the burden of Empire.

While the previous board had been reluctant to increase the number of branches and agencies faster than was entirely safe, and almost every decision to open at a new place took several years to clinch, some expansion did take place in response to the rapid growth of trade and transport. The branches at Accra, Freetown and Calabar have been mentioned. In the early years of the century branches had been established at Cape Coast, Axim and Sekondi along the Gold Coast, and Bathurst in The Gambia. A branch at Kumasi, in the heart of the Ashanti forest, was opened in 1907 after several years of hesitation and a final delay when the door of the strong-room fell overboard from a surfboat on landing. In 1909 another Gold Coast branch was opened at Tarkwa, close to the goldfields and later a source of industrial diamonds. In Sierra Leone a branch was opened at Bo in 1908 after some haggling with the Colonial Government.

Proposals to open at other places were frequently made to the board but the directors took a great deal of convincing. No action was taken on recommendations to set up at Abeokuta, Ilorin and Ibadan in Nigeria. On April 23, 1906, Mr. Paterson thought that there was 'not sufficient inducement' to open at Ibadan – Africa's largest black city. In 1909 Onitsha was suggested, but though this was already an enormous market town the board rejected the idea because the Bank of Nigeria had already opened a branch the year before. In Sierra Leone a branch at Sherbro, the focus of a rich river trade, was discussed in 1904 but not opened until 1912.

In 1904 the directors approved the opening of a branch in Lome, Togoland, but postponed action on the advice of Mr. Coke. A year later it was decided to send Mr. Roy Wilson to Hamburg to find a German firm suitable to act as the Bank's Lome agent, but this was quickly vetoed by the chairman who considered the journey 'too expensive and unnecessary'. Finally a German bank which opened at Lome was accepted as agent.

Extensions into French territory met with resistance. A trading firm was appointed agent at Grand Bassam in 1906 but when the Banque de l'Afrique Occidentale threatened to retaliate by opening a branch at Bathurst the BBWA quickly withdrew. Agencies continued in Grand Lahou and in Monrovia, Liberia. In Hamburg, an important centre of West African trade, the Bank was content to let Elder Dempster act as its agency. In 1907 a plan to convert this into a full branch was first approved and then cancelled. There were several branches to be opened at various places but the directors were 'in favour of establishing agencies for the time being'. Agencies were appointed between 1905 and 1909 in Obuassi, on the Ashanti goldfield, in Fernando Po, in several inland places in Sierra Leone and in New York, where the African Banking Corporation had offered to be an agent for BBWA. Some other agencies outside British West Africa were at Abidjan, Dakar, Madeira, Matadi, Las Palmas and Tenerife. In 1910 the Bank had fourteen branches and seventeen agencies.

An important aspect of the Bank's services was that it offered a place of safety for African savings. This was a real innovation. Like the offer of cash advances to African traders for their export produce, the facility was eagerly taken up. African deposits were sometimes the mainstay of local liquidity. As the Bank would for many years pay interest only on term deposits fixed for six or twelve months, and the smaller Africans did not like to tie up their savings for so long, a large part of the money came in on current account, interest free. The Bank was always afraid that sudden withdrawals might find a branch short of cash. The term condition probably limited the flow of African deposits, at least until 'savings accounts' were started later on, but still the total was substantial. And there were some large deposits as well. In 1904 an African customer in Lagos deposited £30,000 on current account. This was considered important enough for the chairman to write to the customer to persuade him to accept 4½% interest for a five-year deposit. The man agreed, but within a few months he died and his heir renewed the deposit for only three years at 4% per annum.

For deposits fixed for six months the usual interest was 3%. But it seems likely that interest was less important to the Africans than safety and convenience. In 1911 the Lagos branch reported to the board that its deposits had reached £100,000. It had 463 African and 26 European depositors.

The reverse of the Bank's activity, its lending policy, was not so well defined. Discussions by the board of directors were nearly always concerned with the type of loans which ought not to be made. Coast managers were frequently criticised for making advances which the board did not approve of. In 1905 the directors agreed that lending should be secured as much as possible on 'liquid securities' which could be used to raise money from the large banks in England. At any rate no other fixed-period loans must be granted without all the directors being consulted first. In 1907 the board found that too much had been advanced to the West African gold mining companies (the Ashanti Goldfields Co. had been going since 1897) on the security of either bullion or mining company shares. Such loans were to be immediately reduced. As for loans or mortgages on property of any kind they were highly unpopular with the directors, and managers were warned time and again to avoid them. The reason was that property titles were not clearly defined by law or even by custom. But it was not always easy for the man on the

F

spot to refuse finance to a good customer if the only collateral he could offer was the title to a building.

In 1907 the chairman wanted a limit of £10,000 laid down for any one loan, and some such instruction seems to have gone out to managers; but the facts of life were winning and larger loans were often approved, including one of £40,000.

On the other hand advances were freely made by the Coast branches against produce, particularly cocoa, rubber and timber. Usually the loans were fixed at 75% of the local value. Some advances were made against cotton, with a limit of £5,000 set in 1909 A system of agricultural loans was considered and discussed with the Colonial Governors but failed at the time because the farmers could not produce satisfactory titles to their land.

The limited scope of the lending policy has always been a source of African criticism against the Bank. African businessmen badly needed loans for the medium term in order to finance stocks, buildings, capital equipment and so on. They never accepted the situation in which the BBWA used deposits only for short-term advances. They had no capital market where they might have raised equity finance as their European competitors were able to do.

This was a real difficulty, but it could not be resolved on the terms of British banking practice. It was not until after the Second World War that a technique for medium-term loans to African businessmen was evolved. Term loans were then gradually developed – and became profitable despite an increase in bad debts.

The physical work of distributing silver money throughout the territories had grown enormously. Large amounts of cash were needed by the trading firms to pay for produce at sharply defined periods of the year, and in many different places. For a long time the traders obtained the money in the few existing bank branches and carried it themselves to the inland trading stations. As neither gold coins nor notes had ever become popular in West Africa cash consisted almost entirely of the traditional £100 bags of shillings, florins or sixpences. Shillings were favoured in Nigeria, florins in the Gold Coast. The carriage of these bags by head-load, rivercraft and the early road trucks – and in the north by donkeys and mules – was cumbersome and expensive. The big trading firms often set up their own money centres by installing strong-rooms in their larger factories. Specie cars were built by the railways to carry silver money over the greater distances. They had to be escorted by police, and even so they were sometimes lost on the way, though they were invariably recovered intact.

It was a constant and growing problem for the Bank and the traders to forecast how much coin would be needed at particular times in particular places. An elaborate system of advance estimating was worked out. The large trading firms asked for the predictions of their local, district and regional agents, assembled them at the head office in each colony and sent the resulting calculations to London. There arrangements would be made with the Bank both for overall credit lines and for the despatch of appropriate amounts of cash to the branches. In 1910 the Bank ordered shipment from England of new silver coin worth £1,182,900, plus £80,000 in French silver money to Bathurst. This new coin was of course additional to the stock of silver money already in West Africa, from which only a certain amount of worn coins and occasional seasonal surpluses were skimmed off.

The system did not always work perfectly. Sudden shortages and seasonal gluts of cash caused both local ill feeling and concern to the board at home. Thus in December 1909 Lagos was criticised for allowing silver stocks to fall 'dangerously low'.

END OF A RIVALRY

In 1910, after the death of Sir Alfred Jones in the previous December and the appointment of Lord Milner as chairman, the conflict between the B B W A and the Bank of Nigeria suddenly subsided. In February a last echo of past hostility came from the Coast when the Lagos manager suggested that the rate for Bank of Nigeria cable transfers should be increased to $\frac{3}{4}$%. The board replied that no action was to be taken because the Bank's general policy was under review. In April two letters from the Bank of Nigeria referred once again to the supply of silver coin, but that seems to have been the last time this controversial issue was raised.

Lord Milner soon came to the conclusion that confrontation

between the two banks should be brought to an end. Talks began in the autumn and led with surprising ease to a draft agreement providing for the business of the Bank of Nigeria to be taken over by the BBWA. The agreement was approved by the board in April 1911 and signed by the two banks on May 5, 1911. Everything went without a hitch: in the following October the Bank of Nigeria gave formal notice of its intention to implement the sale agreement and fixed the date of transfer as June 30, 1912. The entire staff of the BN was offered employment with BBWA and all of them transferred to it, though the London manager, Mr. Osborne Wilmot, left after one year.

On May 22, 1912, the board approved a press announcement and notification to the Colonial Office: 'The Bank of British West Africa Limited has entered into a provisional agreement to purchase the business, assets and goodwill of The Bank of Nigeria Limited.' The formal agreement was sealed on June 20. A few days earlier the shareholders of BBWA had authorised the issue of shares to Bank of Nigeria shareholders. One hundred shares each were allotted to George Miller and Mazzini Stuart and they, together with Clifford B. Edgar, were elected directors of BBWA. (In addition they received BBWA shares in exchange for their private BN holdings).

Altogether 13,000 shares (£4 paid) of BBWA were issued to BN shareholders. The transfer of premises, building sites and other assets on the Coast was handled by David Paterson who had been given Power of Attorney by the BN and was later voted a grant of £105 for his handling of the takeover.

There was no 'merger' of the two banks in a legal sense as the Bank of Nigeria Limited was wound up. Later a new company of the same name was formed by BBWA merely 'to retain the name'. The BN was the smaller of the two banks. Its authorised capital had remained £150,000 from the foundation in 1899. Although the 'subscribed capital' had risen by 1912 to £120,000 only £61,000 had been called up. This was the capital of the BN when it was taken over.

At the time of the takeover the BN had ten branches and a number of agencies. In line with its close association with the Niger trading firms the branches were chiefly in that region. Those at

Lokoja, Onitsha, Warri, and Zungeru remained open and added to the strength of the BBWA. The branches at Burutu and Jebba were closed and those at Calabar and Lagos, where the BBWA was already established, were absorbed. In the Ivory Coast there were branches at Assinie and Grand Bassam which BBWA continued to operate for a time, but they were closed in 1914 and 1919 respectively.

Several of the agencies later became branches but those at Bonny, Brass, Buguma, Degema and Egwanga continued as agencies of BBWA. They were operated by trading firms and their main function was the collection of Bills of Exchange.

How did Lord Milner bring it off? It was all very well to put on paper that he had 'concluded' that the confrontation with the other bank should stop. Sir Alfred Jones had tried the same thing many times since he first raised the possibility of a merger with BN in 1906. In 1907 Lord Elgin, the Colonial Secretary, had strongly recommended that the two banks should amalgamate. Discussions and correspondence on ways of peaceful cooperation, sometimes mentioning the merger idea, had taken place frequently in the intervening three years. Always the Bank of Nigeria had been aggressive, laying down conditions which it knew the other bank could not accept. Yet in 1910 these high spirits seem to have evaporated. On the first approach by Lord Milner the directors of the BN conceded defeat. No more awkward conditions were raised and the sale of the entire business went through as quickly as the legal formalities allowed.

During the years of conflict the resentment of the BN against the silver import privilege of the BBWA had always played an important part. By 1910 this could no longer have been a problem. Although the silver arrangement had been renewed once more in 1909 it was generally accepted that it could not last much longer; in fact it was terminated at the end of 1911. In January 1912 when the London manager of BN, Mr. Wilmot, gave evidence to the Currency Committee he did not even mention the silver controversy; and he gave no hint that the BN was having any financial or other difficulties.

The key to the mystery may well lie in the profit and loss account of the Bank of Nigeria for the year 1911, which showed a net profit of no more than £1,167. Personalities may have played a part. Sir Alfred Jones was not good at diplomacy. He was used to getting his own way. In several instances he provoked people with whom he could not really afford to quarrel. Above all he was a shipowner, and the men behind the Bank of Nigeria were traders who had always felt at the mercy of the shipping lines.

George Miller, one of the two original Miller Brothers who had built up a powerful West African trading group (without ever visiting West Africa) had been in the van of the opposition against Alfred Jones for many years. He was among the chief supporters of the Bank of Nigeria and in 1911, in the middle of the takeover negotiations, he temporarily assumed the chairmanship of the BN. He was then seventy-two years of age, and though he remained hale and active for many more years he may well have felt, like Gibbon in the evening of life, 'the abbreviation of time'.

But the main factor was probably the superb negotiating skill of Lord Milner. He had the confidence of the Colonial Office – it was Mr. Joseph Chamberlain who had sent him to South Africa – and had great experience in gaining the cooperation of opponents. The fact that three of the most personable directors of the BN joined the BBWA board seems proof enough that the deal was clinched in a friendly manner.

So the Bank of British West Africa was once more the sole bank in the entire region. It was the only Government banker. In practice, it was hardly inhibited by the existence of the new supervisory agency, the West African Currency Board. Perhaps the directors would have preferred something nearer the French scheme, under which the Banque de l'Afrique Occidentale was appointed the sole monetary authority for French West Africa; but the price of that status was strict government supervision from Paris. From 1912 to 1917, when the Colonial Bank first appeared on the scene to offer competition, the BBWA had the field to itself.

Chapter Six

A CURRENCY FOR
WEST AFRICA

LORD EMMOTT'S ENQUIRY

IN November 1910 a new Colonial Secretary, Mr. Lewis Harcourt, succeeded the Marquess of Crewe who became Secretary of State for India. Lewis Harcourt was the son of the formidable Sir William Harcourt and like his father a leading Liberal politician. Within a few months of taking over at the Colonial Office he made two decisions of great importance to the Bank. First, he gave notice that the formal agreements on which the Bank's silver import monopoly was based were to be terminated in all the Colonies and Protectorates at the end of 1911. (In practice the change was deferred for a year because of other events.)

Secondly, he appointed a committee, under Lord Emmott, his Parliamentary Under-Secretary, to look into the currency of British West Africa. The report of this committee, published in June 1912, led to the creation of a special silver currency for West Africa, to be managed by a West African Currency Board.

The appointment of the Emmott Committee was a response to two separate pressures. On the one hand the colonial governments were still hankering after the minting profits of the silver currency. In 1900 the Barbour Committee had concluded that some of these profits ought to be used to contribute to the cost of colonial administration, and the balance to build up a West African gold reserve; but the Imperial Treasury had brushed that advice aside. A second and more urgent motive was the Treasury's growing anxiety over the massive absorption of English silver coin by West Africa. Gone were the days when the English shilling was regarded – even by the Treasury itself – as having an imperial mission. Mr. S. Armitage-Smith who represented the Treasury on the Emmott Committee explained the change of view in his evidence:

From the point of view of the Imperial Government the sooner the change from sterling to local silver currency is made the better. I regard the contingent liability connected with a coinage which is not, strictly speaking, a token coinage, because it is not submitted to a limit of legal tender, and which is being absorbed at such an enormous pace by a semi-civilised community, as *a distinct danger to our currency arrangements*. . . . So far from forcing sterling on the Colonies I should be inclined to move for substituting a local system.

The urgency with which the Treasury desired such a change becomes quite understandable when one looks at the figures of silver coin issued for West Africa in the previous few years, quoted by the Emmott Committee:

Silver issued for West Africa, the United Kingdom and other Territories

Period	West Africa	United Kingdom	Other Territories
Annual Average	£	£	£
1886–1890	24,426	920,088	255,939
1891–1895	116,323	761,039	124,461
1896–1900	257,090	796,425	367,233
1901–1905	262,786	234,150	231,504
1906–1910	666,190	781,073	325,347
1911	874,850	1,219,766	286,575

The five-year averages in the table do not even show the full extent of the trend: in 1909 and 1910 the amount of silver coin issued to West Africa (£1,259,450) actually exceeded the amount issued for use in the UK.

This was dangerous, said the Treasury witness, because for various reasons there could be a sudden repatriation of large amounts of silver from West Africa. One such reason might be a poor crop year; another might be the temptation of a colonial government to demand silver beyond the legitimate needs of trade, especially if it was given a share of the issue profits. There was nothing to stop such a government from letting its coin fall to a slight discount 'and the whole floating balance will come back to the United Kingdom'. The redundant silver would then depreciate. 'There might possibly be a panic; there would certainly be a demand for a fundamental change in our currency system. We should be asked and perhaps compelled to make silver a promise to pay in gold. *We might be compelled to keep a gold reserve.*'

Silver money was not legally convertible into gold in Britain. Any coin brought back from abroad had to be sold in the money market, though in practice the Bank of England was ready to take reasonable amounts at a small discount. The Treasury had an informal agreement with the Bank of British West Africa limiting repatriation of silver to £100,000 in each year. But in view of the vast volume which money circulation had now reached in West Africa a more fundamental safeguard was needed.

It was largely on these grounds that the Emmott Committee recommended the creation of a special currency for West Africa. The decision helped to solve two subsidiary problems: the sharing of the minting profits; and the argument about banking arrangements. As the Colonies were assuming responsibility for the new currency it was conceded in principle that they had some claim to a share in the profits. And as in the view of the Treasury a privately owned bank was not an adequate authority for the management of such an important currency, a new statutory body was proposed – the West African Currency Board. The Board was to receive the new profits of issue and use them to build up a separate reserve fund in gold and securities convertible into gold. The interest income from this reserve was to be distributed to the Colonial Governments.

The Emmott Report (Cd. 6426, June 5, 1912), written very smoothly by a junior official called 'young' John Anderson – who rose to be Chancellor of the Exchequer, became Lord Waverley and never lost his rather pompous command of literary English – is a masterpiece of constructive policy-making. For five months the Committee heard evidence from a large number of officials, bankers and traders, and their tales make up a unique picture of West

African conditions at the time. The questions were searching and persistent; witnesses were often asked to describe local customs and historical background. Anyone trying to get away with a glib answer was promptly pulled up. And in all this the Bank of British West Africa played an important part.

By the time the Emmott Committee was set up the former irritation of the Colonial Office with the BBWA had faded away. The silver monopoly had been formally terminated before the Committee met. Since 1910 the BBWA was no longer directly associated with the shipping interests, and the merger with the Bank of Nigeria was well on the way. Though some of the old grudges against the Bank were still brought up by various witnesses the Committee did not take them seriously:

The evidence shows that in point of fact the Bank, during the years in which it has been entrusted with the control of the currency, has interpreted its obligations in a liberal sense to the advantage of the Governments and the merchants.

The good opinion of the Colonial Office was made plain when Lord Harcourt asked the board of the BBWA to allow Leslie Couper, the chief manager, to serve as a member of the Currency Committee. The board agreed and Couper became one of the seven members. Evidence for the Bank was given by David Paterson, who had, as he told the Committee, nineteen years of experience with the Bank, much of it on the Coast.

The key passage of Paterson's long, detailed evidence was that a change of currency would 'have no bearing on the Bank's earning powers', and that the Bank would 'loyally cooperate with the Government in any change decided on, just as it has always done with regard to the existing currency'. Paterson naturally defended the Bank against the charge that it was making too much profit out of its silver monopoly. He described the costly business of handling and storing the silver. He disclosed, to the surprise of the Committee, that whenever the Bank brought surplus silver home it had to 'persuade bank after bank to take a little from us', and the balance had to be taken to the Bank of England which charged a commission of $\frac{3}{8}$%. That was on top of the freight and insurance charges paid by the Bank. He disclosed too that something like half the produce shipped out of British West Africa was financed through the BBWA.

Another point that emerges from Paterson's evidence is the conception which the Bank had of its own status. Asked by Mr. Couper whether the BBWA in West Africa was in any way comparable to the Bank of England in England, Paterson replied:

The Bank of British West Africa has aimed at being, and in reality is, the National Bank in British West African colonies. It has been supported by the Colonial Office and the different West African Governments, and now holds the confidence of the populations, European and Native. It is in daily touch with trade and traders to whom it has introduced the existing currency. It is known to be the custodian of Government funds, and has played an important part in the development of business methods and the growing prosperity of the West African colonies.

Three other items from the proceedings of the Emmott Committee throw some light on the monetary problems of the period. One is the uneasiness which all the Commissioners seemed to have felt in dealing with a large currency area which used silver as its money without any backing of gold. Almost every witness was pressed to explain why gold coins should not be introduced into West Africa. Everyone gave the same reply: gold had never become popular except in places like The Gambia or at Kumasi, where French cattle dealers asked for gold because they could not take British silver into the neighbouring French colonies. Quite recently a demand for gold had also come from cocoa growers at Accra who wanted it for hoarding. Despite the great physical drawback of using silver coins for large-scale payments, gold had never caught on. Whenever gold coins got into circulation they tended to be melted down for jewellery.

This intrigued the Commissioners. Gold had been acceptable in West Africa in slave trading times, and it was widely used in the French territories. Why not in British West Africa? There was a suspicion that the terms for gold coin issues were less favourable than those for silver, either by design or by default. No satisfactory explanation emerged. The Committee had to be content to link the proposed new currency to gold through a reserve fund that would be potentially convertible into gold.

Similar questions were asked about the possibility of issuing notes as a subsidiary means of payment. Here again the logic was all in favour of such a scheme. Why should anyone want to take something like £50,000 (not an unusual sum at the peak produce-buying season) out of the Bank in five hundred heavy jute bags filled with silver coins and carry them dozens or hundreds of miles inland by primitive means of transport, when the same amount in paper notes would be so much easier to pack and handle?

The unanimous answer of all the witnesses was that the Africans just would not accept paper as money. It had been tried; the Bank of Nigeria made a note issue and kept it going for a few years. But notes were used mainly in the coastal centres for payments between European firms and to the Government. So the idea of a note issue was placed in reserve for possible future use.

Finally, the 'seignorage' profit which caused so much argument between all British colonies and the Home Government was explained in great detail by Mr. Armitage-Smith. At the time of the Coinage Act 1870 an ounce of silver was worth 60½d. and it was minted into coins with a face value of 5s. 6d. The difference of 9·09% was the profit or 'seignorage'. It barely covered the cost of minting, distribution and particularly of re-coining worn coins. Since 1870 the price of silver bullion had fallen to less than half. The average for the year 1910 was just over 24½d. an ounce. The seignorage had risen from 9·09% to 165·49%. Mr. Armitage-Smith neatly covered up the actual amount gained in the previous year or so by quoting the 'average' gross profit between 1872 and 1910 which worked out at £278,589 per annum, with a net profit after all expenses of around £200,000. As the figure was obviously very much smaller in the early part of that period it must have been a great deal larger in 1910. The Colonies were not asking for chickenfeed.

The recommendation of the Emmott Committee was that a special silver currency should be introduced into British West Africa and a Currency Board be set up to control it. This was accepted by the Government of Mr. H. H. Asquith in September 1912. It turned out to be a fortunate decision for the Bank.

THE WEST AFRICAN CURRENCY BOARD

The Board was appointed in November 1912 and held its first meeting in that month. The first chairman was Sir George Fiddes of the Colonial Office. Other members were W. H. Mercer, one of the Crown Agents, and Leslie Couper, the general manager of the Bank of British West Africa. Couper had played his part in the creation of the new system as a member of the Emmott Committee. When the Colonial Secretary asked the directors of the Bank to release him for service on the new Board they raised no objections.

The post did not in fact involve very heavy duties. The Board did not establish its own offices or engage its own staff. From the outset it made use of the Crown Agents for both. Only the Secretary was a full-time employee and he was drawn from the Crown Agents' staff. While the Currency Board fulfilled an important constitutional function its organisation in England was rather shadowy. Its expenses were negligible. The remuneration of the Board's members was nominal (Couper received £100 per annum), and later on ceased altogether. Yet at first it held weekly meetings at the Crown Agents' offices in Whitehall Gardens with the Secretary, Mr. D. L. H. Baynes, in attendance. It had to buy silver bullion, approve the design and order the coining of the new currency at the Royal Mint, and make arrangements for shipping and payments.

Perhaps as a gesture of independence the Board decided not to use the Crown Agents as its bankers. In July 1913 it opened an account with the London Joint Stock Bank (later Midland Bank) and this bank financed the Board in the minting of coin and other initial expenditure.

The first Constitution of the Board was laid down in a memorandum by Mr. Lewis Harcourt, the Colonial Secretary, dated December 6, 1912. It set out the duties of the Board, in particular the introduction of the new silver coinage and the creation of a 'gold standard reserve' in gold and securities. The minimum proportion of gold in the reserve was to be fixed by the Colonial Secretary from time to time.

Besides issuing the new coins which ranged from the two-shilling florin in silver down to the tenth of a penny in nickel-bronze, the Board had also to arrange for the gradual withdrawal of the British silver coinage from West African circulation and its shipment home. Rules for an issue of currency notes were also provided but this matter was left in abeyance. (The need for paper money arose quite suddenly three years later, at the end of 1915, when war conditions produced an acute shortage of silver coinage.)

The reason why the new Currency Board was able to function with a minute organisation was that it entrusted the operation of the new system in West Africa to the BBWA. Four currency centres were established in Lagos, Accra, Freetown and Bathurst. In each of them a Currency Officer was appointed from the local colonial administration. The business of receiving, storing and then issuing the coin in exchange for sterling coins or drafts on London was to be discharged by the Bank of British West Africa acting as agent for the Board.

The new coins were legalised on May 7, 1913. Shortly afterwards a press notice announced that the currency could be obtained either at the branches of the BBWA in West Africa or by applying to the Board in London for coin to be delivered on the Coast. The Board offered to deliver at any ocean port in British West Africa served by Elder Dempster steamers in exchange for pre-payment in London, with a premium of 15s. per £100 (¾%) 'towards the freight cost'.

The terms on which the Bank would act as agent of the Board in West Africa were agreed after an exchange of letters. First the Board explained in a letter dated December 9, 1912, what was immediately required: the Bank's branches at the four currency centres should offer safe custody of all coin held by the Board in West Africa. Each branch was to undertake the delivery, exchange or redemption of currency. It would keep accounts of all local transactions on behalf of the Board under the supervision and control of a Government official. The funds of the Board were to be kept entirely separate from those of the Bank. No machinery was required outside these four centres (that is what the Board thought at the time).

On April 16, 1913, the Bank replied that it would be glad to act as agent for the Board. As to terms, the Board was to pay for all necessary out-of-pocket expenses such as freight, insurance, porterage, specie boxes and bags, labels, seals, etc. Government guards were to be provided for the four branches free of cost. If the Bank's strong-rooms proved insufficient the Board was to pay for extra storage facilities. For all used silver coin returned to the Bank a commission of $\frac{1}{2}$% was to be paid for counting, sorting and storing, and if necessary, shipment to England. For shipping the Board's coin 'from port to port in West Africa as directed by the Board' the Bank asked for $\frac{1}{4}$% commission.

The Board accepted these terms on May 6, 1913, and the arrangement came into force on July 1, subject to six months' notice of termination by either party. From the point of view of the Bank the remuneration which consisted entirely of commissions as a percentage of turnover, without any fixed agency charge, was an experiment. Receipts fluctuated heavily from year to year, and it was not long before the Bank asked for a minimum annual fee.

The new West African silver coins were quickly designed and minted. Before the end of 1913 £889,000 of the coinage was shipped to the Coast but Imperial silver was also still being sent out, the amount for 1913 being £539,700. In the course of 1914 silver held by the Bank for the Board steadily rose towards £1,000,000.

The first report of the Currency Board for the nineteen months ended in mid-1914 recorded that the new currency was being accepted in West Africa without difficulty. The Bank soon got accustomed to its additional duties, though there were occasional arguments with one or other of the Currency officers. The first rumblings were also heard of a complaint which became familiar later on, about the extra duties imposed on branch managers, cashiers and accountants in handling the Board's coin separately from the Bank's. The local work-load was made worse by a sudden rise in the demand for coin during 1913 when the Gold Coast cocoa crop soared for the first time to over 50,000 tons.

The outbreak of the First World War in August 1914 abruptly cut off trade with Germany, reduced the number of ship sailings and caused a heavy fall in West African commodity exports. Produce prices slumped, and currency needs dropped accordingly. The Board was landed with large amounts of surplus coin. Those who had handed in this coin demanded payment in English currency or gold in London. The Board had not enough funds to pay for this; so it had to ship the silver home despite the wartime rise in freight rates. Between July and November 1914 £530,000 worth of silver coin was repatriated.

In the following December the trend was reversed; prices recovered and the Board had to pay out £100,000 of new silver in West Africa. This see-saw pattern was typical of West Africa and had always caused acute problems to the traders and the Bank. The Board was simply being introduced to a local malady.

In the course of 1915 the nickel-bronze coinage of pence, halfpence and tenth-pence which had been introduced in Nigeria in 1907 and in the Gold Coast in 1912 was transferred to the Board.

All this might suggest a large number of officials burning the midnight oil to cope with exasperating new problems. But the fact was that the real work was done by the Bank of British West Africa whose Coast staff seem to have taken the additional pressures in their stride. The proof lies in the following sentence from the Currency Board's second annual report: 'The cost of administration in England, i.e. salaries, furniture, stationery and miscellaneous expenditure in the year under review was £576 16s.' In the following year the sum rose to £1,075.

A SEESAW OF MONEY SUPPLY

In 1915 a serious shortage of silver coin arose in the United Kingdom. The West African Currency Board had just found silver supplies in the Colonies abundant. So it arranged once again for an extra repatriation of sterling coins from the Coast. That turned out to be unfortunate. At the end of the year the situation suddenly changed: the demand for cocoa on the Gold Coast soared and prices rose steeply; in Nigeria a large crop of groundnuts appeared on the market for the first time. Unexpectedly there was plenty of shipping available. An 'unprecedented demand for silver coin' found the Board's stock insufficient.

The repatriation of British coin was stopped and more of the new West African coins were urgently ordered in London, but the Mint could not promise early delivery. To deal with the crisis the Board decided to introduce English currency notes. In November 1915 the new Colonial Secretary, Mr. Bonar Law, issued an amended Constitution of the Currency Board to authorise a note issue. A total of £257,000 of UK notes was distributed. That seems to have been sufficient to meet the crisis, especially as the BBWA imported some gold coins at the same time. Most of the notes were withdrawn again by June 1916. By then the Royal Mint had been able to produce and ship a further supply of West African coins and the panic had subsided.

In the twelve months to June 30, 1917, the Board sent £1,500,000 worth of coin to West Africa, bringing the total amount shipped since the introduction of the West African coinage in 1913 to £3,900,000. In the same four years some £800,000 worth of sterling silver had been withdrawn and sent to England.

The crisis of 1916 made the Board think more urgently about the issue of special West African currency notes. Again the notes were designed, printed and shipped in a short time. On July 11, 1916, the first issue was made in Nigeria, and in September the new notes were experimentally introduced in the Gold Coast and Sierra Leone.

PRODUCE RANGE WIDENS

As the war drew to its climax the demand for West African produce, and the prices offered, increased sharply. Apart from the palm products which still formed the largest part of the outward shipments, cocoa had become important and a new crop, groundnuts, now showed a spectacular growth.

Some varieties of groundnuts (or peanuts) had been grown in West Africa as a food crop for a long time. Around 1900 African farmers in Senegal and The Gambia began to cultivate the crop deliberately for sale to export traders. As an annual crop it did not need as much capital as cocoa, though the preparation, packing and collection at inland centres for transport to the ports became a complex commercial task once production had grown beyond a certain volume.

In Northern Nigeria, which eventually became the largest production area, groundnut growing for the market was started by Hausa traders around 1910. These men had all the commercial skill,

G

organisation and capital required. Their traditional trans-Sahara trade was in decline and the kola nut routes from the south had shifted elsewhere. It seems that a group of Hausas persuaded farmers, starting around Kano, to grow groundnuts for sale. They financed them and guaranteed the purchase of the crop. The buyers then sold the crop to European firms who shipped them to Europe where the nuts soon gained a large market.

The groundnut industry was thus initiated by Africans. It was particularly suited to the conditions of Northern Nigeria. The savannah country was the right kind of soil and the farmers of the region had long been accustomed to growing crops for the market, such as grain and cotton. It was common for them, or their women-folk, to be traders in the dry season. The result was that within ten years some 45,000 tons of groundnuts, worth well over £1,000,000, were being exported from Northern Nigeria alone, and by the 1950s Nigeria, Senegal and The Gambia together produced more than three-quarters of the world's supply of groundnuts.

After this digression we must return to the problems of managing the West African currency.

In 1917–18 a record groundnut crop was harvested in The Gambia. Until then the handling of groundnuts in that colony had been financed largely by the importation of French five-franc pieces, locally known as dollars. Now it became impossible to obtain new franc supplies from France. British silver was introduced and was accepted both by the local farmers and by those from the surrounding French territories.

Throughout West Africa the demand for currency was heavy in that year and £1,350,000 worth of new silver coin was paid out. The year brought the first loss of silver at sea. A ship bringing £4,800 in threepenny pieces was lost through enemy action.

BANK AND BOARD

The brief episode of the English currency notes distributed in 1915–16 and the subsequent issue of the new West African notes had involved the BBWA branches in a good deal of work and worry. The Board tried to pour oil on the waters by proclaiming that it was 'indebted to the BBWA for the ready cooperation which they have offered with a view to popularising the notes in all the Colonies concerned'. The Bank was not taken in. In January 1917 it asked for an additional fee of £500 per annum for handling notes, and the Board agreed.

In December 1917 the chief manager of the BBWA wrote to the Currency Board outlining a new agency agreement based on the experience of the first five years. While percentage commissions were to be retained the idea of a fixed annual minimum fee appears for the first time. The new terms were accepted by the Board as from January 1, 1918, and in the following July the minimum agency fee was set at £1,500 per annum, to come into effect on January 1, 1919. A year later the minimum fee was raised to £3,000 per annum on the grounds that the Bank was building a number of expensive new strong-rooms. (A new one at Lagos cost over £10,000 and the interest on this alone at 6% was £600 per annum.) The Board once more accepted the new fee but turned down the Bank's further request for a ten-year agreement. Although the Board appreciated that a large capital expenditure was required from the Bank for a number of additional strong-rooms and specially strengthened buildings it did not feel able to give any guarantee for more than one year at a time.

It may be of interest here to pursue this subject of the Bank's remuneration for its agency work a little ahead of our general history. In January 1921 the Bank asked for the minimum fee to be raised to £4,000; the Board refused but offered to raise the commission on the value of silver coin shipped to the UK to $\frac{1}{4}$%. David Paterson wrote that this was quite inadequate: 'The withdrawal of the notes from circulation, now that coin is more plentiful, is imposing a very severe tax upon the staff and considerable expense for transporting the notes to Currency Centres.' Yet for 1922 the basic fee was again fixed at £3,000, plus commission of $\frac{1}{8}$% on homeward consignments of silver with a maximum of £1,000. These figures remained unchanged until 1927 when the overall maximum was consolidated to £4,000 per annum and a new addition of £1,000 was agreed as rent for the use of the Bank's strong-rooms. Gradually as more strong-rooms were built at more

branches the idea that 5% of the actual capital cost would be added
to the Bank's annual fee as rent became accepted.

Oddly enough the agency agreement between the Currency
Board and the Bank on which the entire supply and control of
currency in British West Africa depended was based on little more
than an exchange of letters which took place once a year. Sometimes
the Secretary of the Board had to remind the Bank that it had not
sent in its usual letter asking for the agreement to be renewed for
another twelve months on the same terms. It was a typically English
arrangement. But it worked.

At a later date, when the general manager of the Bank felt that
the Currency Board did not properly appreciate the heavy and costly
burden undertaken by the Bank's branches in West Africa in dealing
with the rapidly expanding currency, the Secretary of the Board
simply inserted in its next annual report a charming tribute to the
invaluable work done by the Bank, and as that seemed to be the best
reward obtainable, it was quietly accepted.

Chapter Seven

THE FIRST WORLD WAR

A CHECK TO EXPANSION

W HEN the First World War broke out in 1914 the Bank had fully recovered from the unsettling events of 1912 – the introduction of a new currency under the control of an official board, and the takeover of the Bank of Nigeria. The arrival of several new directors on the board strengthened its hand. Sir Owen Philipps who had joined in 1911 had his chief interest in shipping but gave valuable service to the Bank. He was a man of imagination and vigour. Incidentally he showed his confidence in the future of the BBWA by becoming an increasingly important shareholder. He acquired 2,000 shares from Elder Dempster on joining the board in 1911 and took up further allotments in succeeding years until in 1919 he held 5,250 shares, on which £21,000 had been paid up. These shares he held then for 15 years. The shareholding in BBWA which the new Elder Dempster Company had acquired in 1910 from the estate of Sir Alfred Jones was also increased in 1913 and 1917 when it was 21,448 shares, paid-up £85,792 – out of a total issued capital of 140,000 shares, paid-up £560,000.

The three directors who had come over from the Bank of Nigeria, C. B. Edgar, George Miller and Mazzini Stuart, were successful businessmen in their own right and brought a large store of experience to the Bank. With the death of Mr. Henry Coke in December 1913 the last of the original directors had passed away and only Harrison

Williams and George Neville were left of those who had worked under the chairmanship of Sir Alfred Jones.

The minutes of board meetings in the years just before the first war indicate that the responsibility for the running of the Bank both at home and in West Africa was gradually shifting from board to management. Leslie Couper, the Chief Manager, had been with the Bank from the beginning, and had gained much personal authority. With him were David Paterson and Roy Wilson who had also long experience of the Bank's affairs. Among others who formed a strong management team were G. A. Lester and W. H. Gaman. Increasingly the directors confined themselves to discussing and deciding the larger issues of policy.

The Bank was doing well. The paid-up capital was now £292,000. Net profit for the year ended March 31, 1913 was £43,955, and in the year ended March 31, 1914 when the paid-up capital had been increased to £400,000 it was £60,800. More branches and agencies were being opened, the volume of business increased, the work for the Currency Board proceeded smoothly and profitably. Some thought was given to the pay and living conditions of the staff on the Coast; a good deal of work was done on improving accommodation besides building new Bank premises. Two small symptoms of a new attitude towards staff might be quoted. In 1912 the directors promised £5 to any member of the staff who passed the examinations of the Institute of Bankers. In March 1914 it was decided to pay a bonus of £25 per annum to European staff members who became proficient in one of the native languages. The year 1912 also saw the beginning of an annual staff magazine.

At the outbreak of the war the BBWA had a total staff of 214 Europeans and 115 Africans. Almost at once twenty-one men from Head Office, eleven from Liverpool office and eight on the Coast joined the forces. In West Africa a campaign was launched against the two German colonies of Togoland and the Cameroons. In the former there was a powerful radio station at Kamina which helped German submarines to hunt allied merchant ships. Both British and French forces invaded Togoland, and the German Governor who commanded a force of some 300 Europeans and 1,200 Africans withdrew from large territories to defend Kamina. There a stiff battle had to be fought and the Germans surrendered only after blowing up the station.

The Cameroons were invaded by a British force from Eastern Nigeria and a French force from Equatorial Africa. The Germans had 500 Europeans and about 6,000 Africans under arms, with a dozen field-guns and many machine-guns. The first invasion attempt failed but on a further effort the capital and chief port of Duala surrendered. British and French forces advanced slowly with many battles and heavy casualties. Reinforcements had to be sent. It was February 1916 before the last of the German forces surrendered after many of them had escaped into the Spanish territory of Muni.

The Royal West African Frontier Force, which had been formed in 1897 with Sir Frederick Lugard as its first Commandant, was the instrument of British power in these campaigns. It was then expanded and sent to East Africa to help in the subjection of the German colonies there, and it was 1918 before the survivors returned.

Staff shortages naturally worried the management both in England and in West Africa, particularly after more people had left for the services in 1915. A circular letter from the Head Office in August 1915 requested all managers and staff to make the greatest possible economies. It was fortunate that the staff on the Coast had been reinforced in 1912 by the absorption of the Bank of Nigeria. To recruit an additional man now required a special permit from the government which was hard to get. However the work of the Bank seems to have been carried on efficiently throughout the war.

All staff members joining the forces at the outbreak of war received full pay for six months, and later received the difference between their army pay and bank salaries, as did those who were conscripted later. Where these rules did not fit a particular case the board was liberal in sanctioning special payments. In 1915 a sum of £3,300 was set aside to pay a war bonus to European and African staff – 10% of annual pay, with a maximum of £50, for Home staff, and 5% for coast staff. A further war bonus was paid in 1917 and yet another in 1918, each costing £10,000. These were separate from various cost of living bonuses and increases in pay scales.

Other arrangements for the staff during the war years included the formation of a Staff Fund into which the Bank would pay an annual sum to finance pensions for those retiring after long service. A new Pension Scheme and a profit-sharing scheme were discussed at length during 1917, but it seems that the first allocation to the latter was only made in 1920.

A number of BBWA employees were killed or wounded in action and several died when their ships were torpedoed. Memorial plates were erected in the Bank's buildings at London, Liverpool, Manchester, Lagos and Accra.

In the Bank's branch at Hamburg the British staff was interned and weekly food parcels were sent to them throughout the war. Some of them however were allowed to return home on exchange against Germans interned in England. Among them were S. H. Urry, who became manager of Manchester office, and J. E. Sparkes, who became manager of the Liverpool branch of the National Bank.

Meanwhile economic conditions in British West Africa were not as seriously affected by the war as many had feared. Despite shortages of imported goods and shipping difficulties production and trade expanded in fits and starts.

One problem which troubled the Bank at an early stage of the war was the marketing of palm kernels. These had become very valuable as a raw material for both margarine and cattle cake. In the years immediately before the war exports from Nigeria, the Gold Coast and Sierra Leone had reached £4,250,000 per annum, but 80% of the shipments had been going to Germany. Kernel-crushing mills had been established in north Germany many years before, and while the cattle cake was sold to German farmers much of the edible oil was exported to other countries including England. The war stimulated the demand for margarine but there was little processing machinery or marketing organisation in England. Mr. Leslie Couper suggested to the Colonial Office that an official enquiry into the problems of West African edible nuts and seeds should be set up. He mobilised the London Chamber of Commerce in support of the idea, and Sir Owen Philipps stirred up the West Africa Committees of the Liverpool and Manchester Chambers of Commerce.

In July 1915 the Colonial Secretary appointed a Committee of Enquiry. Under the chairmanship of Mr. Steel-Maitland, the Parliamentary Under-Secretary, the members included Sir Frederick

Lugard, then Governor-General of Nigeria, Sir Hugh Clifford, Governor of the Gold Coast, and Leslie Couper himself.

In June 1916 the Committee recommended that an export duty should be imposed on all palm kernels exported from British West Africa but refunded on all kernels shipped to, and crushed in, any part of the British Empire. This was done, and the expansion of crushing and processing facilities in England followed quickly. There was a satisfactory recovery of palm kernel production in West Africa.

The episode of the Edible Nuts Committee showed the growing personal influence of Leslie Couper outside the Bank itself. As a member of the West African Currency Board he was not merely associating on terms of official secrecy with senior members of the Colonial Office and the Crown Agents, but he was taking part in the formulation of official policies. He was also elected chairman of the West Africa Committee of the London Chamber of Commerce, an influential body. At the end of the war when the British Overseas Banks Association (now The British Overseas and Commonwealth Banks Association) was formed Couper was made Chairman of it in 1920.

The British territories in West Africa remained generally calm during the war period but there was one exception. In mid-1918 the people of the Egba Kingdom who live around Abeokuta rose in revolt. The Kingdom had been expressly excluded when in 1895 a Protectorate over Yorubaland was proclaimed. The British authorities signed a Treaty of Independence with the Alake of Abeokuta. But this was terminated in 1914 and 'indirect' British administration was installed. One of the principal results was that the Egbas became liable to government taxes. It was later said that dishonest clerks had been sent in to enforce this. At any rate resentment gradually built up until it burst into open revolt, which was suppressed with military force.

CHANGE OF LEADERSHIP

For the Bank as a whole the event which made the most direct impact at this time was the departure of its chairman, Lord Milner. In December 1916 Lord Milner was asked by Mr. Lloyd George to join the War Cabinet. He at once informed Leslie Couper that he intended to accept the invitation. On December 21, 1916, the board received a letter from Lord Milner announcing this decision and resigning the chairmanship and directorship. Lord Milner had been responsible for adapting the Bank's policy to the serious challenges which it faced after the death of Sir Alfred Jones in 1909. He had given the Bank a quality of leadership which was probably crucial to its success.

The progress made by the Bank under Lord Milner's leadership may be summarised by a few figures taken from the annual reports of the period.

Between March 31, 1910 and March 31, 1916 the paid-up capital was doubled from £200,000 to £400,000, and the Reserve increased from £80,000 to £150,000, plus £50,000 set aside in 1915 for War Contingencies. Deposits (current accounts and fixed-term) rose from £1,075,000 to £2,523,000. Cash went up from £302,000 to £1,021,000. The growth of turnover is seen in the rise in advances from £297,000 to £638,000 and in Bills for Collection from £52,000 to £153,000.

Profit, as published, had nearly trebled from £20,570 in 1909–10 to £60,800 in 1913–14 before the impact of war reduced it to £48,000 in 1914–15 recovering to £59,000 in 1915–16. (The return on capital employed had thus increased roughly from $7\frac{1}{2}$% to 11%.) Dividends were 9% free of tax from 1910 to 1913, $9\frac{1}{2}$% tax free for the first half of 1913–14 and $9\frac{1}{2}$% less tax for the second half, when war had broken out; the rate was reduced to $6\frac{1}{2}$% less tax for 1914–15 but restored to 8% less tax for 1915–16.

When Lord Milner came in the Bank had fourteen branches and seventeen agencies. When he left it had thirty-four branches and twenty-nine agencies.

One of the personal gifts for which Lord Milner is remembered to this day was his extraordinary ability to find the right man for a difficult job. It is safe to assume that he applied his talent to the problem raised by his sudden resignation. Within a few days the directors elected his successor. He was Lord Selborne, a close associate of Lord Milner over many years.

The second Earl of Selborne was born in 1859; after Winchester and history at Oxford he became an MP and was, like Milner, 'adopted' by Joseph Chamberlain. From 1895 to 1900 he was Under-Secretary for the Colonies. In 1900 he was appointed First Lord of the Admiralty, and the next five years were highly constructive for the British Navy. Next he succeeded Lord Milner as High Commissioner for South Africa where he did much to smooth the path for the Union, returning home in 1910 a Knight of the Garter. He again became a Minister (of Agriculture) but resigned in June 1916 over the Irish policy of the Asquith Government. As he was not asked to join Lloyd George's Government he was free to replace Lord Milner in some of his private positions.

The Bank of British West Africa once again had a chairman of authority and experience, a great public figure, and a man steeped in African affairs. He took his seat as chairman on January 5, 1917.

There is no evidence of any immediate change in policy or style of management. The Bank had been in an expansionary mood for two or three years, and plans simply went forward in the customary way. The opening of new branches was proposed, studied, discussed – and then sometimes approved. Thus in 1914 branches were opened at Kano and Port Harcourt. In 1915 a branch was opened at Koforidua; in 1916 one at Kaduna and another at Nsawan. In the following year a branch was opened at Jos, on the tin-mining plateau. The agency at Fernando Po was turned into a branch.

In 1915, at the end of the Cameroons campaign, a branch was opened in Duala but when in the following year that port was transferred to a French administration the branch was closed again.

Twice during the war Leslie Couper paid lengthy visits to West Africa. In 1917 he went to Liberia and concluded with the Government an agreement giving greater scope to the Bank. Large ideas were discussed jointly with an American group for the development of Liberian roads, railways, harbours, etc. As the expected UK Government guarantee was not forthcoming only modest progress was made along these lines.

OPERATIONS OUTSIDE WEST AFRICA

Even before the war ambitious plans for expansion into areas outside West Africa had been discussed. Schemes for Algeria and Tunisia were considered for several years, but despite various studies on the spot the Bank never opened in either of these countries.

Plans for extending operations to Morocco were more successful. The board had first discussed Morocco in April 1910 and the subject came up frequently in 1912 but 'no decision was reached'. On April 1, 1914, a definite scheme was put up for forming a new bank in Morocco in conjunction with a leading German financial house. The board turned it down as too ambitious. In 1915 however Leslie Couper paid a visit to North Africa and in the same year branches were opened in Casablanca and in Tangier. In the course of 1917 branches were opened at Fez, Saffi and Mazagan, another branch at Mogador was authorised but not opened until 1921. Hopes for Moroccan prosperity were running high. Mr. Couper arranged for two experts, W. B. Harris and W. Cozens Hardy, to write a book entitled *Modern Morocco* for the Bank. It was published in 1919. A branch at Marrakech was opened in 1918 and in April of that year Leslie Couper addressed the British Chamber of Commerce in Tangier.

The Bank also opened its own agency in New York in 1916 after a visit by Roy Wilson. The growing ambitions of the board can be seen in wartime discussions about opening branches in Paris, Rotterdam and other places in Europe. Meanwhile in its West African birthplace, Lagos, the BBWA in 1916 acquired a large plot of freehold land at Ikoyi, where several houses for managers were later built.

In the French West African colonies, where the wartime difficulties of the French Government and the heavy demand for the local products seemed to offer a good opportunity for the Bank to employ some capital, it was inhibited by the old market-sharing agreement with the Banque de l'Afrique Occidentale. Indeed when the BAO enquired in 1915 whether the agreement still held the London directors replied loyally that 'it would only be fair that competition between the two institutions in their respective spheres should be mutually avoided'.

The possibility of extending into Egypt and the Sudan was much considered in 1917. In the end one agency was approved, but action was delayed until the end of the war and in 1918 and 1920 branches were opened at Alexandria and Cairo.

ENTER THE COLONIAL BANK

For four years the Bank of British West Africa had the banking field in the British territories to itself. In 1916 a powerful new competitor appeared on the scene. The Colonial Bank, which had been granted a charter to operate in the West Indies as long ago as 1836, decided to enter West Africa. We have one clue to the riddle why this bank suddenly felt, after eighty years of reasonably profitable work in the Caribbean and in the middle of a world war, that it must seek wider horizons. Its deputy chairman in 1916 was Sir W. Maxwell Aitken, MP (soon to become famous as Lord Beaverbrook), the Canadian who had come to England to launch a crusade for the re-birth of the British Empire. Although in 1916 the chairman of the Colonial Bank was Mr. Cyril Gurney, Beaverbrook took the chair in 1917 and held it until the following year when he joined Lloyd George's Cabinet. The Colonial Bank obtained from Parliament a revision of its charter permitting it to work anywhere in the British Empire, and on October 4, 1916 the chairman announced that the bank was about to open branches at Accra, Lagos and Zaria.

At that time the Colonial Bank had a capital of £2,000,000 of which £600,000 was paid up; and a reserve of £150,000. For comparison the BBWA had around the same time (March 31, 1917) an authorised capital of £2,000,000 of which £560,000 was paid up. The reserve was £220,000. The two banks were thus of similar size. The BBWA had the advantage of well-established links with the Colonial Governments, the West African Currency Board and the business community on the Coast. To set against this the Colonial Bank had that unique human engine: Beaverbrook. What this meant was soon seen. Within a few months of the new charter being approved the Colonial Bank had opened its first branches and installed management and staff. The manager sent out to Lagos to direct the West African operations was Mr. E. Hyslop Bell who had been Joint General Manager in London. He was an able and experienced banker, generally regarded as a 'gentleman banker', who later became chairman of the Niger Company.

The BBWA watched the offensive of its new rival with some concern. Almost at once Leslie Couper, who was then in Lagos, reported that the Colonial Bank was trying to poach staff. Mr. Unwin, the Lagos manager, had received an offer, and another staff member had already defected. The Colonial Bank was informed that Mr. Unwin was still under contract for five years, and if they enticed anyone else the BBWA would apply for an injunction in London. Legal proceedings were to be taken for any breach of contract.

That incident did not seem to worry the Colonial Bank. It went on expanding fast, and continued to take customers away from the BBWA. In 1917 it opened offices in Liverpool and Manchester. Soon it was reported that even the British Cotton Growing Association had transferred part of its account to the Colonial Bank. In July 1917 the BBWA offered to make an 'arrangement' with the Colonial Bank, exchanging a number of BBWA shares for the control of the CB's West African business. The offer was promptly declined. In 1918 four further branches were opened, and in 1919 yet another five branches. The bank even opened an agency at Dakar, where the BBWA had stayed out for the sake of good relations with the French. Within two years of its arrival the Colonial Bank was established not only in the three original centres but in Kano, Jos and Port Harcourt in Nigeria, Sekondi and Kumasi in the Gold Coast, Freetown in Sierra Leone and Bathurst in The Gambia. Five further branches and one agency were opened in 1919–20 bringing the number of branches to seventeen.

The balance sheet soon began to reflect the success of the venture. In the year to mid-1916 the Colonial Bank showed a profit of £60,501; in 1916–17 this dropped to £49,832; but in the calendar year 1918 it shot up to £78,143, and in the following year to £126,579. These figures included the West Indian business but almost certainly mirror the expansion in West Africa. By 1918 the reserve had grown to £325,000 and new shares were issued by which the paid-up capital was increased to £750,000. By that time

Mr. C. F. Wood had taken Lord Beaverbrook's place as chairman. The dividend which had been level at 7% per annum from 1915 to 1917 was increased to 8% in 1918 and to 10% in 1919.

There was enough business for two banks, and a touch of competition cannot have done the BBWA any harm. But the directors were soon seriously concerned about the attitude of the Colonial authorities. In Nigeria at any rate the Government gave the Colonial Bank some of its financial business. By 1919 the Governor of Nigeria ordered an equal division of silver coin between the two banks. The BBWA made 'strong representation' but the Colonial Office approved the Governor's action. The new rival was proving to be too strong to be either bought out or subdued. Within a few years it was to grow into a much more formidable shape.

Chapter Eight

UPS AND DOWNS OF
THE TWENTIES

PLANS AND ALLIANCES

The peace of 1918 was followed by a boom in West Africa. World demand for the products of the region was strong and prices were high. For the African farmers it was a time of increasing incomes and rising expectations. The European trading firms were basking in prosperity. The Currency Board found the money circulation growing from £4,400,000 in mid-1918 to £13,600,000 in mid-1920. The Bank's net profit for 1918–19 was £114,267; for 1919–20 it was £171,397.

Presumably it was this trend which made the directors look for a stronger capital base to underpin the further growth they confidently expected. They were hoping for great developments in North Africa and the Eastern Mediterranean. After opening branches in Cairo and Alexandria (where the Bank almost at once advanced £500,000 to the Cotton Control Commission) they sent Leslie Couper east to visit cotton centres in Egypt and the Sudan, and to go on to Beirut and Constantinople, 'to which extensions might now or later be made'. This venture into the Levant did not, in fact, turn out successfully; but the directors could hardly foresee this in the euphoric post-war mood of 1919.

In London friendly personal relations had grown up between the BBWA and Lloyds Bank. Roy Wilson had particularly close contact with Lloyds Bank managers. Sir Owen Philipps seems to have been the first director to suggest a financial link with the larger bank.

(*Top*) First Branch of the
Bank—at Lagos (demolished
1904)

(*Bottom*) Second Lagos
building, of which an artist's
impression appears on the dust
jacket of this volume
(demolished 1950–1952)

(*Above*) Third Lagos building, opened in 1932 and demolished 1975 to make way for larger premises

(*Opposite*) The 'Old Bank' at Accra, but not the first Bank building there (demolished about 1966)

(*Opposite Bottom*) New 200-foot-long Bank building at Accra, opened 1968

Jos Market Branch.
Premises opened 1963

At any rate on January 17, 1919 he was authorised by the board to negotiate 'a general working agreement' with Lloyds Bank Limited. Rapid progress was made. Lloyds Bank agreed to buy 15,000 BBWA shares from Elder Dempster & Co. at £6¾ per share, paid for by 3,750 shares of Lloyds Bank which stood at £27 each in the market. Lloyds Bank also subscribed for a further 15,000 shares for cash at £7¼ each. Thirdly Lloyds Bank was to take 7,500 shares of BBWA as part of a new issue of 40,000 shares to be made at £6 per share. Finally Lloyds Bank agreed to hold all its BBWA shares for five years.

Apart from this capital investment, far-reaching plans for mutual cooperation were agreed in principle. Lord Selborne and Sir Richard V. Vassar-Smith, the respective chairmen of the two banks, exchanged formal letters which were worded like grand proclamations. 'A Treaty of Alliance', they declared, was to be entered into by the two institutions. Each bank was to nominate a director to the board of the other. Each bank was to appoint the other its agent and correspondent. The BBWA would transfer its banking accounts to Lloyds Bank, with some exceptions. Lloyds Bank would finance seasonal and other requirements of the BBWA on terms as favourable as those granted to their own affiliated banks. Both banks would influence all possible business in favour of each other and would 'work in the closest accord'.

The heads of agreement were approved by the BBWA board on July 4, 1919, and Mr. J. Beaumont Pease from Lloyds Bank was elected to the board. An Extraordinary General Meeting was held to approve the scheme, to increase the authorised capital to £4,000,000, and to raise the number of directors to fourteen. Lord Selborne explained the policy behind the link-up to shareholders:

This arrangement is not a sale of your business to a great institution, nor is it an amalgamation with the institution, nor does Lloyds Bank acquire control over your business. What they do acquire is a great interest and influence in your business which is exactly what your directors wanted. Now why? Because in this age of world competition, in a period where great opportunities are open to your bank for expansion and fresh enterprises, and when the clouds are heavy on the horizon we felt it would be of the greatest advantage to this comparatively small bank to be united in close alliance with a world famous institution like Lloyds Bank. We

H

believe that the alliance is a mutual benefit to the small bank and to the great bank.

A circular was issued to all branches explaining the arrangement and suggesting that they should work on close terms with Lloyds Bank and its associated banks. In October a second Lloyds director, Sir Henry Babington Smith, was added to the BBWA board.

The 'Treaty of Alliance' with Lloyds Bank had given the Bank of British West Africa a strong new foundation for its future as an international bank. Yet it did not satisfy the ambitions of Lord Selborne and his colleagues. Within a few months they were discussing similar links with three other powerful banks. On August 6, 1920, 'following negotiations over some months' the directors approved a memorandum of agreement drawn up with these three banks: London County Westminster and Parr's Bank Limited (now National Westminster Bank), National Provincial and Union Bank of England Limited (later National Provincial, and now merged into National Westminster), and The Standard Bank of South Africa Limited (now The Standard Bank Limited – part of Standard Chartered Bank Limited). Lloyds Bank had been kept informed of these negotiations and had concurred in the agreements. The three banks were each taking up one third of an issue of 100,000 new shares at £6¼ per share. Each of the three banks also nominated a director to the BBWA board. Mr. R. Hugh Tennant was appointed for Westminster, Mr. Frederick Eley, MP, for National Provincial, and Mr. R. E. Dickinson for Standard Bank. In April 1921 Sir Frederick Eley (as he had just become) offered to resign as he had left the National Provincial Bank; he was persuaded to stay and Mr. F. A. Johnston was appointed to represent the NP. A few months later Mr. Beaumont Pease resigned owing to pressure of other duties and Lloyds Bank nominated Sir Austin Harris in his place.

The Bank of British West Africa emerged from these negotiations with greatly increased capital resources, a stronger board of directors and firm business connections with four of the largest British banks. In 1920 the paid-up capital was put up from £580,000 to £800,000, and at March 31, 1921 to £1·2 million. But if the intention had been to use the new strength for 'expansion and fresh enterprises' these hopes were disappointed.

In Egypt the branches in Alexandria and Cairo ran almost immediately into losses – for the year to March 31, 1921, about £30,000
was lost – and the directors 'thought the prospects did not warrant
further extension'. Proposals for going into the Sudan were not
followed up. In 1921 Sir Frederick Eley and Mr. Roy Wilson visited
Egypt and reported on the prospects without enthusiasm. It was
decided to maintain the two branches but not to expand further.
Nothing was done about Beirut or Turkey. In fact, by 1925 the
Egyptian business was abandoned and taken over by Lloyds Bank.

The business in Morocco went well for a time, but in 1921, just
when a new bank building at Casablanca – designed by Mr. H. G.
Holt, the Bank's architect – was getting ready for an official opening,
serious irregularities were discovered in the accounts of the branch.
The chief accountant was sent to investigate and a sum of over two
million French francs had to be provided to cover the losses. This
cost the Bank something like £30,000.

Around the same time the Bank's New York agent reported a
heavy loss resulting from 'certain exchange transactions'. It was found
that these deals had been unauthorised and a series of legal actions
followed. The board decided that it could not really control an
independent agency in New York and in 1922 asked the Standard
Bank of South Africa to take over its agency business there. This
was done.

The losses suffered in Egypt, Morocco and New York at the same
time, and at a moment when the post-war boom had turned into
depression, brought the Bank's expansion plans to an abrupt halt.
Once again its attention had to be concentrated on West Africa.

THE POST-WAR RECESSION

It was not long before West Africa itself was hit by a slump. 'The
lands in which we do our business' said Lord Selborne in his usual
stately style 'share the vicissitudes of the old world and not the wealth
of the new world.'

Since the end of the war, in the two years of prosperity, the Bank
had engaged a considerable new staff, built and improved a number
of premises, and opened new branches. Its affairs seemed to be in

good shape. Deposits had risen from £4,700,000 in 1918 to £6,500,000 in 1919 and £11,800,000 in 1920. In the same period the amount of bills of exchange handled (a good measure of trade conditions) had grown from £3,600,000 to almost £10,000,000. In more general terms, the amount of currency circulating in the area of the West African Currency Board had increased from £4,400,000 at mid-1918 to £13,600,000 two years later.

In April 1920 world prices for West Africa's chief commodities collapsed. The change was sudden and unexpected; many thought it would be temporary. The great Niger Company, which had just been acquired by Lever Brothers for a sum of £8,000,000 – a sum based on the booming business of the previous year – decided to support the produce markets by buying at unchanged prices and laying in stocks for recovery. Prices did not revive and in a few months the company found itself with huge produce stocks and little or no cash. Lever Brothers itself was gravely embarrassed and had to postpone for some years a scheme for merging the Niger Company with the African and Eastern Trade Corporation, a group of four large trading houses formed in 1919 by the African Association, Miller Brothers (of Liverpool) Ltd., F. and A. Swanzy, and Millers Ltd. The two Miller companies represented the original Miller brothers, Alexander and George. They had been associated with the Swanzy interests since 1903, so that all three were regarded as 'the Miller group'.

The accounts of the BBWA quickly reflected the decline in trade. Between the year to March 1920 and that to March 1923 deposits, bills of exchange, and the rate of dividend were all halved. The Currency Board's money circulation, too, dropped by almost half within two years. In the course of 1921 some of the Bank's customers fell into serious financial difficulties. An important tin mining company was the first to default. Next a substantial trading firm asked for a meeting with its creditors. In 1922 the Bank had to be represented at more and more creditors' meetings, and there were one or two ominous bankruptcies.

The troubles of the Niger Company, too, made their impact on the Bank: in 1921 it asked the BBWA to agree to a deferred repayment of its debts over a period. Tough negotiations followed.

Several outstanding bills of £60,000 each drawn by the Niger Company were 'accepted' by Lever Brothers. They were in fact all paid within nine months. For future credits to the Niger Company or its subsidiaries the guarantee of Lever Brothers was to be a condition. Even so the Bank was not entirely reassured, as Levers themselves were having difficulty in raising finance for the Niger purchase. Some ill-feeling is suggested by the fact that Mr. C. B. Edgar, a director of the Bank, resigned from the board of the Niger Company. In the event the Bank did not lose any money over this matter, but it continued to keep a weather eye on the Niger Company whose fortunes did not fully recover before it was hit by the next slump in 1929 and forced to merge with its chief rival, the African and Eastern Trade Corporation.

The Bank's profit for the year to mid-1921 was nearly 30% down to £216,000, and in 1921-2 it dropped another 12% to £189,000, although the fall was not disclosed in the published profit figure. In June 1921 nearly £100,000 was set aside as a reserve against doubtful debts. In the following year another £325,000 was added to this contingency fund, and £320,000 was used to write off bad debts. A further £105,000 was provided in 1922 and at the end of that year the General Manager certified that all bad and doubtful debts were now covered by the funds set aside.

Around this time several changes took place in the Bank's senior staff. In 1920, no doubt in response to the problems of bad debts, W. H. Gaman, the chief accountant, was appointed to a new post of Chief Inspector, and his place was taken by W. J. Cook. In the same year the Secretary, J. R. Bingham, had to retire owing to ill-health, and G. B. Bennett became the new Secretary. Finally, at the chairman's suggestion, Roy Wilson was brought from Liverpool to be Assistant General Manager in London.

An effort was made in 1922 to cut costs. Four directors formed an Economy Committee and recommended various kinds of savings. Lord Selborne, in a handwritten letter, instructed the General Manager to report by March on steps taken to bring about these economies. His report seems to have satisfied the March meeting of directors. The savings were probably marginal, such as the closing down of the staff magazine.

The Currency Board, which had been repatriating the old sterling silver coins to England whenever possible since 1913, now found that it had a surplus even of its own special coinage, and it began to ship some of this to London for its bullion value. The Board had by 1920 accumulated a reserve fund of £9,000,000; in that year it distributed a first 'dividend' of £100,000 to the four Colonial Governments – Nigeria, Gold Coast, Sierra Leone and The Gambia – out of the interest from its reserve investments. In the following two years the dividend trebled and it went on increasing for some time after that.

While the financial difficulties of many European trading firms caused a great deal of concern to the Bank a large part of its business went on as usual. The purchase and shipment of the wide range of West African products had to be financed, though on a reduced scale, and imported merchandise needed credit while it spread through the huge country to the ultimate consumers. Relations with African Chiefs and traders were as important as ever. In July 1921 the Emir of Katsina, one of the Fulani rulers in Northern Nigeria, visited London and was entertained at the Head Office of the Bank. He was taken by Leslie Couper to see the Royal Mint, the Bank of England and the Mansion House, where he was received by the Lord Mayor. Such visits of prominent African personalities have always been a feature in the life of the BBWA.

By 1924 the worst of the slump was over, and business recovered gradually during the rest of the decade, though it did not again reach the boom levels of 1919–20. The Bank felt confident enough in July 1924 to open a new branch at Oshogbo, another in 1925 at Abonnema and a third in 1926 at Aba. In 1927–8 the dividend was partly restored from 5% to 6%.

For some reason now unknown a branch was opened at Gibraltar in the troubled year of 1923. It was not a good idea. The branch incurred small losses each year, and when an Inspector was sent in 1925 to see what the trouble was, he wrote: 'Our Bank appears to have a good name locally but the people are conservative and are slow to bring their accounts to us, preferring to deal with old friends.' The Anglo-Egyptian Bank was the 'old friend'; it was well established and had the Government account. It was decided to close the branch again in 1926, but as by that time Barclays (DCO) had taken over the Anglo-Egyptian Bank the closure was delayed until an agreement was reached under which the BBWA would not in future compete in Gibraltar while Barclays undertook to stay out of Bathurst.

Meanwhile at home the Bank lost its assistant general manager, Roy Wilson, when he was elected to a seat in Parliament.

BARCLAYS BANK INTERVENES

The BBWA was now allied with three of the five London Clearing Banks as well as with a leading British overseas bank. But the BBWA directors were not the only ones to look for this kind of reassurance. The Colonial Bank soon caught the same idea, and for much the same reasons. Once it was well established in West Africa it began to think of opportunities in other countries. As it had been operating in the West Indies for nearly a century it was accustomed to an international or at any rate an imperial outlook. During the post-war boom its directors keenly studied the possibilities of banking in Egypt and in South Africa.

Someone else in London was thinking on similar lines. Mr. Frederick Goodenough, chairman of Barclays Bank, another of the 'Big Five' London deposit banks, was intrigued by the idea of forming a bank which would link several parts of the British Empire together. He found that there were two good banks in financial straits: the Anglo-Egyptian Bank and the National Bank of South Africa. The Colonial Bank had made the same discovery and would have liked to take them over but did not have sufficient spare capital.

Barclays Bank had held some shares in the Colonial Bank for some years, and in 1919 it sold half its interest to the National Bank of South Africa (this was reported to the board of BBWA on December 12, 1919). Negotiations began between Barclays, Colonial, and the two other banks which resulted in 1925 in the formation of Barclays Bank (Dominion, Colonial and Overseas).

This was much more than the 'Treaty of Alliance' concluded earlier between BBWA and Lloyds. From the outset Barclays DCO was designed as a single integrated enterprise. It is true that at first the constituent overseas banks – Colonial Bank, Anglo-Egyptian Bank and National Bank of South Africa – were left largely in charge of their regional business, but the aim was clearly the creation of a unified international bank under the leadership of Barclays. Plans for expansion into other territories such as East Africa were already in the air. In practice the Colonial Bank, which was healthy and well managed, continued for several years to use its own name in West Africa; but an advertisement in 1926 was already headed 'Barclays Bank (Dominion, Colonial and Overseas) formerly the Colonial Bank'.

At the time of the 1925 merger, eight years after the Colonial Bank had arrived in West Africa, it was already a strong institution. It had nine branches in Nigeria, six in the Gold Coast, and one each in Sierra Leone, The Gambia, Togoland, Senegal and the Cameroons. In the four British territories it had by then obtained a share of official business and described itself as 'Bankers to the Government'. The name of Barclays gradually became dominant, and with the strong capital backing of the English senior partner the bank continued to expand. Before long it became the most powerful competitor the BBWA had yet had to face.

Chapter Nine

TRADERS – EUROPEAN AFRICAN, LEVANTINE

THE LEVER EMPIRE

THE European trading firms which had introduced a modern market economy into West Africa ran into financial difficulties during and after the First World War, and it took them many years to recover. In the process of reorganisation the name of William Hesketh Lever stands out. The son of a grocer in the cotton town of Bolton, he went early into soap-making and made it successful. He had advanced ideas on living and working conditions for workers as well as on manufacturing processes, marketing and advertising. In 1888 he and his brother James started the famous industrial estate of Port Sunlight where all workers were to have the best possible housing, welfare and amenities.

Palm oil was one of the main raw materials for soap-making, and the Levers soon took an interest in West Africa where it mainly came from. William Lever paid his first visit to West Africa in 1911; his wife went with him and died on their return. In the same year Lever Brothers signed an agreement with the King of the Belgians for the development of the palm forests in the Congo. This led to the introduction of a new kind of cultivated palm and the creation of very large plantations, with oil mills, soap factories and social amenities on the model of Port Sunlight. 'Leverville' was a great success.

In the British territories plantations were not allowed mainly because all land was owned by a family or a tribe, and it was decreed that land could never be alienated from the native owner. After independence plantations were soon introduced. Today one can see estates planted with teak, rubber, palms, bananas, oranges and other crops. Lever Brothers did manage to lease a large territory in Sierra Leone in 1912 to extract palm oil, but the quality of the local palm fruit was poor and the scheme was abandoned after large losses. In the main Levers worked by buying up existing trading firms with access to raw material supplies. The first of these was W. B. MacIver & Company Limited, purchased in 1910. During the next ten years a large number of other firms were taken over, including several in Bathurst, until in 1920 Lord Leverhulme, as he had become, bought the bulk of the ordinary shares of the Niger Company (as described in the previous chapter). He had already taken an interest in the second large combine, the African and Eastern Trade Corporation; and in 1921 he tried to bring it into his fold in order to form a single operating group which could dominate West African production and trade.

The slump of 1920 and the financial consequences for Levers of having bought the Niger Company at the wrong time and price foiled this scheme for the time being. The next step was to integrate the sixty-six separate companies which the Levers had gradually bought up without making any attempt to bring them under a single control. In 1923 Lord Leverhulme gave that task to the Niger Company, after strengthening its board. He asked Mr. E. Hyslop Bell, the general manager of the Colonial Bank, to become Chairman of the Niger Company and brought in as vice-chairman Mr. W. E. Snelling, a financial and taxation expert. Snelling in turn took on a young personal assistant called George Cole who was to become in turn head of the United Africa Company and of the Anglo-Dutch Unilever Company. He is now Lord Cole. It was not an easy task to eliminate overlapping among the constituent companies. Some of them had long traditions and strong personal leadership. It took a number of years to overcome these problems, and it might have taken even longer if business conditions had not become so harsh after 1929 that they favoured the largest possible concentration.

The same process was in fact going on during the twenties within the African and Eastern Trade Corporation, which was taking over one old-established firm after another. In 1929 the two large groups finally merged and jointly set up the United Africa Company, in which Lever Brothers gained an 80% shareholding. In a reconstruction of the UAC in 1939 Unilever (as it had then become) took over the balance of shares in African and Eastern and became its sole owner.

Relations between the trading companies and the Bank of British West Africa in those years were friendly but not as close as they would have been between bank and customer in England. To a large extent the trading firms did their own banking. The methods varied in the different regions, but the essence was that the firms gave credit to the African traders, particularly the women traders, and to the produce buyers. The lending risk was taken by them rather than by the Bank.

In the Gold Coast the usual practice was to give 'buying limits' to African traders. A woman trader might be granted the right to purchase merchandise up to a certain sum, sometimes a very large sum, as long as she made regular repayments out of her cash receipts. Usually she had to deposit some security such as gold, or, more often, strings of beads which most women wore round their waists. These had no great intrinsic value but the women would go to any lengths to pay their debts in order to retrieve the beads. In other cases the verbal or written guarantee of a Chief might be accepted as security. Or if a woman trader was content to start small and to pay in her daily cash-take very regularly, the local manager might steadily raise her buying limit without any collateral. (The writer talked to one lady in Accra, now said to be turning over something like £2,000,000 a year in her own store, who recalled starting with a corner of her sister's market stall and a £20 buying limit at G. B. Ollivant.)

In Nigeria the trading companies often gave credit to produce buyers without security. A large produce buyer might take with him into the bush many bags of cash, perhaps several thousand pounds, a big load of empty produce bags worth many hundreds of pounds, and a good deal of merchandise including salt. When he returned with the produce he would repay and buy more merchandise, perhaps leaving some surplus money on deposit with the company to build up a security for future trips. As the farmers increasingly demanded cash payment they would come themselves into the trading stores to spend what they had received for their produce. The companies sometimes lost money when a debtor disappeared but on the whole they did well.

The trading firms looked to the Bank above all for the supply of cash when and where they needed it. The bigger firms had their own strong-rooms in many places where the Bank had no branch, and in some of these they acted as agencies for the Bank. Many traders had to travel considerable distances to the nearest Bank branch to collect cash. The system by which cash needs in different places and seasons were estimated in advance and agreed between the Bank and the traders has already been described. The Bank supplied credit in the form of advances or overdraft facilities to the trading companies, though it was of course also granting credit directly to African traders and produce buyers.

The Niger Company had always been at the centre of the opposition to the monopoly enjoyed for many years both by Elder Dempster in shipping and by the BBWA in banking. The Niger Company and the African and Eastern group now chartered their own vessels to carry a part of their trade, and John Holt & Company still had two steamers running to avoid dependence on Elder Dempster. Eventually an agreement was made by which the main shipping field was left to Elder Dempster while both the Niger Company and African and Eastern were left with four vessels each. But that was not the end of the conflict.

In banking the traders had fought hard, and often as a group, to break the early monopoly of the BBWA. They had set up the Bank of Nigeria in 1899, and when that was taken over by the BBWA in 1912 many traders remained suspicious. The arrival of the Colonial Bank in 1916 was welcomed by the Niger Company and a number of other firms. This may explain how the general manager of the Colonial Bank later became Chairman of the Niger Company and presided over the integration of the vast Lever interests.

THE WOMEN TRADERS

Women had always played a large part in the commerce of West Africa. They were engaged mainly in the domestic trade, dominating the great markets which abounded throughout the region. They were particularly powerful in the Gold Coast, where they formed associations which monopolised certain trades. In the chief market of Accra the women would hold daily meetings to fix prices and regulate supplies. But their position was strong also in others parts of West Africa.

As the women traders were so largely concerned with the wholesale and retail trade in miscellaneous products they took to the introduction of money quite early. But on the whole they never got used to the idea of banking. To this day they still dislike putting their sales and profit figures on paper, and the idea of revealing the amount of their savings to a bank clerk who will put figures into a book that might one day be seen by a tax inspector is abhorrent to most of them. Instead, they carry a mass of figures safely and clearly in their heads.

Their need for credit is normally satisfied by the trading firms, and their savings are commonly invested in property, particularly dwelling houses from which they draw rent. Some of the richer women traders are said to own considerable property in England and other countries.

In Sierra Leone there are few women who trade on a large scale. One exception, some years ago, was the famous Princess James who started in Freetown but moved to Koidu just in time for the big diamond rush. She sold mainly textiles including the 'oatmeal prints' popular among Sierra Leone women; but her trade spread to general merchandise as well. She had a buying limit of £5,000 a month at the United Africa Company stores and is still remembered both as a good customer and a splendid personality.

At times the Bank inadvertently strayed into a field of business which the women considered their own preserve. Thus it was once engaged in a benevolent scheme for financing farmers in the growing of maize. All went well until the crop came to be sold. The women traders had a corner in the sale of maize and would not let anyone else bring it to market. They made their own buying and selling prices. The cartel could not be broken and the Bank hastily withdrew in confusion from the whole scheme.

An acute description of women traders in the Gold Coast twenty years ago is given by Elspeth Huxley in her book *Four Guineas*:*

Four Guineas by Elspeth Huxley published by Chatto and Windus Ltd, 1954.

The markets of Accra are remarkable for the size, vigour and astuteness of the women traders, who hold a position unique, I should think, in Africa. Strong as buffalos, large-boned, strident, gaily dressed in patterned clothes with little jackets, either plump and soft fleshed as marshmallows or else lean as old leather, their faces look imperious and uncompliant, like the faces of cattle dealers in English country towns.

Their God is money and they adore him constantly.... They are down at their stalls by six in the morning and stay there till dark.... Somewhere a husband is working, idling or trading too. These husbands are, in a sense, adjuncts, like male spiders; it is the market women who make the money and call the tune....

Nearly all the mammies are illiterate and carry in their heads intricate multiple sums. The trading firms have no security beyond the woman's reputation: often they do not even know her address. Yet it is the rarest thing in the world for one of them to default.

Apart from trading in the market stalls, and, more recently, running their own stores as the towns grow larger, women also take an important part in buying produce in the bush and the villages. This practice goes back at least to the early years of this century.

The following description (in the BBWA staff magazine for 1913) moves us to Nigeria, to the market of Onitsha, one of the greatest in Africa. When the first bank branch was opened there by the Bank of Nigeria, later taken over by the BBWA, 'the whole of the trade was virtually in the hands of the Niger Company. The Onitsha traders, principally the women, used to go into the interior for a few days and barter there for palm oil and kernels.'

By 1913 there had been much change. 'Today there are at least a dozen influential and fairly wealthy native traders. Onitsha enjoys the control over a vast and wealthy hinterland. One of the Bank's best African clients, in 1910, had the small paper bags in which he sold sugar, tea, etc. marked "grocer". Today he is known as a "trader"; he has two branches in the interior and two factories on the Onitsha waterside.'

However the women traders all over West Africa are liable to lose their tempers when they feel that some government or other authority tries to impose upon them. 'Mammie riots' are familiar in most of the bigger market towns. The most spectacular confrontation took pace in Southern Nigeria in December 1929. It became

known as the 'women's war'. The Government had taken a population census and a rumour got around that the next step was to impose
a tax on the profits of the market women. At Aba crowds of women
broke into the factories, looted the stores and got away with the
goods by land and river. Canoes loaded with loot were seen
going down river past Opobo. The women, having met with
no serious resistance, had become convinced that the authorities
would not allow police or troops to fire on them. The riots soon
spread over a wide area and lasted for several weeks. In several
places troops were called in, but they were not always able to restore
order.

Some of the incidents are described in the *History of the Royal West
African Frontier Force*. In one place on the Cross River above Calabar
an officer was thrown into the river by a woman ring-leader. At
Okpala a platoon formed a square with bayonets fixed – but though
the square held, the women went on looting. The clash at Aba is
recorded by one who was present:

The District Officer held a palaver with the leaders of a large crowd of
women outside his office. He tried to explain to them that the Government had no intention of levying a tax on women. The leaders – apparently to gain time for more contingents to arrive – asked for this statement to be put in writing, which he did. Then they asked for five typed
copies and went on making frivolous demands.

As time went on the mob increased, grew more excited and pressed
slowly forward. The women, of all ages, were wearing fronds of palm
leaves, emblem of solidarity and warlike intent. They were stripped to
the waist and wearing only loin-cloths. Many had their faces daubed with
red or white clay, also a sign of war. They were armed with stout sticks,
heavy pestles used for pounding corn, and, in some cases, with matchets.

At times the women chanted an Ibo war song: 'What is the smell?
Death is the smell'. They also danced and waved their weapons.

All this took place while the palaver dragged on. At last becoming
more and more excited, the mob reached a state of frenzy. Its numbers
continued to increase, and canoe loads of women were awaiting events on
the river behind the District Officer's office and government buildings.

A platoon of troops had arrived early that morning after an all night
journey. Finally the mob began to surge forward. The officer ordered the
right half of his platoon to fire a volley. The mob still moved on and
some men and women armed with matchets tried to rush the post office.

The soldiers fired two more volleys. After that the crowd broke and scattered, leaving twenty-one dead and nineteen wounded.*

A Commission of Enquiry later reported that the firing at the time it took place 'was absolutely necessary to protect life and property. . . . We have no doubt that had the troops been overpowered, the government offices would have been destroyed and the factories looted. The latter held large stores of gin and other intoxicants.'

AN IMPORTANT AFRICAN CUSTOMER

As a general rule the Bank of British West Africa was involved in the financing of trade in an indirect way – by granting credit to the European companies which in turn financed the African traders, from the large produce buyer to the market women. But there were many exceptions to this rule. A large number of Africans made deposits in the Bank and used its current account facilities – and in some branches this phrase might well mean the sudden arrival of a big customer with a hundred or so bags of shillings loaded on the heads of carriers, on donkeys or in a van. All this money had to be carefully counted by the cashier, all suspicious-looking coins put through the counting machine where forgeries usually showed up, after which the coins were bagged, labelled and weighed before being lodged in the strong-room.

Within days or weeks the customer would probably reappear to ask for his cash in order to start on his next buying journey. Sometimes there was trouble if the man claimed that he had paid in bright new coins and would not be fobbed off by used coins in return. Or he wished to deal only with the branch manager whom he knew, but who might have been transferred elsewhere. There were hundreds of such problems, and the Bank became adept at dealing with them.

The screen of the trading companies was a comfortable safety net which the Bank was content to use for many years. Before the Second World War at any rate it did not often take the initiative to get new African customers. There is a good deal of evidence that this

*History of the Royal West African Frontier Force, by Col. A. Haywood and Brig. Clarke, 1964.

Freetown Branch in 1909

(*Top*) Bank Manager's
residence at Calabar,
Nigeria, 1961

(*Bottom*) Residence of
District Manager for Nigeria,
1949 (demolished for re-
building, 1959)

(*Opposite*) Front entrance,
Tangier Branch, which was
sold to Banque Marocaine du
Commerce Extérieur in 1960

Onitsha Branch, 1921, with
Manager's quarters above

attitude caused some irritation among colonial officers, who were impatient to see the country more fully developed.

At Kano, in Northern Nigeria, the Resident (the senior Government officer) in 1932 was a Mr. Lindsell. He decided to do something in support of the African traders in his area. He called in the agent of the Elder Dempster Lines and made a proposal to him which he was to pass on to his Head Office. The agent wrote to his chief in Lagos and underlined the importance of the matter by asking that it should be treated as extremely confidential. 'I respectfully submit that it is not safe to allow a sight of the letter to any of your African staff.' This is part of the letter:

On the 21st inst. the writer was called to the Residency and was in consultation with the Resident all forenoon.

It would appear that the government are alarmed at the stranglehold that the Pool and the United Africa Company especially are obtaining on the groundnut trade in all out-stations, and it is felt that if some immediate action is not taken, the U.A.C. will soon make it almost impossible for outsiders to operate at all. That position, you will agree, would be extremely harmful to this country and of course to this Company. The policy of the government therefore is to assist the stronger African buyers to survive; and they feel that we may be able to assist to some extent.

It has been agreed that the only African with sufficient capital to stand up to the U.A.C. is Alasan Dantata.

We understand that on shipping credits being opened the Bank of British West Africa would offer Alasan Dantata the fullest possible facilities which would enable him to buy a very considerable tonnage, only limited by the extent of his credits and the shipping available. Mr. Roker, their local manager, is communicating with Mr. Becker [W. F. Becker, Nigeria District Manager] by the next mail with a view to laying the whole position before him. Mr. Becker, of course, knows Dantata and is familiar to a great extent also with the position here at the moment.

We have authentic information that on a conservative estimate Dantata is worth £40,000, and that he usually commences each season with £20,000 liquid cash of his own. From this you will see that he has easily sufficient liquid funds to purchase some four thousand tons of groundnuts at present prices without calling on the Bank for assistance. When operating, however, such an outlay would never be necessary, as, of course, the Bank would advance against railings.

It is suggested that our Head Office approach the Bank of British West Africa London office on the matter if they wish to assure themselves that our information is correct.

I

The whole matter has been discussed with Dantata, who has had a consultation also with the Resident; and he seems very keen to hurry forward the negotiations to enable him to commence shipping. He could easily buy at least twenty thousand tons before the end of the current season as he has control over large areas of farms and innumerable smaller buyers.

We have been asked to ask you to kindly treat this matter as extremely private as it is of the utmost importance that the whole matter is kept from the U.A.C.*

In his effort to break into the UAC fortress the Resident at Kano approached the agent of Elder Dempster Lines because he realised, or had been told, that the first step would have to be the opening of 'shipping credits' at the port of export, based not just on the usual shipping documents but on a purchase contract from a broker or buyer in England. He seems to have decided that such credits were more easily arranged by the shipping company than by the Bank.

Alasan Dantata had come to Kano from the Gold Coast where his mother had been a market trader. He came from a trading family. His father had been engaged in the 'kola nut trek' on which traders from the Kano area and other northern parts had traditionally gone to the Gold Coast where the best kola nuts were then grown. West African kola nuts (a popular stimulant throughout the Islamic world) had been an important export product in the cross-Sahara trade to North Africa and the Middle East for more than a thousand years. The traders would collect their supplies of nuts in return for merchandise that was either manufactured in the north, such as Kano cloth, or had been imported across the desert. Such a tour might easily take two years.

Alasan Dantata settled in Kano in the 1920s and became a leading groundnut buyer. He also sold textiles, salt, sugar and other goods needed by the farmers. For some time he was financed by the United Africa Company. One of their former managers recalls that Dantata might well be handed a cheque for £100,000 as an advance before going out to buy produce, as well as perhaps a thousand jute bags. With the cheque he would knock at the door of the BBWA manager at dawn and ask for a thousand bags of shillings. 'Dantata first came in by camel, then by donkey and later by lorry.' His son,

---

* I am grateful to the UAC for allowing me to quote this letter.

Alhadji Sanusi Dantata, recalls that his father would load the money bags and the merchandise on a donkey train while he himself rode a horse from which he could keep a sharp eye on everything. The same cavalcade would then return to Kano with the groundnuts. The first three-ton lorry was later bought for the eldest son to drive.

Today Alhadji Sanusi Dantata is the head of a greatly enlarged family business which has spread into various branches of manufacturing. He is also a director of the Standard Bank in Nigeria.

OTHER TRADING FIRMS

Some of the other European traders with whom the Bank had dealings in West Africa at various times were both large and old-established. Many of the oldest firms merged into larger groups or disappeared. Nine of them had combined in 1889 in the African Association. Later on the pressure of competition compelled many others to sell out to Lever Brothers. Thus in 1917 Levers bought John Walkden & Company which was founded in 1865 and had been very successful at times. In the following year they bought an even older firm, Richard & William King, founded in 1695 by John King of Bristol and taken into the West Africa trade before 1800 by his grandson Thomas King, who took sides actively against the slave trade and joined the campaign of Lord Wilberforce. His sons Richard and William then took over the West African business and concentrated mainly on the Oil Rivers, the Cameroons and the Ivory Coast. When the firm was taken over by Lever Brothers in 1918 its head was Mervyn King, the son of William, who had already been a director of the African Association and of the Royal Niger Company for many years.

F. & A. Swanzy had been trading with West Africa at least since the eighteenth century, chiefly on the Gold Coast. In 1904 the house ran into financial difficulties and turned to a competitor, Miller Brothers, for help. The two firms then cooperated closely but remained independent until 1919 when they were among the four principal companies that formed the African and Eastern Trade Corporation. Many other trading firms were extinguished when the United Africa Company was formed in 1929, and still more in the following ten years as the UAC absorbed African and Eastern and others. Some, however, have continued to trade under their own names within the UAC fold.

Prominent among the latter is G. B. Ollivant & Company. This firm was established in Manchester in 1858, first to export textiles to West Africa. It prospered and spread into two-way trading until it lost some of its independence in a financial crisis in 1907. For many years after that GBO relied on finance from Elder Dempster & Co. but when the shipping group itself met serious difficulties in 1930 it called in the loans and the chairman of GBO, Leonard Chadwick, turned to the UAC for help. This led in 1933 to a partial takeover by UAC but Leonard Chadwick, and later his son, continued as heads of GBO. A part of the capital was then held by the Bibby Line and was finally bought by UAC in 1946. But to this day G. B. Ollivant is a household name in West African commerce.

Among the independent survivors was John Holt & Company whose intense struggles with Elder Dempster and the early BBWA have been recounted. John Holt, the founder, never tolerated an association or partnership for long, and a spirit of fierce individualism was preserved in the firm, both in shipping and in trading.

Three trading firms which have always been good customers of the Bank and still carry on a prosperous activity in West Africa should now be mentioned. Paterson Zochonis & Company – known throughout West Africa as PZ – was formed in Manchester in 1884. It exported textiles and other merchandise to the Coast and soon developed a return trade of shipping West African produce. For many years it was present only in Nigeria, Sierra Leone, Liberia, French Guinea and the Cameroons, but later it spread into the Gold Coast as well. Today it has an issued capital of over £2 million and owns separate companies in the various West African states. The main business is that of merchants with over a hundred stores throughout the region. In addition the group manufactures soap and cosmetic products, assembles sewing machines, etc. The Zochonis family remains in control and the chairman is Mr. J. B. Zochonis. Also on the board are two members of the Loupos family and one of the Spoudeas family, both of which have long been associated with Paterson Zochonis.

For many years two French trading companies have played an important part in the business of West Africa. The Compagnie Française de l'Afrique Occidentale, known on the Coast as 'The French Company', was started in Marseilles in 1887, taking over from the older Compagnie du Sénégal. It soon opened up in Liverpool, then the centre of the British West African trade. Its activities spread throughout British and French West Africa and into Central Africa. In time it established itself in London and Manchester. From a base of general commerce it went into such branches as vehicle distribution in West Africa (and in Britain) and textile manufacture. In France itself it now owns important supermarkets and shopping centres. The Head Office remains in Marseilles and the latest balance sheet total has been just over Fr. frs. 100,000,000.

The second French trading group on the Coast is the Société Commerciale de l'Ouest Africain, which has its Head Office in Paris and its chief British office in Manchester. It was established by a Swiss–French group in 1907 and gradually spread its activities very widely across West, Central and East Africa, the Far East, North Africa and North America. The SCOA are dealers in many commodities, run shops and supermarkets and have taken their share in the more recent development of manufacturing industry in Africa.

The two French groups have always maintained French senior managements even in British West Africa, but they have been good customers of the BBWA and have remained so after a French bank was established in Nigeria.

TRADERS FROM THE LEVANT

Immigrants from the Levant, particularly Syrians and Lebanese, began to settle in West Africa in the last decade of the nineteenth century. This was part of an exodus from the troubled Middle East which went mainly to the United States and South America. They brought varied Eastern merchandise with them to start trading. Some of them were at first known as 'corals' because they arrived with stocks of coral beads for which they found a ready market. As they were prepared to work hard and live on little – many left their wives and children at home until they had saved enough to provide for them on the Coast – they soon prospered. By 1929 (according to A. G. Hopkins) there were just over 3,000 Levantines in French West Africa and a slightly smaller number in the British colonies.

The people of the Levant have been known as good traders ever since the Phoenicians sailed into the Atlantic. Some of the immigrants into West Africa had already done business in South America and landed on the West Coast on their way home. In some fields they soon out-traded the Africans. This naturally caused some resentment, and the BBWA was often accused of giving preference to Syrian and Lebanese traders over African ones. The charge needs some explanation.

Most of the Levantines remained small traders, shopkeepers and artisans, but a fair number built up substantial businesses. A few of these will be mentioned in this section. Some became customers of the Bank – or later of other banks – and others preferred to look after their own money affairs in strict secrecy. The Bank, as it gained experience with this community, became ready to finance them because they were reliable borrowers. They were accustomed to money dealings, kept books and took bank credit seriously. Quite often when one of them was in difficulties a consortium of his relatives and friends would take over his business and pay off the bank debt.

By contrast, the Bank often found it difficult to obtain proper security on which to make loans to African businessmen. They did not, as a rule, stick closely to the terms on which bank credit was granted. It was a frequent experience that the Bank lent working capital to an African for his business, but the owner would divert the cash into buying or building houses as a private investment. The Bank would then find, when it came to repaying the debt, that the business had been 'milked' of capital and the loan could not be recovered.

Advances were, of course, always made to Africans on the same terms as to others when the security was produce or merchandise in store, on train or ship. There was no argument about that. When it came to lending on more general security a further difficulty was that in most parts of West Africa the property laws were such that the real ownership of land or buildings was hard to establish. For that reason mortgages were not considered suitable backing for finance, though they were, in fact, often accepted despite the legal insecurity.

In Sierra Leone, where the Eastern traders had their earliest successes, another factor came to their aid. The national passion of the local population was (and is) education. Any man who made a success with a grocery or ironmonger's store wanted above all to send his son to high school and university, and if possible to England to become a lawyer. Many African businesses wilted for this reason. Even when a father's plans were more modest he still hoped that his children would become clerks, teachers or ministers rather than take over the shop.

Many of the Levantines prospered through this peculiar lack of African competition; but they also got on well in the other territories where the background was different. Some of them are recalled in the following notes, based on memories of former bank officials.

Yusuf Bohsali came to Nigeria early in the century and started in textiles. His interest gradually shifted to property; in time he owned a great deal of property in Lagos, and when he died, in the 1950s, he was reported to be worth well over £1 million.

Mohammed El Khalil came into prominence in Nigeria during the Second World War and built up one of the largest fleets of lorries in Western Nigeria. His firm, El Khalil Transport Ltd., carried most of the BBWA's cash over a large area, as far as Oshogbo in the north and just short of Onitsha to the east. He did not cross the Niger to Onitsha, which was supplied from Port Harcourt. His lorries also carried large quantities of imported goods to Western Nigeria and brought produce back to Lagos for export.

Arif Barakat, too, made his start in textiles but soon saw the possibilities of the cinema and built up a chain of open-air cinemas in and around Lagos, Abeokuta and Ibadan. He also took several travelling shows into the bush areas.

Then there was K. Maroun, who started a pig farm in Nigeria and made it a success. He sold pork and bacon both locally and for export to Europe. He ran a cold store in Kano, where he also acted as a groundnut buyer and processed some groundnuts into oil. An official of the Bank left to join Maroun and handle his accounts. Oddly enough the second largest contingent of Syrian and Lebanese traders was in Kano, where they prospered despite the keen commercial ability of the local Hausas. In most places Syrians and Lebanese lived in clearly separated areas.

Some of them are well remembered for their energy and enterprise. Michael Elias, who in his old age was regarded as the grand old man of all Lebanese and Syrians in Nigeria, is reputed to have *walked* from Lagos to Kano (where his home was) about 1926, financing himself as he went by selling trade goods. One version is that he rode, but as the road passes the tsetse-fly belt that seems unlikely.

Another 'Levantine', Georges Calil, was said to have been taken out of Smyrna by his mother on the roof of a train (and was therefore probably a Greek). He was partly educated in Paris and came to Nigeria to buy and ship groundnuts for Gueydan Frères of Marseilles, a firm which failed in 1934. Calil later bought groundnuts for the Marketing Board. He retired to London where he died about 1965. Another Kano man regarded as a Syrian who was in fact from Tripoli and carried an Italian passport was Saul Raccah, who became the biggest non-European buyer of groundnuts in the north. He was believed to speak seven languages, and he employed a European manager to keep his books and make his returns.

Moving westwards to Ghana, the majority of Eastern traders there were Lebanese rather than Syrians. Some specialised in such things as Belgian window glass, motor-car distribution and maintenance (R. S. Malek in Accra was agent for Jaguar and Renault and had extensive workshops), road transport for passengers and freight, tailoring, or the operation of saw mills. There were provision merchants, dealers in imported beer and whisky, proprietors of nightclubs and restaurants. Some were professional men: W. W. Saleeby was a dental surgeon who qualified in the USA and practised in Liberia before settling in Ghana; later he also obtained a UK degree.

In the late 1930s, during the 'strike' of the cocoa producers in the Gold Coast, there emerged the significant figure of A. G. Leventis, a Greek native of Cyprus. He was employed by G. B. Ollivant as a local manager and fell out with his superior, Mr. Frank Samuel, one of the three joint managing directors of the United Africa Company. Leventis started his own business, buying and shipping cocoa, importing consumer goods and later engineering products. When war broke out and an official control of both export and import trade was set up which favoured the larger European companies, Leventis launched a public campaign against this aspect of Government policy. It became an historic struggle between him and the UAC. Rumours appeared that he had bribed officials to obtain import licences. A judicial enquiry was set up into the allegations and found that there was some truth in them. Leventis alleged that the tribunal had been prejudiced; and he made his point very publicly by briefing day after day the editor of the Accra evening newspaper whose name was Dr. Kwame Nkrumah. Nothing lifted Nkrumah's heart more easily than a broadside against the big European companies. The campaign succeeded and a second tribunal quashed the original findings and exonerated Leventis. Not unnaturally his relations with the first independent Government of Ghana were cordial. Today A. G. Leventis & Co. has several separate limited companies in West Africa running department stores and shops and acting as agents for engineering products such as vacuum cleaners, air-conditioners, radio and television sets, typewriters and refrigerators.

In Nigeria another Greek businessman, John Mandilas, achieved considerable success. In partnership with a fellow countryman he built up an important trading and agency firm. He then set out on his own and his company, Mandilas Limited, Lagos, now has a capital of over £4 million. It has the agency for Volkswagen cars and Carrier air-conditioners, among others. Mr. Mandilas himself became a Nigerian national and was thus not affected by the indigenisation decrees. In 1974 the Managing Director of Standard Bank Nigeria Limited, C. R. Harding, left the bank's service and became Managing Director of the Mandilas company.

In Sierra Leone several Lebanese families achieved business success. The leading firm was J. Milhem & Sons, started by two brothers and steadily extending over many activities. Other members of the family built up separate businesses, and one nephew, Edmond

Moukarzel, gained control of the original firm when the two brothers came near retirement. Moukarzel introduced a car agency and went into building as well; when he himself retired from Sierra Leone he was a rich man and had his two sons accepted for an eminent English public school. Most of the Eastern traders were of course of much smaller stature and made a modest living chiefly in general trading, especially in textiles.

Wherever a new way of making money emerged, the Levantines would quickly try their hand. An interesting case was the discovery in 1930 of diamonds in Sierra Leone – which is more fully described in another context. Almost at once a group of Lebanese took the lead in purchasing stones found 'privately' and disposing of them through an international family network. That was before mining licences were introduced, and long before the Government purchasing and exporting monopoly was set up. But with each step in official regulation they adapted themselves smoothly: in Koidu, now one of the largest diamond centres, I met a Lebanese dealer who held both a mining and a trading licence from the Sierra Leone Government, and each was numbered 001. He had been first in the field and was so expert in valuing the rough stones brought in by African diggers that he enjoyed popular trust. A dealer like this might well pay £5,000 or more to an African for a single stone, and he will have to walk to the bank to get the cash. Meanwhile his house will be guarded by several heavily armed brothers and cousins.

Indians came into West Africa more recently, particularly after the partition of India in 1948 which had created a large number of refugees, among whom the energetic and commercially gifted Sikhs and Sindhis were prominent. The two most important Indian firms in recent years have been K. Chelleram & Sons, general merchants, dealers in textiles and owners of supermarkets and other stores. Chellerams now have separate limited companies in Nigeria, Ghana, Sierra Leone, The Gambia, Hamburg and London. Their operations are almost world-wide. A similar concern is J. T. Chanrai which is well established throughout West Africa, mainly in trade but also in certain manufacturing activities.

At first the coming of independent African states strengthened the position of the Levantines. The new rulers, anxious to free themselves from British tutelage, often turned to Eastern advisers. Some of these attained important positions for a time, but that phase did not last long. Popular resentment against the obvious commercial success of the Eastern communities had been growing for some time. Although it did not take the violent expression that has recently been seen in East Africa there have been harsh Government measures to restrict the scope of this minority. It started in Ghana in 1967 when certain areas of economic activity were declared reserved for Ghanaian nationals. These included retail trade where the volume of annual sales was below a set figure, wholesale trade on a similar formula, all taxi services and other transport industries which employed less than thirty persons. Processing and extractive manufacturing industries were added to the list. After two years it was decreed that no expatriate would be permitted to work in reserved trades. For the larger businesses not barred to foreigners the 1967 decree laid down that substantial Ghanaian participation was required. At the same time the Government withdrew a concession made in 1963 which allowed Lebanese nationals born in the country before independence to apply for permission to remain in Ghana.

Since then further restrictions have been imposed at various times on all non-nationals carrying on business in Ghana. This affected many Nigerians as much as Lebanese, Syrians and Indians – and of course Europeans.

In Nigeria it was not until March 1, 1972, that a decree was passed ruling that twenty-two kinds of enterprise – including road haulage, retail trade, advertising and broadcasting – would be reserved exclusively for Nigerians from March 1974. Thirty-two other types of enterprise were barred to non-nationals except where the paid-up capital or turnover was above a fairly high figure. A Nigerian Enterprise Promotion Board was set up to implement the decree and heavy penalties were threatened against Nigerians 'fronting' for expatriate owners. The scale of the changes envisaged may be gathered from a statement made by the Lebanese ambassador in Lagos that some 350 firms in Nigeria were owned by Lebanese nationals and many of those regarded Nigeria as their permanent home.

But these events take us well beyond the life-span of the Bank of British West Africa.

Chapter Ten

LIFE ON THE COAST

FIRST WIVES ARRIVE

LIVING conditions for Europeans in West Africa changed enormously during the first four or five decades in the history of the Bank. Before the turn of the century there were only a few centres like Lagos, Accra and Freetown and perhaps Sekondi where a young bank clerk or junior manager could even attempt to lead something like a European style of life. The journey out might take three or four weeks, after calls at several ports. The terrors of the landing by surf boat have been described. Most men lived in single rooms above the bank premises, or in community 'chummeries', with one common room for eating and relaxation.

The initial pay was barely enough for a bachelor to live on. The 'kit allowance' granted for the first tour was usually spent on clothing of doubtful value which was recommended at home to all young Britons moving to a tropical country; heavy khaki shirts and drill suits, woollen underpants ('of undyed wool'), a 'cholera belt', stiff army boots, a sun topee and a few other items that made life more uncomfortable than it needed to be. The 'furnished accommodation' promised consisted normally of a bare room with a table, a hard wooden bedstead, two chairs and a washstand. All that most tenants added was a batch of glasses. There was very little medical knowledge about local diseases, and the 'free medical care' consisted mainly of a supply of quinine. Sanitation was primitive and water was drunk – if at all – only after boiling and filtering. In the larger towns there was at least some social life among the men of different firms or services: golf, tennis, cricket, shooting and fishing, and in the evening card games. At weekends there was much heavy drinking and eating at parties which often lasted well into the next morning. No less an authority than Sir Alan Burns in his *History of Nigeria* testifies that it was the 'almost universal' custom for white men to live with African mistresses.

Outside the main towns, as the Bank extended into the hinterland, opportunities for social life were much more restricted. There might be only a handful of Europeans in the place and unless a man had some hobby like bird-watching or sketching he would find it hard to fill in his free time, and would often overwork just to occupy himself. Fortunately in the north, above the tsetse fly belt, there were horses. One could ride to explore the country, and racing was quickly organised with the enthusiastic support of the Africans. Polo was a popular sport among those who could afford it. There was of course horseracing in Lagos as well, and in a few other places south of the tsetse zone. In 1921 the Bank presented a challenge cup to the Lagos Race Committee to mark its keen interest in the sport.

There was a world of difference between the life of a senior manager, who in some places might arrive at the bank in a hammock carried on poles by four men, and the general run of staff who could at best afford a bicycle. The hammock was fairly common among well-to-do Africans as well as Europeans until 1918 or so, and some survived into the 1930s. Less luxuriously they went by sedan-chair, or in a three-wheeled cart pushed by one man, with the passenger steering – or the still cheaper rickshaw.

In another section of the European community army officers lived generally in 'bush houses' built of mud, with grass roofs and matting doors and window coverings. The visit of the Prince of Wales in 1925 led to the construction of the first roomy and airy officers' messes and even a squash court or two.

Conditions were much easier by the time of the First World War. While such things as refrigerators and electric fans, let alone water closets and air-conditioning were still in the distant future, the first reasonably comfortable staff bungalows were being built in the larger towns. With the arrival of quinine and the gradual adaptation of living habits to local conditions diseases no longer claimed so many victims. From 1910 wives were beginning to join their husbands.

Five years later a Mrs. Frederick Willing, the wife of a BBWA manager at Sekondi, and one of the first Bank wives to go to West Africa, wrote in the staff magazine about her experiences:

I am a great advocate of every man having his wife out when it is at all possible. People who have never been out can hardly realise the difference a woman can make in every way. Apart from the companionship which in itself is invaluable she can do so much to make the bungalow, however small it may be, into a home. She is always there to keep an eye on the native servants, see the food is good, water boiled and filtered, and to relieve the husband of all the other housekeeping worries. Naturally he does far better work for his employers when he is happy and contented, and is far more likely to keep fit and well. One cannot blame the men who take to drink, cards, etc., night after night merely for the sake of something to do; not that they really like it, but what is there to attract a man back to a lonely, dimly-lit bungalow and an unappetising dinner?

More and more women are now coming out every year. Of course suitable quarters is the great difficulty, but this is gradually being overcome. 'Barracks' and double-bungalows are things of the past. Every man, no matter what his position, is having his own private bungalow, even though in some cases it may only consist of one room and a large verandah. . . . I do not think there is any reason why women should not keep just as fit as men, and even more so, for they have greater opportunity of taking care of themselves. Apart from the fact that I take quinine regularly, I attribute my good health on the Coast mainly to early hours. I am always ready for bed at 9 p.m. and like to get up about six o'clock, for I love the early mornings. . . .

A Mrs. R. G. S. Miller who went to Calabar in 1912 reported that the Europeans at that time were generally in good health, and she thought this was largely due to the active use of Calabar's fine nine-hole golf course. She also makes a point of the importance to Europeans of keeping pets – dogs, cats, parrots, monkeys, chickens or even a lizard.

The BBWA hesitated a long time before allowing wives to go to the Coast. No European employee was allowed to marry if his salary was below £150 a year, except with the special approval of the board. In the 1920s the 'marriage bar' was put up to £200 per annum. But permission was not often refused and the Bank could be persuaded to pay at least part of the passage money.

West Africa was not an easy place for a European woman to live in anything like European style. They had none of the elaborate amenities that had for many years been customary in India for both official and commercial European females. Some of the wives who went out to West Africa in the early years to outlying branches had to live in conditions that would have shocked their parents and friends in England. They were the pioneers, and they must have agitated successfully for improvements. In the middle thirties a letter from the wife of a bank manager in Nigeria describes how the first modern comforts had arrived:

Life for a woman in those days was very easy as regards household tasks. We had a steward and a small boy, a cook and a cook's mate. The cook did the shopping and had to produce a meal at any time of day or night for any number of people. Cold store food came by the boat once a fortnight; when this was finished we lived on the country. We also had a washman, a garden boy and several nightwatchmen. If I dropped anything there was always someone to pick it up. . . .

Early morning was the time to write and to receive little folder notes from other wives in the station, making arrangements for the day – games of tennis or golf, walking the dogs, shopping, morning coffee parties or bridge – and arrangements for dinner parties, curry lunches and so on. The wives had plenty of time in these small stations to do gardening, try new cookery dishes, make dresses, or learn to play new games, including even snooker.

Even in the larger towns you could not buy any women's clothes, and all had to be brought out from England. We could buy from the Syrian and Indian shops pure silk and cottons, and as many of us brought out belts, buttons and paper patterns we were able to make quite good dresses ourselves.

When shopping we wore a topee; it was unusual to walk anywhere except on the golf course or when exercising the dogs. Mosquito boots were worn in the evening by the careful ones but they did nothing to help a silk dress. When we went to the beach we always wore our topees when swimming in the sea. Only when 'calling' did the women wear normal hats and gloves.

Often we lived over the bank in the middle of the native town. Very few houses had a W.C. Bath water was heated in petrol tins on the wood stove in the kitchen. Refrigeration was unknown except for ice-plants in a few of the larger towns. There one would have an earth box to keep the ice.

For entertainments there were European clubs which were for many years reserved for officials and the most senior commercial people. Dinner was hardly ever before midnight. On Saturday night the dancing went on till daybreak. There were competitions for golf, cricket, tennis, snooker, shooting and, in Lagos, canoeing. . . .*

Another lady who went out to the Coast with her husband, a BBWA manager, in the 1930s recalls some of the less easy aspects of life. The heat and humidity were overwhelming at times; mosquitoes and other insects caused constant irritation. The effort to live at least partly on European types of food and drink needed much planning. There were snakes, lizards, and sometimes locusts to contend with. In the north the dry heat brought persistent dust, quite apart from the seasonal dust-laden mist of the harmattan. And there was the ban on having children in West Africa: if a woman got pregnant she was sent home. On the other hand most European women took a great interest in gardening, and many were able to grow a variety of marvellous flowers and flowering shrubs around their bungalows. 'My husband went off to Accra yesterday, and left me here to look after the garden', wrote one lady from Sekondi in 1915. 'Last night sixty-odd plants came down from Tarkwa Botanical Gardens for me, so I shall have plenty to keep me busy while he is away.'

Some of the complications of their lives were no doubt the result of the attempt to live in a European way, quite separated from the life of the Africans. This division of communities had hardly existed in the earlier colonial period. It came with the arrival of European women (who insisted on it mainly for health reasons) and persisted for thirty years.

Elderly people who remember what life was like in British West Africa fifty years ago always make a point of stressing that the really rough days of the 'Old Coaster' had passed by then. A few tales by even older men might sketch the contrast. A Mr. T. J. Allridge who went to Sierra Leone in the Colonial Service in 1871 recorded some of his memories in 1914. He first went out in a small sailing ship which took forty-nine days. In Freetown sickness and mortality among Europeans were still very heavy. 'No sanitation, no water supply, no nursing homes, hardly a doctor. No railway, no cable,

*From the files of Barclays Bank (DCO).

no parcel post, no opened-up hinterland, no great steamships, no German competition, no Syrian traders, no bank. . . .'

In a lecture given in 1897 Mr. James Pinnock, the founder of the well-known trading firm, said that it was generally believed among Europeans until the 1880s that the unhealthy mangrove swamps and rain forests of the coastal strip were typical of the country. It was only when the first steamers penetrated the creeks and rivers that a few survivors of diseases and fighting reached the beautiful, hilly country to the north of the forest belt.

When Mr. Pinnock first arrived in Lagos there was still much evidence of the slave trade which was only gradually suppressed. 'Lagos was the temporary home of Portuguese and Brazilian slave super-cargoes as well as a few traders. Human skulls were to be seen on tall bamboo sticks on the banks of the river . . . Cannibalism and human sacrifice were not confined to old Benin . . . Trade was by barter: some millions of gallons of fiery spirits were annually imported into Lagos, largely by French and German traders.' In exchange for gin, rum, tobacco, guns, powder, matchets, some cotton goods, silk handkerchiefs, etc., the traders at first got mainly palm oil, ebony and ivory. The range of exports from Lagos later widened to include rubber and gum copal, benniseed, chilli peppers, palm kernels, coffee, mahogany and many other things.

Mr. Pinnock added that he had spent many years on the Coast, travelled a great deal in the interior, and 'never had a single day's sickness'. That was not a typical experience. Even after the enormous progress made in medical knowledge and sanitation, the Bank had to record for 1923 five deaths from yellow fever, one of the victims being a Bank wife.

A JOURNEY TO VICTORIA

Quite apart from the domestic problems which caused so much worry to the wives men were frequently being posted to different places, and before the days of tarred motor roads and tough trucks such movements were not without hardship. As late as 1949 the Bank's manager in Freetown, Sierra Leone, had some business inland at Bo, an important administrative centre. He drove there in

K

the Bank's Wolseley car which was nearly shaken to pieces by the hard corrugation of the earth track. The general manager himself wrote hastily from London forbidding the manager to expose the precious car any further to such treatment. He was to go by train in future. He did; it took twelve hours each way.

At some earlier point we recorded casually that the Colonial Bank opened a branch at Victoria in the Cameroons. This is how the man sent to run that branch describes his journey. First he and his Liberian servant spent three and a half days in the train from Lagos. Then they went by lorry and river launch to the old port of Calabar for a night. From Calabar there was a weekly launch to Victoria. It was a flat-bottomed river craft mainly used for cargo but carrying some passengers on top of the hatch covering. The bank manager was the only European on board. He had taken his own chair and camp-bed, food and drink. The first twelve hours were through the creeks and not unpleasant. About midnight they came out into the open sea and the movement of the little barge became highly uncomfortable. It rained hard. For another eight hours every passenger was wet, seasick and miserable. So he arrived at Victoria to take charge of the bank.

A few months later the same man was transferred from Victoria to Freetown. That journey took a month by launch, lorry, train and ship!

FRAUDS, FORGERIES AND LOSSES

The history of any bank must include some experience of loss through carelessness, dishonesty, or robbery. The BBWA tried to minimise such incidents by making managers and cashiers personally responsible for losses. Sometimes this rule was harshly enforced. For instance in 1910 a telegraphic transfer of £10 from Bathurst to New York was paid at £175 owing to a coding error. The sender promised to make good but failed to do so and a claim on the recipient was equally unsuccessful. The manager and the cable officer at Bathurst were held to be jointly responsible and ordered to contribute £25 each towards the loss.

In the same year a cash loss of £160 was reported at Saltpond from a safe. This was recovered from the insurance but it led to a rule that 'no bank funds should be placed in a safe which has not two locks, and two officers must be present on opening the cash safe'. In 1912 two forgeries were reported from Lagos and £50 of cash disappeared mysteriously. In the latter case the cashier was held responsible but it was decided not to press the claim against him as he was resigning for health reasons. Among many such incidents there was a loss of £74 at Freetown in 1913 : here the manager and cashier were debited each with half the amount. At Zaria around that time there were frequent small losses and one 'cashier's shortage' of £190 was reported by cable.

The manufacture of false silver coins was a flourishing industry for many years. As cash was paid into the bank every coin was put through a counting apparatus which would reject the more obvious frauds, such as clay coins painted silver, which were too thick to pass. But in the main detection depended on the operator, and some duds went through.

From time to time European bank officials yielded to temptation. In 1920 a former acting manager of a branch in Nigeria was arrested on a charge of forgery and sentenced to eighteen months hard labour. In the following year a former manager of a branch in the Gold Coast was sentenced to two years hard labour. For 'irregularities' a former branch cashier in Nigeria was arrested in London and sentenced to four years imprisonment and a clerk of the same branch received a similar sentence. They were proved to have committed forgery and 'suppression'. The losses were partly covered by insurance.

In 1929 £400 was stolen from the cash reserves at Ibadan, and three men were arrested. The two European officers at Ibadan were held accountable for the loss, resigned and returned to England. In 1932 a deficit of £763 was reported in the cash balance at Bo in Sierra Leone. This was then an agency conducted by the United Africa Company which accepted responsibility for the loss. About the same time a cashier at Las Palmas was found to have embezzled a substantial sum; but when he was found out he agreed to give the Bank a mortgage on his property and no legal proceedings were taken.

These are only selected examples of the Bank's experience with fraud cases. More examples will be recorded in a later chapter dealing with the 1950s. On the whole, the BBWA suffered no more than other British banks operating a branch system thousands of miles away from the London Head Office. One conclusion to be drawn from the record is that while the largest number of small swindles were committed by African clerks a minority of serious frauds were carried out by European officers.

THE WAR AGAINST THREE INSECTS

The three main reasons why West Africa was known until fifty years ago as 'the white man's grave' were two mosquitoes and a fly.

The *anopheles* mosquito carries malaria, one of the most widespread and damaging tropical fevers. *Aedes aegypti* was long thought to be the only carrier of yellow fever, another devastating killer; more recently it was found that other mosquitoes including *anopheles* can also be carriers. The third of the West African scourges is the tsetse fly, *glossina palpalis*, the main carrier of *trypanosomiasis* or sleeping sickness. This disease mainly affects animals but human beings can also be infected.

Malaria was the most frequent cause of sickness and death until the early years of this century. The role of the *anopheles* mosquito in transmitting the infection was discovered in the 1890s but the fact that quinine could protect people against malaria and help to cure it was known long before that time. As soon as Europeans settled in regular towns on the Coast they began to take daily doses of quinine. This became compulsory for the staff of the Bank and in some places the quinine was supplied free. Some of the trading companies whose staff spread more widely into the interior provided them free of charge with liquid quinine as well as with mosquito boots. These measures had reduced the incidence of the serious types of malaria by the time of the First World War.

During the war the Germans, cut off from the main source of cinchona bark from which quinine was obtained (Peru), began intensive research into synthetic anti-malaria substances. One of these, plasmoquin, was produced in the 1920s and another, pamaquin, was known in 1924. Outside Germany the first of the synthetic drugs to be marketed was Atabrine, also known as Erion. During the 1930s synthetic anti-malaria substances were widely studied and produced. Quinacrine (or mepacrine) was especially popular.

The synthetic drugs proved to be effective in protecting people against malaria, and they avoided some of the bad side effects which quinine has on some people. But the early synthetics tended to turn the skin yellow and this had the serious result that many females dodged taking them.

The next historic advance in the fight against malaria came in the Second World War. For some time before its outbreak the US Army Command had recognised that malaria would be one of the principal medical problems in the event of war. At that time America was still largely dependent on Germany for the supply of synthetic drugs. In 1941 the US Army Division of Medical Sciences held several conferences on malaria problems in which many academic and business experts took part. A British adviser, Professor Burns of the British Central Scientific Office in Washington, shared in this work. One result was that the production of synthetic drugs under various proprietary names was greatly expanded. The most crucial advance, however, was the massive application of the new Swiss insecticide, DDT, against the mosquito itself. It was this which gradually made large areas of the world almost entirely safe against malaria. Almost – but not quite. Quinine or one of the synthetic anti-malaria drugs must still be taken daily by every European working in West Africa, though some of the newer drugs give immunity if taken once a week. Cases of serious malaria are now relatively rare.

Yellow fever was the cause of numerous deaths among the Bank's staff until about forty years ago. While the method by which the *Aegypti* mosquito transmitted the infection was discovered in the 1890s – partly as a result of the malaria research of Sir Ronald Ross and others in India – no drug or vaccine was known to give immunity to humans until the 1930s. In 1902 yellow fever was eradicated from Havana by anti-mosquito measures. This approach could not be used in large areas such as South America or West Africa, and research into remedies continued for many years, largely under American leadership. The Rockefeller Foundation in New York

financed an extensive research programme. As part of this, a Yellow
Fever Commission was established in Lagos, Nigeria, in July 1920.
It was led by Dr. R. E. Noble, Assistant Surgeon General to the US
Army; it included Dr. Adrian Stokes of Trinity College, Dublin;
Dr. A. E. Horn of the West African Medical Service, and Dr. W. F.
Tytler, British Medical Research Council. Their work did not lead
directly to the discovery of a preventive vaccine.

In 1925 a West Africa Yellow Fever Commission began work at
Yaba near Lagos under Dr. Henry Beeuwkes. The Commission was
housed in five prefabricated buildings which had been sent from
New York. At that time it was widely believed that the carrier of
yellow fever was a mosquito which had been named *Leptospira
icteroides*. This had been discovered by a Japanese scientist, Dr.
Hideyo Noguchi, who had studied yellow fever in Ecuador in 1918,
and a year later in Mexico, Peru and Brazil. After much further work
Dr. Noguchi claimed in 1920 to have developed an effective serum;
in 1925 he reported on 'some thousands of people' successfully
inoculated in South America. When the West Africa Yellow Fever
Commission started work in the same year it tested Dr. Noguchi's
claim but could not confirm it. Work went on for three more years.
In 1928 Dr. Noguchi himself visited the Commission and, with
three other researchers, underwent inoculation by the experimental
serum. All four died. The other three were Adrian Stokes, William
Alexander Young, and Theodor B. Hayne.

Soon afterwards the first safe serum to give immunity from yellow
fever was produced at Yaba; in 1931 ten people were successfully
inoculated. The method was not practical for large-scale use but
further research led to the introduction of the 17 D vaccine in 1936.
This was given by a single injection and was more dependable. By
the outbreak of World War II it was being produced in very large
quantities, and the Yellow Fever Laboratory shipped millions of
doses to the US Army and Navy as well as to West, East, and Central
Africa. In March 1941 the board of the BBWA decided to make a
donation to the Wellcome Research Institution in support of 'the
valuable services which the Institution had performed without
charge in supplying vaccine and carrying out inoculation against
yellow fever'. Gradually inoculation became a general habit and at

the same time the suppression of mosquitoes in inhabited areas of West Africa achieved considerable success. Today yellow fever has almost disappeared from the area, though milder forms, particularly one resembling jaundice, still occur.

The tsetse fly is found only in Africa and it is thought to inhabit about four and a half million square miles of the continent – largely stretching across West Africa and the Southern Sahara to the northern edge of South Africa, though it is also found in East Africa. The insect lives in well-defined areas known as fly-belts but tends to shift its habitat quite often. It infects its victims by biting and injecting blood parasites called trypanosomes into the bloodstream. The main symptoms of the disease caused by the parasite are anaemia and progressive emaciation. Apart from domestic cattle, horses, donkeys, mules, camels, pigs and dogs are all liable to catch the disease, and in the worst areas large numbers of humans become affected.

The tsetse fly has had a profound influence on the economic life of West Africa. Where it rules there can be no animal transport and no husbandry; therefore no manure to regenerate the soil. Farming has to shift ground continuously as the earth is exhausted; unless artificial fertiliser is introduced the common method is to burn down an area of forest for cultivation, relying on the ash to keep the soil productive for a few years. However, the tsetse fly bites only in daytime so that men and animals can pass safely through the infested zones at night. This has always been a factor in the transport of cattle reared in the northern savannah country to the densely populated coastal areas.

While insecticides can kill the tsetse fly they cannot be effectively applied to the huge area it inhabits. Moreover some animals which get bitten by the fly do not catch the disease or do so only mildly. Some species of tsetse fly like the blood of antelopes, wild pigs and various wild ruminants. As these animals travel they carry the infection with them and other insects biting them elsewhere can pick up the parasite and inject it into other, more susceptible, animals in a new region. It is for this reason that great numbers of wild game have been methodically destroyed in Rhodesia, Zambia, Tanzania, Uganda and also in Ghana. For a time this game destruction has freed areas from the tsetse fly but it is not certain that the method will have any lasting effect.

Human beings can be protected from the insect by fly-screens sprayed with insecticide such as DDT, but this is expensive and time consuming. A more radical remedy is to remove everyone from a village or area that is badly exposed to the tsetse fly. For all the difficulties that have been mentioned great progress has been made in opening new areas to cattle ranching and in making formerly uninhabitable areas safe for man.

So much for the three dominant plagues. A fourth one, blackwater fever, receded soon after the general use of quinine was replaced by synthetic anti-malaria drugs. Whether the two facts are causally linked is not certain. And finally the advance of hygiene and sanitation has virtually eliminated bubonic plague which was sporadic until fairly recent times, though it did not usually threaten Europeans. As late as 1927 the Lagos manager of the BBWA reported that a plague epidemic in the city was 'receding'. As a result of a campaign against rats by a 'small army of rat-catchers' the number of deaths had been reduced to only two a week. Cholera, too, has been effectively suppressed by mass immunisation, and though some forms of food poisoning are bound to persist epidemic dysentery is no longer a threat. Black and white men can live in most parts of West Africa in good health if they take the precautions devised by modern medical research.

Chapter Eleven

THE WORLD TRADE
DEPRESSION

THE BANK UNDER PRESSURE

SUDDENLY, in 1929, the modest recovery in West African production and trade came to an end. World markets for primary commodities crumbled as business activity in the industrial countries was drastically reduced. Between 1928 and 1931 exports from British West Africa shrunk by 50% in money value and by 40% in volume; imports dropped by 59% in value and by 41% in quantity. The currency circulation fell from £15 million at mid-1928 to £9·5 million at mid-1931, and £8 million at mid-1932.

The Bank quickly felt the impact of the economic collapse. Between March 1929 and March 1932 'bills for collection' fell by one half. The published profit, after allowing for sums set aside against bad debts, etc., fell from £128,330 in 1928–9 to £24,568 in 1930–1, and even that figure included the profit on a large sale of investments. The dividend was reduced from 6% to 4%, and it remained at that level until it was cautiously raised to 5% in 1936. The price of the BBWA shares in the stock market slumped from a high point of £4 13s. 9d. in 1929 to a low point of £1 17s. 6d. in 1931; after that it recovered to about £3 10s. in 1933 and £4 in 1934.

Fortunately the Bank had a strong foundation of liquid resources. It was so strong, indeed, that in September 1930 the board's newly established economy committee noted: 'the Bank has at present more capital than it can profitably use in its customary business'. It recommended that more should be invested in government securities to earn interest at between 4% and 5%, as additional revenue was badly needed. The benefit did not last long, as in August 1932 a holding of nearly £1·5 million of 5% War Loan had to be converted into a new 3½% stock.

The annual report of the Bank for 1930–1 grimly describes the turn of fortunes: 'The exceptionally heavy fall in profit reflects the serious depression in trading conditions. . . . With the unprecedented fall in prices in primary products there has been a heavy decline in turnover on traders' accounts, and a large contraction in the amount of loans and advances taken by the Bank's customers during the year . . . but the directors desire to record that having regard to its reserves and strong and liquid position, the Bank will be able to take the fullest advantage of any improvement in trade.'

Retrenchment of overhead costs was clearly necessary, and this time the cutting was drastic. The Bank had been caught by the world trade slump in the middle of an expansion programme. In 1929 new branches had been opened at Takoradi, the new timber and manganese port, and at Oda and Nkawkaw. In May 1930 another new branch was opened at Gusau. But in 1931 a wholesale closure of branches began. Friendly discussions with Barclays led to both banks closing down at Gusau, Bekwai and Nsawam in 1932, each undertaking to give six months' notice of any reopening.

Other branches to be shut were at Opobo, Abonnema, Axim and Lokoja, as well as the agency at Half Assinie. Altogether the number of branches was reduced from fifty-eight in 1930 to forty in 1938. Outside British West Africa the Bank withdrew from the Canary Islands, Fernando Po and Liberia. The retreat from Morocco had already begun in 1929 and in the following years most, but not all, of the branches there were closed down.

In view of the contraction in business the Bank now found itself overstaffed. Between 1929 and 1932 the staff was reduced from 874 to 652. In many cases officers were persuaded to retire and were granted compensation. Those who stayed had their annual bonuses sharply reduced and the general manager accepted a salary cut. The directors' fees were also reduced. Senior staff had no salary increases for several years. In 1933 one of the two auditors, Messrs Price, Waterhouse & Co. was dropped, leaving Messrs Peat, Marwick, Mitchell & Co. as sole auditors.

While the Bank itself thus adapted itself to the straitened conditions, many of its customers ran into serious financial difficulties. The first indication of the pressures to come was in July 1929, when £5,000 was transferred from Profit and Loss Account to a 'Contingency 1929 Account'. Soon very much larger sums had to be set aside against the risk of loss on loans, and so many debtors found themselves unable to pay that in 1930 ten members of the Head Office staff were authorised individually to attend meetings of creditors called by insolvent firms.

At this time the outstanding credits of the Lever group caused much anxiety. The formation of the United Africa Company in 1929 had not solved all the financial problems of the group. Drastic changes had been made in structure, ownership and personalities but took time to produce results. In February 1931 the board of the BBWA heard from Mr. Paterson, the general manager, that the Bank had been offered guarantees for the obligations of the UAC – 55% from Lever Brothers and 45% from the African and Eastern Trade Corporation. He pointed out that they already held guarantees of Lever Brothers for £700,000. The directors decided 'to act in conjunction with the other banks concerned'. In May, after further negotiations, the guarantees of the two companies up to a maximum of £2½ million were received in respect of UAC debts.

Even the largest trading groups had suffered serious financial damage from the slump in trade; many of the smaller and less solid firms went to the wall. The Bank devoted much effort in these years to securing repayment of outstanding advances and avoiding losses. It did not always succeed but it emerged from the crisis with its liquid resources unimpaired and its organisation in good health.

New men were coming up in the Bank staff. In 1930 D. D. Gibb was appointed Manager of Lagos branch. He was much respected; in 1934 he became Senior Manager for Nigeria and was one of the first to inhabit one of the fine houses in Bank Road, Ikoyi. G. Anson Cowe was made Manager at Freetown in 1930; he, too, was a man of parts; in 1931 he was appointed a member of the Sierra Leone Legislative Council, which 'the board learned with satisfaction'. In Accra G. B. Kirk was appointed Manager.

The economy drive had been successful both in saving staff

salaries and opening opportunities for promotion, but it had its drawbacks. The Bank's staff pay fell behind that of the colonial governments. In 1934 a young man who went to the Coast (he later rose to a high position outside the Bank) got £300 a year plus £50 Coast allowance and half-pay when on leave; he lived rent free in a small bedroom over the bank branch and had the use of the communal mess ('a lot of rough, hard-drinking fellows to be thrown in with for a youngster just out from England', he says). His contract was even then only for eighteen months. At the same period a Government servant of similar age and experience had a pay of £400 a year with full pay on leave, a bungalow of his own, and if he married, a comfortable house. Moreover his pay would be raised fairly soon to £600 per annum plus £60 allowances. The Bank's pay and conditions continued to stagnate not only in comparison with the public service but also against commercial companies. It was only after the Second World War that the gap was repaired, and by then the Bank had lost some good men.

AFRICAN REACTIONS

All these financial troubles were, of course, only mirror reflections of what was really going on in West Africa. In half a century the powerful incentives of the money economy had made a deep impact. More and more Africans were drawn into production for export, with all the associated processing, distribution and other services. Important new industries like cocoa and groundnut growing for overseas markets had developed, giving employment and rising material standards to many thousands. In 1920 the hopes and expectations aroused by these achievements had received a profound shock, which found a tentative expression in a series of labour disputes and strikes. The shock was far graver in 1930.

Economic disasters caused by external events were, of course, not unknown in West African experience. The destruction of the trans-Saharan trade in the nineteenth century by such events as the gradual suppression of the slave trade, the rise and fall of the European fashion for ostrich feathers, and the French colonial conquest was a far heavier blow to many large communities in West Africa than the world slump of the 1930s. But the market collapse certainly caused much disillusionment after the high promise of the open market economy fostered by the European connection.

Distress and disappointment were inevitable when the terms of trade turned against the producers of primary commodities – first in 1920 and then, after a temporary recovery, in 1930. A given quantity of exports would buy a reduced volume of imports. Some attempts were made at first to produce more; it was relatively easy to put more land under groundnuts and to harvest tree crops like cocoa and coffee more intensively for a year or two. But the effort to sell more on depressed markets only served to push prices still further down.

The African producers, always quick to react to market changes, soon tried the opposite tack of cutting back production in order to stabilise prices. The first scheme of this kind was organised by the Gold Coast cocoa producers as early as 1921. It had only a passing effect on prices, but it provided experience for the larger-scale restriction scheme of the next decade.

There was a growing suspicion among African farmers and traders that the frequent mergers of European firms during the twenties, leading up to the monolith of the United Africa Company in 1929, were aimed at strengthening the buyers of produce (and sellers of imported merchandise) at the expense of the producers. That was indeed one effect of the mergers, though the chief motive had been financial survival rather than deliberate concentration of trade. The traditional all-out competition between scores of trading companies, which had given African farmers and consumers a certain amount of bargaining strength, was certainly reduced by these amalgamations. The resulting groups still had to fight for their lives; even the United Africa Company showed a heavy loss in its first two years. Economy measures were inescapable, and they involved the closing down of a large number of competing trading stations and stores all over British West Africa.

This development particularly affected the offtake of cocoa. The main cocoa producers in the Gold Coast happened to be commercially alert. Many of them were independent entrepreneurs rather than village farmers. Convinced by now that the European trading firms were combining against them to hold prices down, they organised a series of output restrictions and held out for better prices before they would deliver. It was such a simple idea; no one could be surprised (though many were) that rural Africans were as capable of uniting for the manipulation of the market as were the international producers of rubber, tin, copper and other commodities.

In 1937 the dispute came to a head when cocoa farmers flatly refused to sell their produce. It was the most militant reaction to economic adversity during this period. It led to a British Government enquiry (the Nowell Commission) which reported in 1938 that the African producers had not been entirely wrong to suspect that business practices were being changed to their disadvantage, both in the organisation of the international cocoa market in London and in the market-sharing agreements between trading firms in West Africa. Indeed in 1937 the UAC had succeeded in organising a daily price-fixing agreement with virtually all the big cocoa producing and consuming firms.

The main conclusion of the Nowell Commission, however, was that collective marketing boards should be set up to secure a more orderly marketing of cocoa. This had been an increasingly popular idea, in many forms and for many commodities, in the international efforts to overcome the trade depression. Similar plans to influence the world cocoa market and to stabilise prices by official intervention had been put forward in the Gold Coast since 1931, when one such scheme was rejected by the Gold Coast Government.

About the same time Government intervention in the economy was being considered in the French West African colonies where a number of schemes regulating external trade were introduced from 1931 onwards. In 1934 the French introduced import tariffs and quotas and set up a compensation fund to support producer prices in West Africa for rubber and coffee, bananas and vegetable products. The fund was financed by a levy on imports into France. These and other attempts to stabilise prices had little practical effect but they led the way to the establishment of official Marketing Boards after the outbreak of war in 1939.

In British West Africa no such actions were taken before the war, though official thinking had been well conditioned for the setting up of marketing boards for various commodities in the circumstances of the war emergency.

The cocoa dispute of the 1930s coincided with the outbreak of a devastating tree disease, first noticed in the Gold Coast in 1936. It was known as the 'swollen shoot' disease; by 1938 it was identified as a virus disease. The virus is carried by the mealy bug and can completely kill a tree in three years. For many years the only method of controlling the spread of the disease was to grub out the affected trees. This was established in 1941 but application was difficult even though compensation was paid. The trouble spread. Not until 1952 did the control campaign come into full effect and by then large areas were devastated. Cutting out the infected trees continued until 1962. It was then abandoned in favour of a voluntary scheme without compensation, but this was a failure. Large areas had to be abandoned for cocoa production, though outside these areas swollen shoot appears to be under reasonable control.

DEPARTURE OF THE PIONEERS

In 1929 the Bank suffered a grave loss by the death of Leslie Couper, who had been working for it from the start. The whole business of the Bank had come to depend on him. Although it was still the board of directors that made the policy decisions it was now almost invariably the general manager who recommended a certain course of action to the board. He was appointed Chief Manager of the Bank in 1910 and given the title General Manager in 1918. He was greatly respected both in Whitehall and in the City. His membership of the Emmott Committee on the West African Currency in 1911, and of the resulting West African Currency Board, has already been mentioned. He was awarded the CMG in 1919. Apart from his membership of various City organisations he was also appointed a member of the Palestine Currency Board in 1926. As a result of his dealings with the Liberian Government he was made a Knight Commander of the Order of the African Redemption. His death at the age of fifty-eight was quite unexpected.

Fortunately a strong body of competent managers had been built up both in England and in West Africa. David Paterson, who had joined the Bank in 1893, became the new general manager. He had spent about twenty years in West Africa but had been at Head Office since 1913 and had become a close personal friend of Leslie Couper. W. F. Becker was brought back from Lagos in 1932 to become his assistant. Roy Wilson, who had joined in 1895 and left the Bank in 1924 to become a Member of Parliament, did not seek re-election in 1929 and rejoined the Bank as a director. He took Leslie Couper's place as a member of the West African Currency Board and in turn was knighted.

In the same year George W. Neville, the real founder of the Bank, died at the age of seventy-seven. He had been elected a director on his return to London in 1900 and his profound knowledge of West African conditions had been of great value to the Bank. In 1931 the death of C. B. Edgar occurred; he had been chairman of the Bank of Nigeria when it was taken over by the BBWA in 1912, and had been on the board ever since. In 1931 another old director, W. F. Moore, resigned for health reasons, and in the following year O. Harrison Williams gave up his seat on the board because he was no longer able to travel to London for the meetings. Another important resignation in 1931 was that of Lord Kylsant, who as Sir Owen Philipps had joined the board in 1910 after the acquisition of Elder Dempster and other assets of the late Sir Alfred Jones. Lord Kylsant was engulfed by the financial collapse of his shipping group and resigned.

Yet another director, D. Q. Henriques, was killed in a motor accident in 1932, and in 1934 Mazzini Stuart, who had also come over from the Bank of Nigeria in 1912, resigned for health reasons. After that there were no Liverpool or Manchester directors left on the board. Sir Frederick Eley became increasingly influential. In 1930 he was elected deputy chairman and in the following year he acted as chairman during Lord Selborne's visit to West Africa. In 1936 Hugh Tennant who represented the Westminster Bank on the board died, and Lord Goschen, who had been Viceroy of India, was nominated by that bank as his successor. F. A. Beane, who had been a chief Executive of Lloyds Bank, was also appointed a director in 1936.

A MERGER PROPOSAL

In December 1934, when the stubborn business depression showed little sign of lifting, someone in the Bank of British West Africa conceived an idea far more radical than mere cost-cutting. Sir Roy Wilson approached Sir John Caulcutt, deputy chairman of Barclays Bank (Dominion, Colonial and Overseas) with a 'tentative proposal' that the two banks should cease their 'needless and wasteful competition in West Africa'.

He pointed out that in many of the commercial centres where both banks were established there was hardly enough business for one bank. In recent years Barclays had opened branches in many quite small towns.

His proposal was that Barclays should agree to close all their West African branches; that the BBWA should take over all their premises at an agreed valuation and such of their loans and overdrafts as were considered sound.

In return, Barclays were to acquire at an agreed price such a shareholding in the BBWA as would give them equality with the other four shareholding banks. Barclays were also to nominate one or even two directors to the BBWA board.

No explicit reply to this proposal was received for about ten months. On October 8, 1935, Mr. H. L. M. Tritton, chairman of Barclays (DC&O) and Sir John Caulcutt, deputy chairman, saw Sir Roy Wilson to set out their response. Mr. Tritton said that he and some of his colleagues had given careful consideration to this proposal; but while it had many attractions, they were unable to accept it.

Mr. Tritton added that Barclays, too, were most anxious to avoid foolish and wasteful competition in West Africa. He suggested that the two general managers of their banks should meet and try to find some formula acceptable to both banks, under which useless competition would in future be avoided.

It was a courteous rejection, and far from causing hard feelings the episode seems to have strengthened good relations between the competing banks.

More than three years later, in February 1939, Sir Roy Wilson had

L

another talk on a different subject with Sir John Caulcutt, who had by now become chairman of Barclays (DC&O). He took the opportunity to raise again the proposal that Barclays should retire from West Africa on the terms and conditions suggested in his original scheme. The answer was once again a firm negative; Sir John Caulcutt said that the idea had been twice carefully considered, once in December 1934 by the late Mr. Goodenough, and again by Barclays' full board in October 1935. On both occasions it had been turned down, and this must be taken as their final decision.

The main subject of the 1939 meeting was interesting enough. It was the damage caused to both banks by the determined efforts of the United Africa Company to do without their services in West Africa. The UAC was offering financial facilities during the produce seasons to customers who hitherto had done their business with the banks.

Sir Roy Wilson cited some instances. The UAC had persuaded the West African Currency Board to handle some of its outward transfers of funds to West Africa. They had made arrangements to supply all the cash requirements of three important BBWA customers (Swiss African Trading Co., Busi & Stephenson, Sierra Leone Coaling Co.). They had arranged with the Gold Coast Government to pay their duties and rail freights in London to the Crown Agents, thus avoiding the need for bank financing on the Gold Coast and reducing the amount of cable transfers which the Government made through the banks.

Barclays had suffered similarly, and it was agreed that Sir Roy was to put the following suggestion to the Currency Board (of which he was a member): In order to put the Currency Board in a position to refuse to grant transfer of funds to or from currency centres to anyone but the banks, the banks should offer to make such transfers to any firm, person or company at rates not higher than those charged by the Currency Board.

Sir Roy should also interview the deputy chairman of the United Africa Company 'and ask him why such an old and valued customer should seek to do without the services of the banks and to compete with our business'.

The short-cuts taken by the UAC had caused much concern to

the BBWA for some time. In May 1938 Sir Roy Wilson had explained in a note to his fellow directors that 'owing to the advent of Levers the method of financing the West African harvests has radically changed. Outward cable transfers are now used to pay for exports from West Africa instead of the produce shipments being financed by Bills of Exchange drawn and discounted in Africa.'

It should be explained that under the traditional procedure the shipper of the produce would draw a bill of exchange, with bill of lading and other documents attached, which would then be purchased by the Bank at a higher rate than that for Telegraphic Transfers. The rate included an interest element as well as a negotiating commission. This was part of the Bank's normal business, and when the UAC found a way of doing without it the Bank lost a good deal of revenue.

The dispute with the UAC was resolved on compromise terms patiently negotiated by Sir Roy Wilson. First he persuaded the Currency Board to agree not to issue transfers in future to any one but the banks, so long as the banks' rates for such transfers were not higher than those charged by the Board to the banks. (There is no record of the Board actually amending its rules to that effect, but Sir Roy was able to report to the directors, and presumably to Barclays, that his formula had received 'full support'.)

Next, he offered the UAC reduced rates in return for an undertaking that the company would not compete with the banks in future. (Again there is no detailed record of what happened, but an agreement was eventually reached on some such terms. He had been asked by Barclays not to mention that the two banks had discussed this scheme beforehand, so that no suspicion of a joint threat could arise; in the event the agreement covered both banks.) In fact, relations between the BBWA and the United Africa Company became very friendly from that time onwards. The UAC never joined in the common practice of other trading firms of 'selling' any surplus cash directly to other traders, thus by-passing the Bank. 'Street Exchange' was the local name for this. In the 1950s the UAC actively helped the Bank to expand into the areas from which the company was gradually withdrawing. The short-lived friction of the 1930s never arose again.

The close cooperation between the two banks in resisting the U A C offensive was by no means the first case of joint consultation and action. Many years earlier they had agreed, for example, not to open or reopen branches in certain places without giving an agreed period of notice to the other bank. Understandings about maintaining the same rates for the principal transactions had existed in various areas, and a habit of discussing points of potential dispute had grown up. On January 1, 1945, these matters were codified in a formal agreement headed 'Cooperation between banks in West Africa'. It refers to no fewer than forty-four 'matters agreed between the two banks' and states that 'no deviation or exception shall be made unless by mutual consent of the head offices in London'. Six months notice in writing was to be given by either bank if it wished to cancel or modify the agreement, though 'current rates in force from time to time' were to be agreed separately within the framework of the agreement.

All these arrangements did not prevent the two banks from competing sharply in seeking business or extending their services. The agreement continued in force until January 31, 1957 (when the British and French Bank was founded in Nigeria it signed the agreement), and was later replaced by separate agreements for the independent countries.

GOLD, DIAMONDS AND OTHER MINERALS

West African production had been spreading over a much wider range during the 1920s and 1930s. In particular, minerals had become a substantial element in output and export. Tin mining on the Nigerian plateau expanded until in the late twenties tin made up about 10% of Nigerian exports. In the Gold Coast both panning and quarrying for gold had been substantial and technically fairly advanced at least since the eighth century when the overland trade with the Arab world and southern Europe became large. The main deposit in the British colonies was in the Ashanti area and the Ashanti Goldfields Company was formed in 1897 to exploit it.

The B B W A, particularly its branch at Tarkwa which had been opened in 1909, was heavily involved in the financing of gold, lending against bullion deposited in its vault. This was a reasonable risk in peacetime when assaying was done locally and the Bank, after receiving an official certificate of gold value, could be certain that it would soon be shipped to England. But during the war shipments were at times suspended. In 1916 £176,000 worth of gold bullion was stored at the Tarkwa branch and £74,000 had been lent against it. It was uncertain when this gold could be shipped to England. The problem was put to the Bank of England in London, which agreed to purchase the gold directly while it was lodged at Tarkwa. After that agreement purchases took place regularly without the gold moving out of the Tarkwa strong-room. On May 25, 1917, it was recorded that gold held at Tarkwa on account of the Bank of England had risen to a value of £1,030,180.

A number of other minerals became important elements in production and trade. A manganese deposit was opened up in the Gold Coast; by the late 1920s mineral shipments from that colony already made up 5% of its exports. In Sierra Leone a very large iron-ore deposit was found. Iron had always been known to exist in West Africa. Iron ore mining and smelting was quite extensive as long ago as 500 B C. Even then it was not simple pig-iron but puddled or forged steel made in clay kilns, and iron weapons and implements were manufactured at a very early stage. The discovery of really big ore deposits in the 1920s made modern extraction methods possible. The Sierra Leone Development Corporation was formed in 1929 to take on this task. By 1939 minerals accounted for over 60% of all exports from Sierra Leone. Naturally the BBWA played its part in these growing industries, but mineral products did not escape the world slump in commodity prices.

THE GEMS OF SIERRA LEONE

The discovery of gem diamonds in Sierra Leone took place at the worst point of the world depression. In 1930 some very large diamonds were found in the Kono district and prospecting started in earnest in 1932. The Sierra Leone Selection Trust was granted exclusive mining rights in 1935 and news of some spectacular finds soon attracted many African fortune seekers who were undeterred by the lack of official mining licences. Both the company and the

Government have been trying ever since to suppress 'illicit diamond mining'. Success has been erratic. On the whole the company has dominated the mechanised mining activities and private diggers (who had no licences until 1956) have more or less defied prohibitions outside the mines. Before and during the Second World War illicit diamond mining was still ancillary to the organised extraction; it was after the war that the monopoly was effectively undermined. By then the centre of mining had shifted to the richer Tongo field.

Before the great diamond rush of the 1950s the BBWA was only indirectly involved in the trade. During the retrenchment period the branch at Bo, the earliest centre of the diamond trade, had been closed down and it was not reopened until 1950. The headquarters of the Sierra Leone Selection Trust was first established in Segbwema, then the final point of the railway; the mine was further on at Yengema. It was the BBWA main branch at Freetown which came into touch with these activities quite early, and chiefly for the purpose of providing safe custody. Thus the Selection Trust deposited its original mining rights titles with the Bank in 1936. The Bank also had to supply cash to the Trust for its up-country requirements. This alone needed much organisation and was not without risk. Then there was the importation of machinery and supplies for the mining operations for which bank financing was arranged.

The Bank was sometimes accused of encouraging illicit diamond digging. That charge was quite unfounded. In the late 1930s the Bank was asked by the Colonial Office to organise a regular outlet for the African diamond winners in Sierra Leone. At that time the stones were mainly industrials with a very small proportion of 'cuttables' of less than one carat; they were sent to London, cleaned and graded by a Hatton Garden expert, and then sold by open tender by the Bank. The operations were successful for the Bank and helpful to the African diggers. Conditions changed, of course, after the discovery of large gem diamonds in Sierra Leone in the 1950s; then, too, the Bank acted within Government regulations and in close touch with officials. That period will be described in a later chapter.

In the Gold Coast diamonds were also discovered in commercial quantities during the 1930s. In the Ashanti goldmining region irregular production of small diamonds developed. The Bank's branch in Tarkwa was making advances against diamonds as early as 1935. A branch return for the period April 1937 to March 1938 shows that in the twelve months 111 consignments of diamonds with a total weight of 16,255 carats were accepted, and advances of £3,288 made against them. The diamonds were shipped to London and sold; the proceeds, after deduction of a 7% commission, worked out at £5,633. Thus the branch had on average advanced about 60% of the sales value to the miners who brought in their findings.

This business steadily grew until Tarkwa branch was as deeply involved in diamonds as in gold. One of the older African clerks recalls how the miners – mainly Nigerians – would come into the banking hall, throw their bags on to a large counter, show their mining licences and wait while the stones were being cleaned by shaking, tested through magnifying glasses and weighed on an elaborate pair of diamond scales with a great assortment of weights down to a minute piece of silver foil.

This area has continued to produce mainly small diamonds for industrial use. The Tarkwa branch of the Bank, now housed in a new building, no longer deals with diamonds but the 1949 ledger shows that the business was still in full swing then. Individual miners were bringing in large numbers of stones adding up to a small number of carats and yielding only a modest cash return. To pick a single case, one Y. J. Aminu is shown to have brought in an estimated 12,440 stones which the branch manager judged to have a total weight of 311 carats. On this the Bank made an immediate advance of £350. It noted the number of the miner's licence and paid the royalty of £38 17s. 6d. to the 'Stool' (the Paramount Chief). After the stones had been sent to London and sold in the diamond market for £514, a customs duty of 9%, a commission of 7½% and interest of nearly £6 were deducted. The miner was paid another £74 to add to his advance.

In this case the miner received an advance of just under 70% of the amount which the stones finally realised in London. The general rule was that the Bank would advance up to 75% but the amount depended a great deal on the judgement of the branch manager as to the market value of the stones. It is remarkable that the Bank almost never made a substantial mistake in estimating the price which these tiny diamonds, delivered encased in dirt by the bucketful, would fetch in Hatton Garden. Much later, by 1953, the volume of diamonds grew so large that the London valuers were overwhelmed and sales were delayed at a time when prices were falling. The diamond diggers were disappointed, and the Government withdrew the banks' dealing licences.

The man who introduced the diamond business to the Tarkwa branch of the Bank in 1935 was C. J. Green, a colourful personality who deserves a place in these annals. Born in 1887 he joined the Bank in 1911 and after serving in Nigeria was transferred to Accra in 1916, and appointed manager of the branch at Bekwai in the Gold Coast in 1919. He remained there for thirteen years, until the branch was closed during the world slump. He became highly popular with the African community and was regarded as the mayor of the town. When the branch was closed the Paramount Chief or Omanhene wrote to the District Manager expressing his regret at the leaving of his old friend C. J. Green. Writing in the name of 'my elders, people and I' the Chief said that 'by his convincing personality and commendable services Mr. Green has endeared himself to all his customers and nonetheless to me'. He hoped that when business improved Mr. Green might be sent back to them.

But in 1933 he was instead sent to Tarkwa branch where he was manager for fifteen years and stayed on for seven years after his retirement. It is not recorded whether he was formally appointed a Chief, but there is no doubt that his status was equivalent. He was so regarded by both Europeans and Africans. His close relations with the local Africans probably helped him to develop the diamond business of the Bank which depended a great deal on mutual trust.

Chapter Twelve

THE SECOND WORLD
WAR

DEFENSIVE PRECAUTIONS

WHEN war broke out in 1939 the Bank had stabilised its position in West Africa. Since 1935 deposits had grown again: from £6·7 million to £7·4 million, £8·7 million and £9·9 million on March 31, 1938. Liquid resources in cash and investments had fully recovered, and the dividend was raised from 4% to 5%. West African business conditions had gradually improved and the effects of the world slump were wearing off. The money circulation increased from just under £10 million in the year to mid-1935 to £12·5 million at mid-1936 and £19·3 million at mid-1937, though in the following year, owing to the cocoa troubles, it fell back to £16·4 million – but even that was higher than in any pre-slump year.

All the earlier problems with bad and doubtful debts had been cleared up: in 1938 there was a balance of £184,000 left in the Contingencies Account.

But the directors, like many others, felt war approaching, and thought the City of London might become a precarious place in the event of air raids. Lord Goschen offered the Bank his country house, Seacox Heath at Hawkhurst in Kent, as an alternative head office in case of need, rent free. The offer was gratefully accepted and arrangements were made for offices and living accommodation for some sixty bank officials. All the head office staff except single men were in fact moved to Hawkhurst just before war began. This precaution proved its value during the main bombing of London, but early in

1943 the staff was moved back to the City. Kent, the garden of England, was soon on the main line of the German 'flying bombs' which were being shot down all around the lovely orchards.

Before long the war made a deep impact on the business of the Bank. The branch in Hamburg was lost, but this time all the British staff were able to get home. In West Africa the commercial channels changed: the British Ministry of Food took over the purchase of the cocoa crop in 1939 and in the following year the West African Cocoa Control Board was set up. This was followed in 1942 by the formation of the West African Produce Control Board which purchased the main export crops, fixed prices and arranged the marketing. Private firms continued to purchase the produce but they had to sell it to the statutory boards, which paid on or before shipment. The Government was also the only seller of the controlled products in Britain.

Under this system the Bank's customers needed less finance than before. As deposits (including those of the control boards) steadily increased the Bank found itself with more cash than it could profitably employ in West Africa. Less credit was also required to finance imports, as supplies of European goods were restricted. Between 1940 and 1945 deposits rose from £7·4 million to £19·3 million while advances remained static around £2·4 million or a little less, and bills for collection dropped from £532,000 to £413,000. But the money deployed in London brought in good interest, and the published profit increased apace:

Year to March 31	Profit £	Dividend % (less Tax)
1939	42,878	4
1940	36,649	3
1941	58,887	4
1942	70,942	4
1943	74,463	4
1944	117,304	4
1945	126,232	5

Over this period the reserve fund increased from £400,000 to £600,000. The trend was reflected in the price of BBWA shares, which fell to below £2 in 1941 and recovered to £6 in 1945.

The Bank's work for the West African Currency Board continued throughout the war years. The agency fee paid to the Bank had been fixed as long ago as 1927 at £4,000 a year plus a commission on silver collected and shipped home, with a maximum sum of £500 a year. In addition the Board paid rent for the strong-rooms installed by the Bank in an increasing number of branches at 5% of the capital cost. Only this rent went on rising because more and larger strong-rooms were being installed; the two basic fees were confirmed without change at the beginning of each year by a simple exchange of letters. In December 1939 the Colonial Office suggested that the Bank should reduce its transfer rates, but the directors pointed out that it was unfair to expect them to accept a cut 'at a time of rising costs and the unsettled state of trade in West Africa'. No change seems to have been made.

West Africa was not as far removed from the active theatres of war as a map might suggest. One aspect was mentioned by the chairman of the Bank in 1942: 'West Africa, the chief sphere of our operations, has become an important highway between Great Britain, the United States and the Middle East.' A mirror effect was that the branches at Freetown and Lagos arranged to pay out local currency to travellers with Letters of Credit from certain banks.

But it went much farther than that. In August 1940 – when France had been overrun – Sir Roy Wilson set out some wider considerations in a memorandum to the Currency Board.

Certain branches of the Bank in West Africa, he pointed out, were exposed to potential danger:

Bathurst is probably the most vulnerable of our branches, being within a few hours' motor run of Dakar. It has an excellent aerodrome, formerly used by the transatlantic planes of the German Lufthansa company. In enemy hands it would be a menace to our shipping. It has no land defences . . . the total garrison for the entire Gambia territory is a company of West African Frontier Force. On the other hand it is within twelve hours' fast sailing of the fortified naval base at Freetown.

Kumasi . . . is liable to attack through the Northern Territories. There is a good road to Tamale and the French frontier. But the Ashanti country is covered with dense forest, and the capital is strongly defended. There are no air-fields or likely landing places.

Keta on the Togoland border might easily be attacked by troops from the Mandated Territory. The branch makes substantial losses and could with advantage be closed.

Kano might possibly be attacked by land or airborne forces, but it would be a hazardous operation. It has an excellent airfield but it is 1,800 miles from Dakar, the nearest French air force base. . . . The Nigerian troops at Kano, which could be reinforced in a few hours from Zaria, Kaduna and Enugu, could easily cope with any likely land invasion.

Maiduguri: this is within 200 miles of Fort Lamy, where there is a garrison of not less than 2,000 French native troops, with a good airfield and a squadron or so of military aircraft. Maiduguri has an aerodrome and usually a company of the WAFF. Little would be gained by raiding this place.

Calabar . . . usually has half a battalion of the WAFF: a surprise attack by land or sea would be almost impossible.

THE TOLL OF WAR

Directors and senior officials, then, had a good deal more to worry about than the procedures for dealing with the official control boards, the difficulties of shipping enough coin and notes to West Africa, and the shortage of staff as men joined the services. The number of staff declined from 582 on March 31, 1938, to 511 on March 31, 1942.

The strain of working under wartime conditions probably undermined the health of a number of senior men. On the board of directors it began in 1940 with the resignation of Sir Alfred Lewis; he was replaced by the Hon. Jasper N. Ridley, nominated by the National Provincial Bank.

In 1942 the Bank suffered a heavy double blow. On February 26, 1942, Lord Selborne, chairman of the board since he followed Lord Milner in 1916, died. Throughout this period he had given active leadership to the Bank, and his long experience in British political affairs, as well as in Africa, had been of great value. He had presided over the link-up with the four large shareholding banks which had greatly strengthened the foundations of the BBWA, and he had seen the Bank through the difficult depression years of the twenties and thirties.

The second grave loss was the death of Sir Roy Wilson on August 27, 1942. He had been taken ill with a heart complaint the year before, and in December he was granted three months' leave of absence. In June 1942, as he had not recovered, he resigned his directorship. He died after an abdominal operation. Wilson had been with the Bank almost from the beginning, rising steadily from a junior position towards the top management and finally to the board. On the way up he had gained an intimate knowledge of the business. His years as a Member of Parliament had widened his horizon, and his twelve years' membership of the West African Currency Board must have given him both knowledge and influence well beyond the normal bank manager's experience.

The death of Sir Roy Wilson led to a vital change in the composition of the West African Currency Board. When his illness compelled him to retire, W. F. Becker was invited to attend in his place, but without having a vote. In July 1943 the Colonial Office decided that in future commercial banks should not be represented on the Currency Board. Instead the Colonial Secretary appointed Mr. R. N. Kershaw, MC, an adviser to the Bank of England, as a member. The link with the Bank of England, 'on a personal basis', continued until 1969 and was no doubt helpful when central banks and separate currencies came to be introduced into the new West African states. But in 1943 Mr. Becker was still 'invited to attend the Board's meetings in a consultative capacity'.

Sir Frederick Eley, the deputy chairman, was elected chairman on March 4, 1942. He had been a director since 1920 and had acted as chairman on several occasions, so that there was no difficulty of transition. There were now only six directors left. Only in 1944 were two new directors appointed: Sir Frank Baddeley and Mr. Sydney Parkes.

The war years also brought many changes among the management and senior staff. In 1943 the chief accountant, W. J. Cook, was granted leave of absence for health reasons, and in 1944 he retired. His successor was Frank Edey. The London manager, G. S. C. Child, retired in 1939 and was replaced by the accountant, W. Johnson. At Lagos the senior manager in Nigeria, D. D. Gibb, fell ill in 1944 and came to England, where he died in July. He had served the Bank for thirty years on the Coast. K. M. Oliver took his place at Lagos.

In the same year F. G. Wright, who had held several managerial posts in West Africa, was brought home and became Joint Head

Office Manager together with W. F. Becker, who had also served many years on the Coast. For some years these two men played a leading part in the central management. In 1945 Geoffrey Redmayne was recalled from Africa to assist the London manager at Head Office. He, too, became a member of the chief management team.

There were, of course, many other changes in management and staff, and during the war years it became difficult to recruit good new men or to provide adequate replacements at all levels. The consequences of these lean years were felt well into the fifties.

Although the Bank's business in Morocco had been much reduced during the 1930 depression, the branch at Casablanca continued to look after substantial deposits and to carry on normal banking. Two branches still existed at Saffi and Mazagan. The branch in Tangier had also remained open and moderately active. In some other places including Marrakech the offices had long been closed but the bank buildings had not been sold. The entire venture into Morocco had been unsuccessful from the start. Losses had far outweighed profits, and with the gradual decline of the once thriving trade with Britain and of the British mercantile community the Bank saw no prospect of a change for the better. It had been considering the closure of the remaining branches and the sale of the premises even before the war broke out.

In June 1940 some cables had been exchanged with Casablanca branch through the Foreign Office, and in October five members of the Casablanca staff were removed to the interior under police supervision. The branch in Tangier was sealed by the American Consulate. A French lawyer, Maître Bonan, wrote that French depositors were likely to take legal action against the Bank for recovery of their claims; and in Tangier the Société Générale started action to recover the amount of a cheque for Fr. frs. 4 million drawn on June 6, 1940, by Casablanca branch on Westminster Foreign Bank in Paris. As this payment had been blocked by the German authorities it was decided to defend the action. In the following year the Société Générale was, in fact, paid Fr. frs. 800,000, a fifth of its claim, and had accepted an undertaking that the balance would be paid within six months of the end of the war, with interest at 3%.

In 1941 Sir Roy Wilson wrote to the Tangier manager with directions in the event of a German invasion of Spain. Local customers were to be invited to remove securities left with the branch for safe custody. In 1942 the remaining eight members of the Casablanca staff were removed to the interior 'and were staying in well-known hotels'. At the request of the board P. G. Saffrey agreed to stay in Casablanca and was permitted to do so. Customers were offered a partial repayment of deposits, and by May 1942 two payments of 20% each had been made.

In November 1942 Casablanca was occupied by American forces. French and foreign banks did an active business, but the BBWA branch remained closed, though after a few weeks all the interned staff had been released and Mr. Saffrey, who had remained in the town throughout, cabled home to urge that he should be allowed to reopen the branch. The board wanted first to be sure that all claims of former depositors could be met, and there were legal and currency problems. The Bank of England, which had been consulted, offered in January 1943 to help with the French authorities and to arrange a transfer into Franc currency amounting to Fr. frs. 30 million, the counterpart of the Bank's franc funds, blocked in the Westminster Bank, Paris, by the German control.

This was accepted, but the branch was instructed to reopen only for the purpose of liquidating the old deposit liabilities. No new business was to be taken on. In June 1943 Casablanca branch re-opened, advertising that it would remain open only for forty days. The BBWA resumed negotiations for the lease or sale of the bank premises at Casablanca, Marrakech, Saffi and Mazagan; the entire business in French Morocco was to be brought to an end. Willing buyers came forward for the properties but no way could be found of converting the purchase price into sterling, so that the matter dragged on until after the end of the war.

At every stage of these events the BBWA management had been in close consultation with the Bank of England, and sometimes with the Treasury and the Foreign Office, to make sure of keeping within the complex wartime regulations. But something had gone wrong.

On September 29, 1943, Sir Frederick Eley, the chairman, was asked to call on the Governor of the Bank of England, Mr. Montague Norman (later Lord Norman). His record of the interview has survived, and is summarised here to illustrate that during the war bank managers and directors had to face highly unusual policy complications.

The Governor, noted Sir Frederick, expressed surprise that the Bank was closing down its branches in French Morocco. The Bank could not close down branches in foreign territory just as it wished, because British prestige had to be considered. 'The Governor intimated that he was speaking for the State or Government rather than for the Bank of England.'

Now there was at that period no more formidable public personality in Britain, except Winston Churchill, than Governor Norman. The Governor, without knowing it, was standing on a rug of which Sir Frederick Eley held the corner in his hand. Sir Frederick was a brave man – he pulled it. He read out a memorandum in which Mr. F. G. Wright, the Bank's General Manager, had recorded the content of several interviews with the official of the Bank of England in charge of French-African affairs. This showed that the Central Bank had not only approved the closing of the Moroccan branches but had arranged the payment of Frs. 30 million to repay depositors.

Mr. Norman was not so easily put off. At his request Frank Wright and the official concerned were called in and confirmed their agreement. It emerged that two months earlier the BBWA had quite properly sent to the Governor a copy of the latest annual accounts containing a statement by the chairman informing the shareholders of the board's decision to close the branches finally. The Governor said there must be some unfortunate misunderstanding. He had only just heard of the decision.

Next, Sir Frederick Eley explained that the BBWA had suffered substantial losses in Morocco ever since it first opened up, and there were no prospects ahead to justify keeping open at a heavy annual outlay and loss. The Governor was not impressed: if the Bank made losses they ought to be borne by the large shareholders. 'This apparently was said seriously,' reported Sir Frederick. He then

Kano Branch. The silver-painted dome became a landmark for aircraft bound for Kano (demolished for re-building, 1974)

BANK OF BRITISH WEST AFRICA Ltd

(*Above*) Ceremonial
opening of new premises
at Gombe by the Emir
of Gombe, May 5, 1956

(*Below*) Ibadan
Branch, completed 1969
(strong-room block at
right background)

Ikeja Airport Branch, Nigeria, where the first drive-in bank in West Africa was installed, 1960

pointed out that the Bank had dispersed its staff, it had sold the Marrakech premises and might have an offer for the Casablanca premises at any time. In reply the Governor said grimly that 'consent to the sale of any properties would not be given'.

After this broadside the directors decided that 'efforts to obtain Bank of England approval for the sale of the Marrakech premises should continue'. The matter was pursued at a 'departmental' level, and a month later the consent was quietly given.

However, the larger question whether the Bank should entirely withdraw from Morocco or give it another trial after the war remained in the air. In April 1945 the Bank of England made a final effort. A meeting took place between Cameron Cobbold (a director who later became Governor and is now Lord Cobbold) and Sir Frederick Eley, with officials present.

Mr. Cobbold expressed the hope that the BBWA, in view of the expectation that the war would end shortly, would be willing to adopt a 'wait and see' policy for long enough to make certain whether or not there was real scope for a British bank in Morocco. He mentioned that the Bank of England had recently been in touch with the Foreign Office 'whose views might not necessarily coincide with their own', and that a confidential report had been obtained from His Majesty's Consul-General in Casablanca.

Sir Frederick Eley replied that the Bank had entered Morocco in 1915 and could speak with the experience of twenty-five years during which eight branches had functioned. Those years had not been fruitful. The business handled was highly speculative, with profits depressed by the competition of eleven other banks, and more than eclipsed by bad debts and administration expenses. In June 1943, when Morocco was liberated and the Casablanca branch reopened, the Bank had purchased Frs. 30 million to repay depositors; it had cost them £150,000. This had been done because the Bank's franc funds were lodged in Paris, blocked by the enemy authorities.

Since then no real business had emerged and none was in prospect. They had no names of substantial customers left on their books. If the branch were kept open it would cost the Bank something like £10,000 a year. Sir Frederick then pointed out that the principal shareholders of the BBWA were four of the large banks, who

M

knew that it had a sound business in the West African colonies and
would deprecate any action involving further losses in foreign territory such as Morocco. Surely they would expect the board of the
BBWA to take 'the view of a prudent banker'.

That put the Bank of England in a dilemma: it was their duty to
see that British banks were prudently conducted, but they had also
been asked by the Foreign Office to see that something was done for
British prestige. The first duty was uppermost, and Mr. Cobbold
said that while he hoped that the BBWA directors would wait and
see what the future held for them in Morocco, he would no longer
'insist' and leave the final decision to the board. The decision to
withdraw was, in fact, confirmed by the directors and Mr. Cobbold
was informed.

As a postscript it should be recorded that after the liberation of
France the blocked balances in Paris were released and the Bank
sold Frs. 30 million to the Bank of England, realising £149,906, and
reducing the loss of the Casablanca pay-out to only £94.

The conditions created by the Spanish Civil War led to the closing
down of the branches in the Canary Islands, at Tenerife and Las
Palmas. This had been decided in 1937 but the winding up and sale
of premises to the Banco Hispano Americano was delayed until 1945.
The manager (Mr. J. B. Shipley) and a senior clerk were kept on full
pay throughout the war years simply to supervise the collection of
bills.

WARTIME COMMODITY CONTROLS

International demand for West African produce was stimulated by
the war. In the thirties the export of edible oils and nuts had met
with increasing competition from Far Eastern sources but now the
shorter distances from the European and American markets favoured
West Africa. Shipping however was much disrupted, and at first
prices on the produce markets fluctuated widely – except for cocoa,
which was controlled from the start. The supply of consumer goods
on which the African producers normally spent their earnings became scarce. The situation encouraged inflation – too much money
chasing too few goods. These facts played some part in the policy

by which the Government control boards set up after the outbreak of war tackled the control of marketing and exports. While cocoa was at once taken over by the British Ministry of Food the control of palm oil, palm kernels and groundnuts developed more gradually until in 1942 the West African Produce Control Board was formed. The Board fixed buying prices for each season. The bills of lading relating to shipments had to be delivered to its officers in West Africa and payment would be made in London on cable advice from the Coast. The cables would include information on advances made by the banks in West Africa against each lot, and these would be repaid by the Board.

While the main control board handled the range of staple products already listed, control arrangements existed for some other commodities as well. For example, hides and skins were shipped to Britain for the account of the Leather Controller; for shipments to the USA the bills of lading were sent to the British Supply Mission in New York. Coffee was shipped from the Gold Coast and Sierra Leone under directions from the British Ministry of Food, which had credit lines with the BBWA for this purpose.

Like most Government controls at all times, this system favoured the established trading companies and particularly the larger firms on whose advice the controllers had inevitably to rely. It needs no emphasis that the smaller traders, as well as the African producers, strongly resented this aspect of wartime control.

The fixing of purchase prices by the control boards raised an even more profound problem. It soon became the Government's policy to fix prices for staple exports well below international levels. The idea was partly to shield the African farmers from the ups and downs of world markets, building up surplus funds in high price years so as to even out incomes in bad years. Another reason was that higher incomes at a time when imported consumer goods were short because of unavoidable shortage of shipping would only lead to more inflation. For some years these arguments were widely accepted as reasonable. Indeed the policy of 'stabilisation' was maintained for a number of years after the war. And in different forms the marketing boards became a permanent institution and were taken over by the African governments on independence.

The power of officials to fix prices was of course highly unpopular from the start among African farmers who knew perfectly well that the controlled prices were almost invariably well below world market levels. They suspected, not without justice, that the bulk of the large reserves that were being piled up by the control boards and their peacetime successors would never be returned to them, but would be spent on a remote thing called economic development. This hostility on broad political grounds was added to the popular discontent against the additional power which the controls gave to the big merchant firms. In the circumstances of the war some form of Government intervention was probably inevitable as West Africa was physically cut off from its foreign markets and sources of supply, except in so far as the Allied navies and airforces could protect the shipping lanes. But when trade was not returned into private hands at the end of the war it became open to argument whether the marketing boards did in fact stabilise prices or did the opposite.

The leading critic of the policy has been Professor P. T. Bauer whose book *West African Trade* appeared at Cambridge in 1954. Bauer argued on the basis of the record that the boards, while fixing prices for each season, had not succeeded in stabilising prices from one season to another, and had entirely failed to stabilise incomes. Bauer maintained that incomes were more unstable under the Marketing Board system than they would have been without it. The dispute went on with some heat for a number of years and by now it is fairly safe to say that the critics won the argument. One can contend that organised marketing and price fixing is a useful way of raising funds for Government-planned economic development; but it will now be hard to show that official price fixing, for whatever motive, ever succeeds in stabilising markets.

A measured judgement was passed in 1966 by Sir Sydney Caine, a former distinguished colonial civil servant, and more recently Head of the London School of Economics. In a paper on *Prices for Primary Producers* (Institute of Economic Affairs, London) he wrote that 'Government actions have been the cause of most of the major disturbances in commodity prices. . . . Most of the West African Boards set up after the war began by accumulating large funds in their early years as a result of wrongly guessing the trend of prices.

The African producers were thus subjected to an involuntary levy. Later the Boards or their Governments diverted a substantial part of the surpluses away from the growers to various public purposes. The Boards have become at least partly tax collectors.'

Sir Sydney Caine's conclusion was: 'Cutting off producers from direct contact with markets and encouraging the habit of attributing all responsibility to Government must prejudice long-term development by delaying the growth in the African peasant of a real commercial and entrepreneurial sense.'

OTHER WARTIME CHANGES

Another lasting set of changes brought about by the war was in *communications*. A commercial airline linking Kano in Northern Nigeria with Khartoum, where it met the main route from South Africa to London, had been opened jointly by Imperial Airways and Elder Dempster in 1936. A proving flight London–Khartoum–Kano was successfully carried out. The 1,700 mile journey from Khartoum to Kano, with seven refuelling stops, took fifteen hours' flying time at a speed of about 115 miles per hour. Regular services were then introduced and extended to Lagos and Accra. The line was managed by Elder's Colonial Airways, which proceeded to install internal flights on a number of routes.

In June 1940 the whole operation was taken over by the British Government. Even the pre-war beginnings of air communications had done something to break down the relative isolation of West Africa from other continents. During and after the war the growth of both domestic and international airlines brought the area for the first time fully into the world economy.

Airmail services began in a small way just after the 1939–45 war. The Bank's branch at Bathurst (now Banjul) was the first to use the airmail as a service to and from South America called at the nearby port of Dakar in Senegal. Before long direct air services from the chief West African cities to London and other world centres developed. Well before 1960 all the Bank mail to West Africa was being despatched by air. It was a drastic change from the earlier processes: before 1946 most letters between the Bank's Head Office and its West

African branches went by surface mail. This took fourteen days or more to Lagos and a reply could not be expected in less than a month. Cargo vessels could take six weeks, through loading and unloading at intermediate ports, and might have to wait for a berth at Lagos.

There was always the possibility that mail would be lost in transit; so duplicates of all letters were sent by the following mail. On arrival they had to be checked to confirm that the original had been received, and then destroyed. In practice this was not always done carefully and some 'confidential' duplicates did not get the security rating they deserved. One such copy, thrown into the waste-paper basket and picked out by a clerk, led to serious embarrassment – as will be told later. After that, from the late fifties onwards, highly confidential messages were dictated into a tape recorder and the tape was sent to the addressee who had the use of a play-back instrument.

Cable communication between England and West Africa had existed before the turn of the century, and the Bank's first private cable code was compiled soon after 1900 by Roy Wilson; this was replaced by a more professional code in the 1920s. Yet another private code was constructed in 1952 and this was in use until recently. The Lagos Cable Station was linked to Accra by radio and thence direct to England in 1929; in that year there were ninety-eight telegraph offices in Nigeria alone. A wireless station was built in Lagos by the Eastern Telegraph Company in 1929. Radio telephones had to wait until the late 1950s and the first commercial telex network was introduced in Nigeria in 1960, the Bank being one of the first six subscribers.

Just how much of this communications development was generated by the war one cannot tell, but the fact that certain key points in British West Africa were of crucial military importance for naval and air strategy no doubt helped to speed the arrival of technical innovations on the Coast. For the Bank these changes meant a great deal: staff could be moved about more quickly while the control of operations by Head Office was strengthened by the rapid exchange of reports and instructions.

The steady reduction in staff numbers has already been mentioned. As for pay, modest rises were approved each year, but from 1939 only those with salaries under £350 a year received rises; senior officers got nothing, at least for the next two years. In the year to March 31, 1942, the total salary bill was £125,270 against £152,391 for the year to March 31, 1938. A modest cost of living allowance was added from 1940 and a cash bonus from 1941, but it was only in 1942 that the directors approved a new salary scale for Europeans in West Africa, starting with £310 per annum for the first year plus duty allowance of £60 per annum, and rising to £405 p.a. plus allowance of £72 p.a. for the sixth year. 'This improved scale would affect 26 people and would bring salaries more nearly to the level of Barclays', says a note. Relatively low pay was at that period a weakness of the B B W A for which it paid dearly after the war. Four junior members of the European staff at Lagos refused the 1942 rise as inadequate, and a small concession was made. In future full pay would be paid on voyages and on leave. In 1943 a special cash bonus was paid to European staff both at home and in West Africa, and this was repeated in the next two years; in 1945 a grant of £30 was paid to married staff on the Coast plus £15 p.a. for each child. In 1946 a 'victory bonus' of 12½% plus a non-recurring 5% was paid to European staff.

As for African staff, the Bank fell in with a decision by the Nigerian Government to pay cost of living allowances to its African employees. The extra cost to the Bank was £1,839 in the first year. All along the Bank's policy was 'to conform with what other employers are doing'. In September 1945 the directors decided to increase the maximum salary of Africans promoted to European appointments (this would include cashiers) from £300 to £450 per annum. Retirement gratuities to such Africans were raised from six to twelve months' salary.

On the whole, the Bank came through the Second World War without serious damage. It managed to adapt itself to massive changes in economic and financial conditions. The more difficult changes had to be faced when peace was restored.

Chapter Thirteen

THE PROBLEMS OF
PEACE

A WIDER HORIZON

AT the end of the war the Bank was in a strange financial condition.
Its deposits had increased since 1939 from £7·3 million to £19·3
million, but much of the extra money was simply lodged with the
Bank because it could not be constructively employed in production
and trade. Almost 40% of the Bank's resources was held in cash,
about 50% in Government securities and little more than 10% was
used in loans and advances to customers. This picture of stagnation
reflected the wartime problem of West Africa: isolation from world
markets and sources of supply had held down commerce while high
prices had inflated holdings of money. The total supply of currency
in West Africa had more than doubled from £11·7 million to
nearly £30 million.

But from 1946 onwards the Bank's figures begin to look differently; not only deposits but advances and 'liabilities for customers'
expand; and the profit is rising vigorously. The table on the next
page shows this trend.

The reserve fund increased comfortably from £600,000 on
March 31, 1945, to £1 million on March 31, 1951. Incidentally the
price of BBWA shares on the London Stock Exchange fluctuated
widely in this period, from a low point of £6 3s. 9d. in 1946 to a
peak of nearly £10 in 1948 and down again to £5 15s. in 1950, to
recover to £9 in September 1951. (These were the old shares of £10
each, £4 paid.) It was obviously difficult in the early years of peace

Year ended March 31	Deposits	Advances (In £ millions)	Liabilities for Customers	Profit after tax, etc. £	Dividend %
1946	23·8	2·7	2·9	130,974	6
1947	25·9	4·4	4·9	145,582	7
1948	38·0	4·1	6·3	143,472	7
1949	38·1	4·5	6·7	144,932	7
1950	44·6	7·8	5·3	154,268	7
1951	52·7	9·2	10·5	183,321	9
1952	54·6	14·4	9·3	212,029	9
1953	58·8	12·3	7·6	242,506	10

to judge the prospects of the BBWA – as indeed those of all the British overseas banks.

World demand and prices for West African products were in fact very high in the immediate post-war years and economic development was rapid. In financing it the large surplus funds piled up by the Produce Marketing Boards as soon as wartime controls were eased, as well as British Government aid and loans and bank financing, all played their part. The dramatic changes of the post-war decade were well described by a World Bank mission reporting in 1954 on Nigeria:

In less than ten years the economy has grown and strengthened to such an extent that it bears little resemblance to the pre-war economy. The initial impetus for this growth came from the wartime and expanded post-war demand for Nigerian exports. World-wide shortages of vegetable fats and oils and a strong demand for cocoa, tin and columbite resulted in high export prices. This permitted not only a substantial rise in living standards ... but also a large increase in government revenues and substantial savings by both the government and the Marketing Boards. The government revenues and the profits of the Marketing Boards, supplemented by Colonial Development and Welfare grants from the United Kingdom government, in turn permitted the substantial expansion of public health and education services and of such public facilities as roads, ports and water supplies. ...

The private section of the economy has likewise participated in and benefited from this expansion. The production of foodstuffs for domestic consumption has kept pace with the growth of income originating in the export sector. Foreign firms have expanded their commercial operations

in Nigeria and have started manufacturing enterprises. Africans in growing numbers have entered the field of foreign trade and many have found
employment in managerial and clerical positions in government and
business.

Similar comments might have been made at the time on the
economies of the other West African colonies. For British West
Africa as a whole the money circulation increased from £34 million
at mid-1946 to £94 million at mid-1954.

These economic changes – leaving the even more drastic political
changes aside for the moment – presented the BBWA with a serious
challenge. In 1947, for example, the Nigerian Government put to
the Bank's acting manager at Lagos a 'tentative proposal' for a long-
term development loan, possibly for a sum of £3 million. At once
the chairman called a special meeting of the board 'as the granting
of long-term facilities of such large figures represented a new
departure in the Bank's policy'. The proposal would have to be
clearly explained to the shareholding banks, who between them held
more than half the BBWA's capital. They seem to have raised no
objection. It was decided to send W. F. Becker, the joint general
manager, to Lagos to make a favourable response to the loan proposal.

Mr. Becker, to give him greater authority, was elected a director
and released from the management. He was asked to take up two
other questions with the Nigerian Government. One was the con-
tinuation of the Government account, the agreement for which
expired that year. The other was 'a new departure into long-term
commercial loans similar to what is being done by Barclays Overseas
Development Corporation'. (Barclays (DC&O) had formed this
Corporation in 1945.)

Mr. Becker duly went to Lagos and soon reported that he had
reached agreement with the Nigerian Government on a number of
topics. The Government account would continue to be with the
BBWA, but finer rates had to be conceded. On the long-term
loan, Becker had agreed that the Bank would underwrite or subscribe to £3 million of a 20–25 year stock provided the terms were
reasonable. The Bank would also grant a loan of £850,000 to a new
body, the Cameroons Development Corporation, which was to

purchase from the Public Custodian the formerly German plantations in the British Cameroons. Repayment would be over 35 years.
Finally the Bank would make a loan of £100,000 to the Ibadan Native
Administration for an enlarged waterworks scheme. The terms were
approved by the board and the agreement with the Nigerian Government was signed in Lagos on June 2, 1947.

Once the breakthrough was made, more long-term loans were
granted in the other colonies. In Freetown a five-year loan was made
to a private customer to complete the building of a local cinema.
In the Gold Coast a loan of £24,000 was granted to the Sekondi/
Takoradi Town Council for the purchase of twenty buses to replace
worn-out vehicles. In January 1948 Accra Town Council obtained a
loan of £42,000 for 20-25 years for the building of a new bus
garage, workshops and stores, to be secured by a mortgage on
revenue. Interest was at $3\frac{1}{2}\%$ p.a. Another loan of £66,000 for a
maximum of 15 years was granted to the same Town Council for
the purchase of new motor buses. It was noted that the Council
already had an advance of £40,000 for the same purpose from
Barclays Development Corporation.

These are merely examples of many similar loans made from 1947
onwards. They show that the BBWA was playing its part quite
early in the financing of economic development, even though it did
not form a special institution for the purpose or make any public
declaration of a new policy.

Another shift of emphasis occurred in 1947 when the West African
Produce Control Board handed over its functions to marketing
boards set up at Lagos and Accra. The new boards decided not to pay
the buying merchants any longer against fortnightly declarations of
tonnage bought and held in warehouses awaiting shipment, but to
pay only after loading on board against shipping documents. This
meant that the traders needed more finance, and the Bank had to
provide it. In July 1947 four large European firms arranged additional facilities of £4·5 million for the next season. Others, of course,
followed.

By 1950 the new system of produce buying and marketing compelled other adjustments in the Bank's policies. Advances against
produce in store rose to very high figures, and African names began

to appear much more often in the lists of customers for whom credits were arranged. The pace of economic development is also reflected in the growing number of contracting firms among the Bank's borrowers. Loans to co-operatives began even earlier to play a substantial part. In 1946 a credit of £500,000 was opened for the newly formed Gold Coast Co-operative Bank to help with the financing of that season's cocoa crop. In the same year a limit of £300,000 was agreed for advances to the Association of Nigerian Co-operative Exporters, jointly with the Registrar of Co-operative Societies. These limits were raised in later years.

All these examples indicate that the more expansive policy adopted by the Bank in the fifties was not a sudden change of course but a natural development of steady post-war adaptation.

FILLING THE DEPLETED RANKS

The board of directors had been much reduced during the war years by retirements and deaths. Many more changes took place in the post-war period. First R. E. Dickinson retired after twenty-one years as a director. He had been a nominee of the Standard Bank of South Africa, and that bank now proposed J. F. G. Gilliat, who was elected. Next Sir Austin E. Harris resigned in 1946 after twenty-five years of service on the board. E. Whitley-Jones, a chief general manager of Lloyds Bank, was elected as his successor. He had been with the B B W A before, serving for seven years in Egypt. When the Egyptian business was taken over by Lloyds Bank he went with it, transferred to England, and rose to the chief managerial post. He brought valuable practical experience to the board and was later elected a deputy chairman.

In June 1946 knighthoods were conferred on Jasper Ridley and Sydney Parkes. In 1947, as mentioned above, W. F. Becker joined the board and retired from management. In 1948 Mr. J. F. G. Gilliat died, and the Standard Bank nominated Lord Harlech as his successor.

In December 1948 Sir Frederick Eley resigned 'owing to increasing years and declining health' after twenty-eight years as a director and six years as chairman. Sir Francis Beane was elected chairman and

Sir Sydney Parkes deputy chairman. In July 1949 Lord Goschen, a director since 1937, retired. Mr. Sylvester Gates, a barrister with banking experience, was elected a director by nomination by the Westminster Bank. Early in 1951 Lord Milverton, on retiring as Governor of Nigeria, joined the board of the BBWA. About the same time Major-General Sir Edward Spears, who had long-standing business connections with West Africa (particularly in goldmining) was elected to the board.

1951 was a year of important changes. The chairman, Sir Francis Beane, retired in May; soon afterwards Sir Jasper Ridley was given leave of absence for health reasons; in October he died and was succeeded by Lord Inchcape on the nomination of the National Provincial Bank.

Lord Harlech was elected chairman in July 1951. He was an eminent public figure deeply involved in the affairs of the British Empire in Africa. As Mr. William Ormsby-Gore he had been a Conservative Member of Parliament from 1910 to 1938; in 1917 he became Parliamentary Private Secretary to Lord Milner and then assistant secretary of the War Cabinet. Lord Milner stimulated his interest in Africa and in 1922 he became Under-Secretary of State for the Colonies; in that period he paid his first visit to West Africa. Much later, in 1936, he was for two years Secretary of State for the Colonies and in 1941 he was sent to South Africa as British High Commissioner for three years. It was after his return to England that he joined the board of the Standard Bank of South Africa and was also elected a director of the Midland Bank where he became deputy chairman. Soon after becoming chairman of the BBWA he was also elected chairman of the Midland Bank and held both posts concurrently for some years. It did not seem to matter that the Midland was not one of the three London clearing banks which had substantial shareholdings in the BBWA.

Lord Harlech was regarded by the management as an excellent chairman who kept a keen eye on general policy and left the running of the Bank to the managers. He had a warm sympathy for Africans and a gift for getting on with them. Incidentally his deepest personal interest was in art: he was for many years a Trustee of the British Museum, the National Gallery and the Tate Gallery, and the three books he published were all on artistic subjects, including one on *Florentine Sculptures of the 15th Century*.

Frank G. Wright, since 1947 general manager, was elected to the board while remaining in his managerial post. This made the board very strong in experienced bank managers but it left the management team somewhat weakened; at any rate the problem of finding the right men to succeed to the senior management posts in the next few years was brought into the open.

Many of those recruited after the first war were becoming due for retirement. Some had left the Bank's service – one became Accountant General of Nigeria. The good men who remained were needed as much in West Africa as in London, especially as a period of expansion and intense competition in banking had just begun. As early as 1945 the joint head office managers (Becker and Wright) were aware of the succession problem. In that year W. A. Evans who had become redundant in Morocco, was appointed Assistant Manager in London; unfortunately he died within a month of taking up the post. It was decided to recall Geoffrey Redmayne from the Coast. He was to assist the London manager temporarily, but in 1946 he was appointed London Manager to succeed W. Johnson, and his stay at head office became permanent.

About the same time E. G. Butterworth was appointed assistant to the joint head office managers. He had been accountant at Accra, a senior post at the time. He did not stay long at Head Office, possibly because he did not get on well with Frank Wright who had become sole General Manager. Butterworth returned to West Africa as an inspector; not long afterwards he left the Bank to join first the Ghana Trade Commission in London and later a similar Nigerian body. Presumably Butterworth had been regarded as a future general manager, and his departure left a gap which was not filled for twelve months. On August 11, 1948, Geoffrey Redmayne was appointed Assistant General Manager and was highly regarded in that position for twenty years until he retired.

Another appointment in 1948 was the promotion to chief accountant of L. J. Kerridge, who had been manager at Casablanca after previous service in Hamburg and the Canary Islands. He, too, did not last. In 1950 he was sent to Hamburg as manager, possibly because he had mastered several European languages. The new chief accountant was Allan Walker.

That was the background against which Lord Harlech, when he became chairman in 1951, had to consider the managerial succession. He decided to seek the right man outside the Bank. He had just become chairman of the Midland Bank as well, and that is where he looked for his candidate. Mr. John C. Read, who was chosen, had twenty-six years of experience at Midland Bank head office and branches as well as in America. He was first appointed an Assistant General Manager of the B B W A in February 1952 and on September 1, 1955, he became the General Manager, which he remained for over fourteen years. Those were years of fundamental change for the Bank, and John Read led the management team throughout the period.

This seems the right place to mention the names of some men prominent in the Bank's service in West Africa in the post-war years. In Lagos the much respected manager, D. D. Gibb, was invalided home during the war and was succeeded by K. M. Oliver, who retired soon after the war. In 1947 W. F. Cable became Lagos Manager and in 1948 he was made District Manager for West Africa. He was highly regarded by his colleagues but seems to have felt unhappy in his post. He resigned in 1952 and went to Canada, where he achieved a senior position with the Bank of Montreal. E. J. McQuin succeeded Cable as Lagos manager and later as District Manager. He was called to London early in 1957 to be appointed an Assistant General Manager, a post he held with considerable ability until his retirement in 1968. In Accra D. H. Medcalf succeeded G. B. Kirk as manager in 1947; later he became District Manager and executive director for Ghana and retired from that position in 1966.

STAFF PROBLEMS ON THE COAST

It was not only the board and the senior management that needed fresh blood. The rank and file of the staff had been allowed to run down. During the depression years, which lasted really from 1921 to 1939 with only short recoveries, the Bank was not doing well and was forced to cut down expenditure. Staff numbers and salaries

were curbed. This caused many European officers to seek employment elsewhere. During the war, from 1939 to 1945, it was virtually
impossible to recruit new staff; at the end of 1945 the total staff on
the Coast, Europeans and Africans, numbered 461. Soon afterwards
many of the older men serving in West Africa reached retirement
age. And while the shortage of experienced staff became acute, the
amount of work increased very rapidly.

In 1951 a senior inspector, J. R. Wilkinson, was given the task of
looking into an abnormally large number of frauds at the Bank's
Nigerian branches. His detailed report, dated January 5, 1952, on
seventeen cases involving probable losses of over £25,000 closed
with an instructive comment on staff conditions, which he considered the main cause of the trouble.

The growth of the workload, reflecting (with some inflationary
exaggeration) the expansion of economic activity in Nigeria, was
illustrated by a few figures relating only to Lagos:

Year	Current A/c Turnover £	Bills Collected £	Telegraphic Transfers Paid £
1938–9	12,972,775	251,585	1,630,953
1945–6	48,369,201	453,268	3,610,058
1950–1	117,091,542	4,063,808	12,829,596

For the reasons given above, there were few European officers left
in the Bank's service with five or more years' experience. Since the
war a number of young men had been recruited but many of them,
coming out of the services, were restless and left before they could
gain technical banking experience. In 1951, out of fifteen European
officers in Lagos, ten were on their first tour in West Africa. (A 'tour'
was then twelve or eighteen months, and while the employment
contract was normally renewed there was no undertaking to do so).

Why were so many juniors leaving? It was 'neither salary conditions, though there are some complaints, nor dislike of the country....
The principal causes are extension of tours beyond the contract
period and uncertainty of leave dates, coupled with long hours of
work at the branches to which juniors are usually first sent' (J. R.

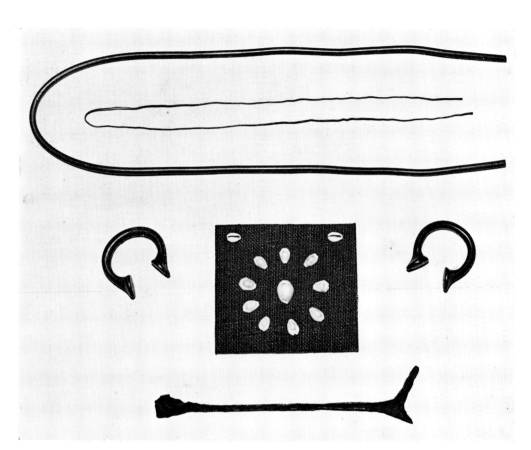

Early forms of currency.
Top: brass rod and copper
wire. Centre: cowries and
manillas. Bottom: 'Kissy'
penny (photograph by
courtesy Standard Chartered
Bank museum)

(*Above*) West African
Currency Board coin
(photograph by courtesy
Standard Chartered Bank
museum)

(*Opposite Top*) West
African Currency Board notes
(photograph by courtesy
Standard Chartered Bank
museum)

(*Opposite Bottom*) Specimen
BBWA note prepared by
Bradbury, Wilkinson & Co. in
1897; no note issue made.

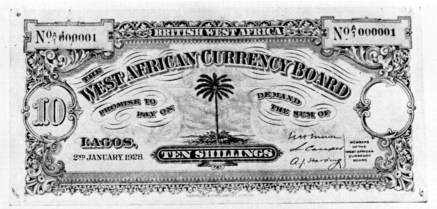

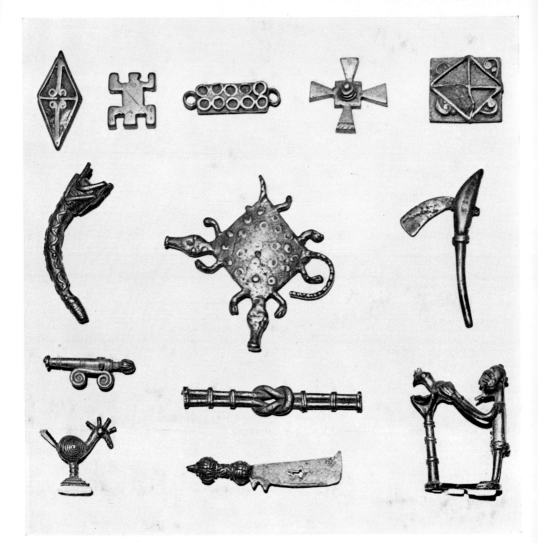

Ashanti gold weights
(photograph by courtesy
Standard Chartered Bank
museum).

Wilkinson's report). Many of the young arrivals had no previous knowledge of banking. Yet some had to be put in charge of branches, and not all proved satisfactory. As a result of their inexperience or inadequacy 'clerical staff have felt that they could do as they pleased'.

As for African staff, 'boom conditions in West Africa since the war have caused a big demand for clerical labour, which has exceeded the supply of efficient applicants. . . . A large proportion of the clerical staff is inexperienced. Out of a total of 110 at Lagos on December 31, 1951 as many as 32 were engaged during 1951.' Moreover 'boom conditions have enabled some Africans to make considerable fortunes since 1946, inducing a "get-rich-quick" mentality in others'.

The inexperience of many Europeans and Africans had thrown a heavy weight of responsibility on the senior staff, the report went on. Their hours of work, and to a lesser extent those of the juniors, would be considered long in the United Kingdom and in the tropics might be deleterious to health.

These conditions were not easy to change overnight. Accommodation for Europeans was strictly limited, and it would take time to build new houses. Smaller branches, too, had no room to house an extra European for practical training. Meanwhile a number of recruits had been arriving from Europe at the age of twenty or twenty-one, when they could hardly have had even elementary training in office work, let alone in banking procedures.

The inspector who wrote this report and judged that salary scales were not a major cause of complaint had been brought up in a hard school. Others did not agree. Around the same time, on October 25, 1950, a European branch manager of the Bank was being sentenced at Port Harcourt to thirteen months imprisonment for defrauding the Bank of money, and Mr. Justice Abbott, delivering the sentence, had some harsh words to say about the salaries paid by the BBWA at that time:

I find it difficult, if not impossible, to understand how your late employers expect a man in your position, who has a certain standard to maintain, to keep up that standard or even to do more than merely exist, on the salary which was being paid to you. To my mind, the Bank is very much to blame in this respect. The manager of the Bank of British West Africa

N

here is in a very responsible position, with millions of pounds passing under his control in the course of each tour. I cannot do better than describe your salary as a niggardly, wretched salary for the manager of a branch of the importance of the one in Port Harcourt. . . . I am satisfied further that you earned and more than earned every penny of your salary, considering the long hours you worked.

The salary which provoked this outburst of indignation was a basic pay of £920 per annum, a duty allowance of £72 p.a., a car allowance of £50 p.a. and an annual bonus of 15% equalling £138 – a total income of £1,180.

Living conditions of the staff, certainly outside the few large centres, had not kept pace with the general growth of prosperity. Around 1950 a young man sent to manage one of the up-country branches would have to live in a tiny bungalow without running water or electricity; the rickety house might well be blown away in a storm. One tall man remembers that as late as 1955, as a small-branch manager, he had such a minute bedroom that there was space only for a five-foot bed, and he had to lie crossways to sleep. Next to his bungalow was a maternity hospital, its delivery room facing his bedroom window across a narrow passage!

Most of the younger bank officers at that time were bachelors, but some wives lived in similar squalor. One lady recalls how she went to Northern Nigeria about 1950 to join her husband, a junior branch manager. They had, of course, no running water and no electricity (therefore no fans); they cooked on a wood fire, and she went shopping in the local market as they had very little money. Her husband had to travel about the region a good deal, sometimes by donkey or camel. Once she fell ill with malaria when he was away. But of course 'one got to know the people very well in a small town, and they were very kind'. Her first baby was born in Kano as she refused to follow the custom for wives to go home to England to have their children. In the outlying places there were usually very few Europeans. A manager sent to a branch like Nguru, close to the desert, before the motor road and airfield arrived, might be the only white man there twenty-five years ago, except perhaps for a missionary. Yet his responsibilities would be serious. He had to judge which of the African traders to trust with loans, to finance the produce buyers, and to know all about the business of his local customers, one of whom earned substantial profits from buying Korans for seven shillings and selling them to the faithful at twenty-four shillings.

Taking in deposits might involve considerable sums. Many years ago one African customer of a small branch in the north had a current-account balance of nearly £500,000. The manager invited him in and offered to pay interest; the man did not know that he had so much money and did not want interest. To store the cash there was no strong-room, not even a safe, but only a wooden box. Security rested in the knowledge – never admitted by the Bank manager – that any thief need only be reported to the local Elders to be executed without hesitation.

So much for the persistent belief that colonial Europeans lived in easy comfort. It is as well to record that the BBWA was not alone in expecting its staff to live in rough conditions. In June 1951 Barclays (DC&O) opened a new local head office for their West African business. J. C. D. Cox was the first local director, appointed to administer branches in Nigeria, the Gold Coast, Sierra Leone and the British Cameroons, a total of nineteen offices. The following description of what Mr. Cox found in Lagos is quoted, with permission, from the files of Barclays (DC&O):

Cox and his one assistant were located in two rooms over the old 55 Marina branch, and from the point of view of premises and amenities this was probably the least attractive of any local head office ever established by our Bank. Those were the days before air-conditioning. Working conditions, always very trying in the South of Nigeria, were particularly obnoxious in Lagos where the business had long outgrown the capacity of the sordid old building.

It soon proved impossible to continue taking up space so urgently needed by a branch 'bursting at its seams', and in May 1953 local head office moved to what must surely be the all-time low in administrative offices in our Bank. This was on the fourth floor of a grocery and general merchandise store. Access could only be obtained by entering the main public door of the store, elbowing a way through the milling customers, mounting dusty concrete stairs and stepping over the recumbent forms of Africans resting from their labours in the comparative cool of the staircase well. Having negotiated these obstacles the visitor, emerging suddenly from the gloom into brilliant sunlight, found himself teetering on the edges of a concrete roof with no parapet, whence a sharp turn took him to the rooms which formed Local Head Office, West Africa. All this had one merit. Few customers tried to visit the local director over a manager's head – it was too difficult.

The rooms were of plain concrete and faced due West with nothing to shield them from the sun. The heat in the afternoon had to be experienced to be believed. . . . Yet these conditions did not deter Cox, who was joined by L. C. Daldry in 1952, from pressing on with the mandate to expand representation in West Africa.

To return to the BBWA's general staff policy around 1950, the conditions revealed by the Wilkinson report and more harshly by the comments of the Port Harcourt judge posed a serious problem. For an institution with a far-flung branch network, operating on a system of dispersed decision-making, a reliable staff is vital. Staff can never be completely reliable unless it is contented. In 1950 the BBWA's staff was not contented. Too many men had grievances and felt that the Bank's leadership did not care about them. There is plenty of evidence, from talks with older men who recall the period, that (to quote a typical reminiscence) the staff 'felt underpaid, overworked, badly housed, and badly treated in such matters as length of contract and pay when on leave'. In all these matters the Bank had fallen behind the level of pay and conditions prevailing among large European firms on the Coast, let alone the civil service.

When the importance of the human problem was at last recognised in London a new attitude towards the staff emerged. But it took several years to reverse the trend by more active recruitment and training, new salary scales, a large building programme and so on. In 1952 Lord Harlech, the chairman, visited West Africa for three weeks and reported that there were great opportunities for expansion. That would need 'new buildings both of Bank offices and houses for our European staff . . . these are some of the best investments we can make'. By March 1953 the Coast staff had been expanded to 1,107 of whom 428 were Europeans and 679 Africans.

New ideas about the scale of expenditure needed in West Africa if the Bank was to hold its place in a fast-changing era had been slowly developing even before 1950. It fell to John Read, when he joined the Bank early in 1952, to focus and implement the new policy which was quickly to lead to a radical change of course: the decision of the Bank to break out of its traditional role of Government banker and guardian of the currency into fully fledged commercial banking.

THE POST-WAR BUILDING PROGRAMME

In tentative outlines the board and management in London had realised soon after the end of the war that a great deal of money would have to be spent on building or rebuilding bank premises in West Africa, and putting up new accommodation for managers and staff. In February 1947 the board was told that Lagos branch would have to be rebuilt within the next few years, and that a London architect, Ronald Ward, had been asked to prepare draft plans for a new building on modern lines. The directors authorised the managers to 'continue the discussions' but were reluctant to commit the Bank at that stage. By July 1947 they were informed that the new Lagos building might cost £100,000, and in November they approved the plan at an estimated cost of £124,000, exclusive of strong-room and office equipment. (The final cost was twice that sum.) In the same year the building of a residential block of four flats was approved. A year later, in November 1948, the General Manager, Frank Wright, 'reminded the board that a substantial, but necessary, building and rebuilding scheme was contemplated. New proposals would be submitted.'

In 1948 plans were approved for three houses at Kumasi, one for the accountant (to cost £4,100) and two for junior Europeans (at a cost of £6,200). They were to be designed by Ronald Ward, who was becoming the Bank's regular architect. In 1949 a bungalow for the Freetown manager was completed; it cost £9,000. As the demolition of the Lagos branch did away with the staff quarters it was decided to build two semi-detached bungalows and a detached one at Ikoyi – on the Bank Road site where the successor bank still has its directors housed.

A formal programme of 'building and rebuilding' was submitted to the directors by the General Manager in August 1949. It listed for immediate action: a new bank building at Tarkwa, Gold Coast, with flat above, and two semi-detached staff houses. New bank buildings with living quarters above at Koforidua and at Bo, Sierra Leone; and one without living quarters at Cape Coast. A bank office at Jos was to be extended. A new house for the manager was to be built at Takoradi, the new Gold Coast port.

For less urgent action ('from 3 to 5 years hence') the plan asked for new bank buildings with quarters above at Bathurst (also a manager's house) and Kumasi; a new bank office and manager's bungalow at Maiduguri, and an extension of the branch building in Freetown. All these schemes were approved in 1949, and others were soon added. In 1950 a new 'chalet' was approved for Sapele to house a second European; at Apapa, the Lagos port, the Bank had applied for a plot and the erection of banking premises was approved. In 1951 the Apapa building plans were authorised at a cost of about £30,000 including a Currency Board strong-room but excluding architect's fees. At Ibadan a staff bungalow was purchased from the Government. So the rebuilding gathered pace; but for several years it met only a small fraction of the need.

Chapter Fourteen

A DECADE OF EXPANSION

THE POLITICAL BACKGROUND CHANGES

AFRICAN dissatisfaction with the colonial system had been growing rapidly during the war. It was not merely a reflection of the new spirit of independence that appeared all over the continent. In West Africa the discontent was strengthened by adverse economic conditions and specific wartime grievances. The promise of steady progress towards prosperity of the European type, which had been implicit in earlier decades, had lost much of its glitter in the years of the slump. When the war brought shortages and inflation; when official bodies cut African producers and traders off from booming world markets and set low prices for the main cash commodities popular resentment became widespread. A number of serious strikes, culminating in the Nigerian general strike in 1945, emphasised the mood of disillusionment. Pressure for African participation in government and, as time went on, for full independence from colonial rule became irresistible.

The British Government, while always keeping a step behind the growth of political pressure, began a strategic retreat as soon as the war was over. Nigeria, indeed, obtained virtual independence in the 1946 constitution which gave African members a majority in the Assembly where they could outvote the Government. African Ministers were functioning by 1951 when the Macpherson constitution was enacted, and a Council of Ministers was formed in 1954, with regional Councils soon afterwards. Looking back one can see that real power left the Colonial Office in 1951, as soon as a non-government majority emerged in the Assembly. For a few years Britain held on to its final say in Nigerian affairs at the centre, but the regions were able to exercise increasingly effective African power. The approach of independence came a little later in the Gold Coast (which was then renamed Ghana) and Sierra Leone, and even later in The Gambia. The timing of the stages and the final transition to independence were different. But the shift of power took place throughout British West Africa during the 1950s.

The Bank of British West Africa was fully aware of these changes. Up to that time its resources had consisted largely of official deposits, and the great bulk of its loans were made to the European trading firms, though some long-term commitment to African development had begun as early as 1947. It was obvious that the Government account would before long go to new African banks, and that the care of the currency would be taken over by national central banks. These matters were then the subject of intensive study and argument. Experts from the Bank of England and other official bodies were visiting West Africa to advise on the regulation of the banking system and the setting up of central banks. At first their reports were still tentative. The *Report on banking in Nigeria* by G. D. Paton of the Bank of England which was published at Lagos in 1948 (see page 217) dealt mainly with protecting the public from irregular banking practices.

Next, the report on *Development and control of banking and agricultural credit facilities in the Gold Coast* published in Accra in 1952 dealt with rather different aspects, as no private African banks had yet appeared in the Gold Coast. Expert opinion at that time thought that it was too early to set up central banks in West Africa, but was concerned with the need for long-term development capital. In 1952 Sir Cecil Trevor submitted a report that went nearer the nerve centre: *Banking conditions in the Gold Coast and the question of setting up a National Bank.* This was quickly followed by Government action, which was described by Lord Harlech in a speech to shareholders of the BBWA in 1953:

The people of the Gold Coast have achieved a long cherished aim in the establishment of their own National Bank entitled the Bank of the Gold Coast, which has been opened with feelings of justifiable pride under the aegis of a board of directors composed mainly of Africans. It commences business with the guidance of experts and has highly trained African staff available in the eleven officers taken from our Bank's service and ten from another British bank. Our feelings are those of goodwill and friendly co-operation towards this new institution, with whom we desire to work in harmony.

The Bank of the Gold Coast was launched with a capital of £300,000 put up by the Government, and a British Governor, Alfred Eggleston. It was not difficult to recognise the future pattern of events in this early experiment. What happened later in the 1950s will be recorded in another section (*The Rise of the African Banks*, page 215).

If the BBWA was to have any real future after independence, it had to go all out for local deposits to create a base for a big commercial loan business. To secure deposits it had to build up a much larger network of branches, spreading out for the first time from the chief centres of administration to the market towns and the growing points for future economic development. It had to devise ways of encouraging Africans, as well as European and eastern traders, to open bank accounts. New lending techniques had to be developed and more attention paid to financing African-controlled business, which was beginning to spread through a variety of trades and light industry. And before all this could be done the Bank needed a much larger and better trained staff and many new buildings both for offices and for staff quarters.

The Bank was later criticised for being slow to adapt itself to the new era. In retrospect it may be thought that the radical changes in the general policy of the Bank which took place around 1952 might well have got under way three or four years earlier. But the first few post-war years were a deeply troubled time in Britain and Europe; it was not easy to be farsighted. The Bank had its hands full in reconstituting its board of directors and senior management, and, as we have seen, it had a difficult task in replenishing the depleted ranks of its staff.

Taking, for instance, the balance sheet for March 31, 1949, one can still see signs of exhaustion. Deposits had doubled since 1945, the year the war ended, but loans and advances were only 12% of deposits. To explain why vast sums were immobilised in cash and rapidly depreciating Government securities the chairman, Sir Francis Beane, said rather unconvincingly that 'these figures emphasise the degree of liquidity which the Bank deems it advisable to maintain to provide the finance required for the purchase of high priced West African produce at seasonal intervals'. In the year to March 1950, when the ratio of advances to deposits had risen to $17\frac{1}{2}\%$ – still a very low figure – the chairman again admitted that this might 'suggest unnecessary liquidity' but repeated that 'ample cash resources were essential'. In the following year the ratio was still only $18\frac{1}{2}\%$ but a new chairman, Lord Harlech, had come in. It was too soon for him to have influenced policy in the year to March 1952 when the loan ratio jumped to 27%; but he had already brought in J. C. Read from the Midland Bank as prospective general manager, and he seems to have been conscious of the need to speed up the changes which had been set in motion, or planned, in the preceding years.

Meanwhile the Bank was in close touch with the emerging African administrations and personalities. In 1951, when Lord Harlech paid a visit to West Africa, he reported: 'I was able to meet many of the new Ministers of Government and was impressed by their keenness and goodwill.' One of the Bank's managers was almost invariably a member of the central and regional administrative bodies. The senior managers were frequently consulted by African politicians and civil servants on monetary and banking matters, and when the central banks came to be set up they drew heavily on the experience – as well as on the staff – of the BBWA.

THE BANK TRANSFORMED

Seen from London, the principal reason for transforming the BBWA into a fully fledged commercial bank was the certainty that with the approaching end of colonial rule the functions of government banker and guardian of the currency would soon be taken over by African institutions. But there was more to it. Another change was going on in West Africa during the 1950s and it opened up a brilliant new opportunity to the Bank at the very time that its traditional purposes were seen to be fading out: the withdrawal of the European trading companies from the hinterland. The Produce Marketing Boards which had replaced the wartime Control Boards between 1947 and 1949 gradually took over the buying of produce in all four colonies from the trading companies. The move was clearly inspired by the wish to transfer the lucrative business of produce buying entirely to Africans, who had up to that time operated mainly as agents of European companies. The process had several stages and went on for a few years until the Marketing Boards had achieved the desired position of sole produce buyers. The Boards then appointed the buying agents and at first included the European firms already in the business.

But for the trading companies this involved a vital change. When the Boards took over they were buyers only. The companies had always made a large part of their profit from linking the buying of produce with the selling of merchandise in their widespread network of 'factories'. This became more and more difficult. The Produce Boards paid their buying agents in the form of commissions, and the rate was too low to make the business worthwhile for European firms. When their traditional retail trade in the produce-buying areas was increasingly hampered by the new arrangements – as well as by growing public complaints that Europeans were blocking the Africans' advance in retail trading, one of the functions they could most easily perform – the companies had no choice but to withdraw.

As a result, large areas of West Africa which had relied on the trading companies for banking services were going to be deprived of them. The companies, and especially the large ones like UAC, had built up an elaborate system of cash and credit. In some places the UAC acted as agent for the BBWA, in others it acted as if it were a bank itself and relied on the BBWA only for two services: the grant of an overall credit facility which was arranged in England and distributed in West Africa by the company's own organisation; and the supply of cash at the nearest BBWA branch. On this basis the UAC acted over vast areas of West Africa like a bank. Its general manager in each colony issued a 'credit authority' to a team of district managers who in turn granted smaller credit authorities to branch managers.

The branches, or agencies, or factories, would advance cash to produce buying agents and other traders when they went to the villages. They would also lend them thousands of jute bags brought from India for transport of produce. Repayment was made when the buyer returned with his goods, sometimes after several weeks. It was the trading companies therefore who fulfilled the retail banking function and took the financial risk in these areas. The prospect of their withdrawing and leaving a vacuum was of crucial importance to the BBWA just when it was looking for new fields of work.

The banks were drawn deeper into this process in Nigeria in 1954 when the regions of the new Federation acquired substantial autonomy and set up their own Marketing Boards. The large assets which the previous single-product Marketing Boards had accumulated were divided among the new Regional Boards and on this security the Boards raised bank credit in London to cover their seasonal requirements. The BBWA, Barclays and the British and French Bank all shared in this financing. The produce was marketed through the Nigeria Produce Marketing Company in London. Similar companies were also formed by the Gold Coast and Sierra Leone. A few years later the credit arrangements had to be changed as the Boards used up their accumulated surpluses and new forms of collateral had to be devised.

ATTACK IS THE BEST DEFENCE

In the early fifties the historic changes which have just been summarised were still trends rather than hard facts. It is always easy to say after the event that the outcome was obvious, but in 1952 the directors and senior managers of the BBWA could not take the future for granted. They had a very large proportion of the Bank's assets lying safely in London. It would not have been unreasonable – and the thought must have occurred to many of them – to beat a gradual retreat. The decision to do the opposite, to commit the Bank's resources heavily to a rapid expansion of the branch network and the staff, to embark on a massive rebuilding programme and to start large-scale commercial lending to Africans – that decision was as crucial as the decision of Sir Alfred Jones sixty years earlier to launch the Bank itself.

How it happened is hidden in the mist of personal memories – most of them differing greatly in emphasis. There is no record of the choice ever being formally discussed or a decision formally taken. The fact that the Bank chose to throw its resources into the attack rather than to retreat before the tide of history was probably more a matter of temperament than of logical decision. After all, that is how most historic events come about. The process is well brought out in a private note written for the purpose of this book by Mr. J. C. Read who joined the Bank in 1952 and presided over the era of expansion:

I cannot say that I saw the priorities. There were jobs to be done in all spheres and the priorities would be within each sphere, not between them. Deposits had to be developed, staff had to be enlarged and trained, buildings, both offices and quarters, had to be rebuilt, new techniques particularly of lending had to be devised, and we had to present a new image to the public.

John Read, as has been mentioned, was appointed Assistant General Manager of the B B W A after serving the Midland Bank for a quarter of a century. His experience with a bank that was much more active in commercial lending and more conscious of the need to fight for deposits in a competitive market brought a new outlook into the councils of the B B W A. But first of all he was to spend eighteen months in West Africa to get to know the territories, the customers, and the staff.

My travels had to be mostly by car over roads which were then almost entirely laterite. One had to ride the corrugations, which meant going at more than 40 miles an hour, and the thick clouds of dust thrown up meant keeping a quarter of a mile behind anything in front and slowing down hard when anything approached. There were no hotels anywhere, not even in Lagos or Accra. I had to stay with our managers, but this gave me the full opportunity I wanted to get to know them. Late nights on the stoep gave me an insight which I could not have acquired in any other manner. Customers and local African dignitaries often joined us.

Looking back I see that I was just in time to witness the end of the Bank's pioneering phase. The European staff were heavily engaged with the supply of cash [the West African circulation was getting on for £90 million, and much of it passed through the Bank several times a year]. Even in London I was to find that I was involved in directing the overall cash movements for there had to be enough cash everywhere at the right time, but it was expensive to have surpluses lying idle.

We certainly enjoyed the prestige of being the Currency Agents – but at what cost! Much of the branch manager's time was taken up with counting and handling coin in the special Currency Board strong-rooms when he ought to have been free to see the customers. This often took the entire morning. Other members of the staff, too, were diverted from their ordinary duties to deal with official Currency Board affairs.

Incredibly, the annual payment made by the Currency Board to the Bank for all its services as Currency Agent had never been increased since 1927 when it was fixed at £4,000 – though the money supply had increased more than sixfold. The only addition was a rental for the special strong-rooms installed by the Bank for the Board's purposes, at 5% of the actual capital cost.

The Bank's financial resources had been growing steadily for some years. While the paid-up capital had remained unchanged at £1·2 million since 1921 and the reserve fund stood at £400,000 from 1920 to 1943 funds then began to expand. Something was added to the Reserve Fund each year – until it reached £1 million in 1951 (March 31) and went on rising to £1·4 million in 1955 when it was decided to increase the paid-up capital to £2·5 million. A similar trend can be traced in the Bank's deposits. These had nearly doubled from £10 million in 1941 to over £19 million in 1945, and went on rising to £44·6 million in 1950 and £54·6 million in 1952.

Some new outlets had to be found for these rapidly growing funds. The Bank had not done well with its conservative policy of keeping vast sums on deposit in London where interest rates were the lowest in history, or in British Government securities, which were fast declining in value. Here then was yet another motive for launching a drive for expansion.

It should also be mentioned that the Bank was being criticised, in the early post-war years, not merely by African public opinion but by British colonial officials. One who reached high office in Nigeria told me: 'We were always pressing the Bank to open up in the inland market towns and not to stay only at the chief centres. For several years after the dramatic political change of 1946 we had the impression that the BBWA was carrying on much as before, and as we were in friendly contact with their managers we made no secret of our views. Some of us were also concerned for a few years at the Bank's delay in opening up managerial posts to Nigerians or appointing Nigerian directors.'

That view of the Bank from the outside might have been right or wrong or something in between. The civil servant on the spot could not have seen any changes in the policy of the Bank until they were converted into action locally. But it is certain that after the Second World War the British colonial Service supported the transfer of power to Africans in business as well as political matters even though its ideas of timing were dominated by the desire that change should be orderly. During the 1950s the colonial administration also favoured the withdrawal of the trading companies from produce buying – which gave the Bank the opportunity to move in – on the grounds that the companies left too much to the middlemen who made large profits at the expense of the farmers.

John Read returned to London in the autumn of 1953, having acquired the fullest and most up-to-date experience of the Bank's West African affairs of all the Head Office team. Together with Frank Wright, who remained general manager for another two years before he retired and joined the board, Read organised the new policy of expansion. By this time the directors were content to confine themselves to overall policy leaving the general manager and the management committee to run the Bank. The committee met daily, and the general manager kept in almost daily touch with the chairman, Lord Harlech, who was also chairman of the Midland Bank and had his hands full. There were moments in the next few years when the directors became very worried about the initial losses inherent in the drive for new business and the risks that were being taken. But they kept their nerve and backed the judgement of the management.

A NEW STAFF POLICY

Before the bold plan could get off the ground it was essential to restore the morale of the staff. In his travels across West Africa John

Read must have had his eyes opened to the frustration and lack of confidence among the European staff, from senior manager down to junior assistant. To this day the survivors remember the earlier period as one of overwork, underpay, almost intolerable living conditions and lack of leadership. Whether all the grievances that are now recalled were entirely justified at the time matters little; but that the staff was dispirited is attested by many witnesses. A young man joining the Bank was paid less than he might have got from one of the merchant companies; his contract was for eighteen months and it was being said that after one or two tours he might become too expensive and be 'allowed to go'.

Thus they had not even the long-term job security which was the usual offset to low pay in other banks. Complaints and suggestions were hardly ever listened to in London. 'Before John Read's long visit,' one man recalls, 'the London people hardly ever came out and if they did they saw only Governors and government officials, a few African dignitaries and perhaps the two or three most senior managers. A chairman or other director might penetrate inland to open a new branch building but if he talked to the staff at all he would tell them about the latest London society gossip or his nice Friesian herd – he did not want to know the people or their desperate worries.'

These reminiscences might be unjust but they are very typical. By 1952 the staff policy of the Bank had produced a critical situation. This was brought home to the management by the Wilkinson report on the Nigerian frauds in 1952 (see page 174). Though Wilkinson's conclusions on the urgent need for a change in staff policy were not even acknowledged in the reply by the General Manager, Frank Wright, nor mentioned in his subsequent letters, it seems inconceivable that Head Office remained unaware of the crisis. At any rate they realised before long that there had to be more better paid and better trained staff before they could go ahead with the expansion project.

The Bank's Secretary, E. J. D. Kewley, was put in charge of staff recruitment and training, with the main object of reinforcing the overseas staff. In July 1953 Lord Harlech pointed out that the total staff had risen to 1,107 compared with 461 at the end of the war in

1945. 'The present strength is represented by 428 Europeans and 679 Africans, and in both instances includes many youthful entrants who are receiving careful training to prepare them for progressively higher posts when opportunities arise. This particularly applies to the younger generation of Africans, many of whom will be called upon to assume more important duties than their predecessors.' A year later, when Lord Harlech had paid another visit to Nigeria, he referred to the problem again. 'It was very apparent that in all spheres there is a great shortage of trained men, African as well as European, in the 30 to 40 age group. This gap, created by the war, is a serious handicap. We are overcoming it by providing staff training on as extensive a scale as possible.'

At that time only one branch was operated entirely by Africans with an African manager; It was in Broad Street, Lagos. It was decided to speed up Africanisation but this required a good deal of additional training, which was organised both in West Africa and in London. There was another problem, tactfully kept quiet: African customers were at first reluctant to bank with a branch that had no European manager. A half-way house was devised: 'We opened new branches particularly where we could have an African manager supported by regular visits of a European once or twice a week to encourage the customers.' By 1958 thirteen Africans were in charge of branch offices.

As for the recruitment of Europeans, a new salary scale was approved in 1952 and new candidates now had to spend some time at the London office, learning the ropes under the supervision of the Chief Inspector, studying at the same time for the examinations of the Institute of Bankers. First results were disappointing. Then the City of London College arranged a special daytime course for young bank officials and this much improved the results. Even so it took a newcomer some time to master the many different duties he might be asked to perform in a branch on the Coast, quite apart from the novelty of collaborating with Africans and getting used to African living conditions. In the first year or two many of them probably did not earn their keep. The cost of keeping Europeans on the Coast was rising fast, for to induce them to go out the Bank now had to offer better pay, more job security, better housing, fares for wives

o

and children, education allowances, special arrangements for children to join their parents at holiday times or for mothers to return home to the children. Since all these costs clearly had to be accepted the management took another look at recruitment policy, and it began to take in men who had already had ten or twelve years of banking experience in Britain. This was a great success.

A little earlier the provision of pensions and other retirement benefits for the staff had been brought up-to-date. For a long time these arrangements had been very sketchy. The first proposal for a pension fund for staff serving in West Africa had been made to the board as early as 1904. Nothing happened until 1907 when the four most senior men – George Neville, Leslie Couper, G. A. Lester and D. W. Paterson – wrote a formal letter to the directors asking them to establish a pension fund 'without further delay'. In 1908 a provident fund was set up; it seemed that the staff on the Coast preferred such a scheme to a proper pension fund because they expected to return home after some years in West Africa and wanted to preserve their claim on the fund. In 1916 the directors decided to add to the Staff Fund each year so as to establish a superannuation scheme for those retiring after long service. In 1917 a profit-sharing scheme was discussed but not introduced until 1920. Under this an amount equal to the dividend to shareholders was allotted to those eligible as credits payable only on retirement or in certain other agreed events.

After the introduction of the provident fund it was usual for the directors to award an arbitrary additional payment to retiring members, usually £100, £200, or in a few cases £250 per annum; these grants were reviewed annually. In 1938 a report showed that twenty-three former staff members were receiving retiring allowances. As an increasing number of senior men would soon reach retiring age a new scheme was approved for payment of one-sixtieth of retiring salary for each year of service, less the annuity value of Staff Funds. In 1943 it was agreed that up to one-third of Staff Funds could be registered separately on behalf of wives.

In November 1948 the Inland Revenue examined the provident and profit-sharing funds and ruled that neither could be accepted for exemption from tax. Unless they were revised on approved lines the Bank might be assessed for arrears of tax over the previous seven years. It was this intervention of the tax authority which led to the setting up of a real pension fund for the home staff. For overseas staff the previous Staff Funds continued. The Bank's first contribution was £20,000, and later in 1949 a provision of £155,000 was set aside for past service. This scheme was approved by the Inland Revenue in 1950 as a superannuation fund. A pension scheme for European staff serving in West Africa was introduced only in 1962 when the Bank put up £1,605,000 as a basis. A widows and orphans fund which would provide £250 p.a. for a widow and £60 for each child was set up in 1958; this required staff contributions. Provident funds for the African staff had been in existence for many years. There were ten such funds of varying sizes by the time the BBWA ceased to be an independent bank in 1965.

The changes in staff policy were not of course made overnight. They took shape steadily between 1952 and 1955 and were related as much to the emergence of a strong new management in London as to the expanding opportunities for banking in West Africa. ('I always believed that the staff – General Manager to messenger – is the Bank', recalls John Read.) Firm plans were drawn up for future needs of senior staff, potential high-flyers were noted and deliberately prepared for the higher jobs. In particular they were moved around the various territories so as to acquire wider regional and banking experience. Most of those selected at that period have since risen to the top ranks.

Another aspect of the new policy was to create a number of new appointments with a managerial title. This opened up more scope for promotion and encouraged initiative in the ranks. At the same time several heads of departments in London were sent out to Africa either to hold down a job there for a short time or merely to make a brief tour in order to improve their first-hand knowledge. One purpose of these visits was to make sure that the Bank in London – as well as in Manchester and Liverpool – was always well informed on the latest West African developments. A good deal of business was attracted by supplying reliable and up-to-date commercial information.

Among those who were sent out to the Coast for this purpose was J. R. Wilkinson, the Chief Inspector, who took over as District

Manager in Accra for six months. The experience he gathered on the spot led him to undertake the massive task of revising an older *Manual of Instructions* for all branches, originally compiled by W. D. Hopkinson. This remained for long the basic textbook of the staff.

Next, the renewal of branch buildings and staff housing was pressed forward. What this involved is set out in the recollections of John Read:

The main office in Lagos was in course of rebuilding but everywhere else the properties were outdated. A particular lesson to me was not to permit rebuilding on an existing site without moving the business to temporary quarters. The inconvenience to customers and the discomforts to the staff cost far more than setting up some alternative accommodation. We shall never know what the rebuilding of the Marina branch in Lagos cost in lost custom, but certainly the same mistake was not made again. Practically the whole of the bank premises were rebuilt in the next ten years.

Good modern designs were developed with the help of our architect, Ronald Ward, and under the care of our premises manager, E. W. Seaman. At many places staff had been living over the bank. This was stopped. Flats were introduced for the younger men at the larger centres, and good houses with two or three bedrooms were built to a basic design. I was particularly anxious to see the creation of real homes on the Coast. On my first visit I sensed that many men were 'camping out', sometimes with no more interest in their quarters than a bed and a dozen glasses, taking their meals at the club under contract. Could anything have been worse for morale?

More wives to make better quarters more comfortable, better arrangements to ensure that leaves were taken on time, better salaries and allowances, and much improved supplies in the stores were soon raising living standards to a satisfactory level. This showed through in the Bank's business. We were spending around £400,000 a year on our properties and as this seemed to be about the expenditure we could afford and administer we went on at this rate until we had modernised everywhere – except in Port Harcourt. That omission was a stroke of luck; the plans had been outlined but were stopped by the outbreak of the civil war. There was some damage to the old building and a new one might have attracted more attention.

THE SPREADING OF THE BRANCHES

The drive to spread the branch network of the Bank throughout British West Africa began in earnest in 1952. Inside the Bank it is firmly held that the branch expansion was started mainly because of the prospect that political independence would involve the loss of the Government and currency business. Equally important was the beginning of a general withdrawal from 'upcountry' by the trading companies, which in time created a banking vacuum. But there was a third factor which set an edge of urgency on these motives: the aggressive competition of Barclays Bank (DC&O).

Although Barclays was not concerned with the currency and had a smaller part of the colonial government business it took the same decision as BBWA at the same time. Having its main business in Britain and elsewhere outside West Africa Barclays was able to put more resources into the expansion campaign and to start it more quickly once the decision had been taken. Between the two banks a race to open new branches developed in the early 1950s and continued until 1959, when new banking regulations slowed down further expansion. The timing is reflected in the number of new branches opened by the BBWA: In 1950–1 the Bank opened up in three new places; in 1951–2 it spread into three additional towns (one of them Benin City which had been clamouring for a bank for years as its trade had grown and the constant transport of cash by head-load, car or lorry to and from the nearest bank branch at the river port of Sapele had become burdensome). In 1952–3 the number of new branches soared to nine. In earlier years the Bank had often established branches where the Government's regional centres were rather than where big markets offered the best commercial opportunities. Now it was being pressed by the new regional authorities to open up in the political headquarters towns, and this was not always resisted; but the main thrust of the campaign was towards the market towns.

The rivalry between the two banks took some eccentric forms. A plan to open a branch at some place that appeared worthwhile had to be kept a dead secret from the competitor. If a manager drove out of town on a Sunday his movements were carefully reported to the opposition in case he was spying out the land for a new branch. Both banks had a covered lorry loaded with a few pieces of essential office furniture and a sealed box of stationery always standing ready to move out at a moment's notice. One BBWA manager recalls that

on a Christmas Eve he was summoned by the district manager and
told that he would have to leave that night for a place called Yendi
to open a new branch of the BBWA. It was urgent because news
had just come in that Barclays were opening in the same place the
very next day. The young man was told that he would be away from
home for about two weeks (it turned out to be eleven months); he
threw a suitcase and one of the emergency stationery kits prepared at
Head Office in London into his small Austin car and drove into the
night. He arrived at Tamale, sixty-five miles from Yendi, at noon on
Christmas Day to find that the manager was in hospital and the
preparations for opening the branch at Yendi had not been made.

So he went on alone, carrying on the roof of his car a wooden
signboard bearing the name 'Bank of British West Africa'. He had
been told that he could stay at the bungalow of the Assembly of
God Mission until he found more permanent accommodation. He
had not been told that the Mission bungalow had been standing
empty for seven years and was the home of bats. Still, he managed.
The signboard was erected on the galvanised iron roof of a mud-built
house on the outskirts of the town. The young man at once went to
call on the Ya Na, the Chief of Dagomba who was the principal
local dignitary. He told him that the Bank proposed to open a
branch in his town and persuaded him to come and open it in person
the next day.

But Barclays Bank was ready with its own branch a hundred yards
up the road and their manager had also called on the Ya Na and got
his promise to open the Barclays branch. So the Chief opened both
on the same day. The same incident is described from the opposite
side in an unpublished history of Barclays (DC&O) which adds:

Our business was conducted in entirely unfurnished accommodation with
a beer crate for a stool and our cash box as a counter. To run this agency
required a great deal of travelling – sixty-two miles each way on a dusty
laterite road which ran over several narrow wooden bridges. Eventually
a prefabricated building was sent for the sub-manager, but one wild
night the roof was blown off. About the same time we opened in Bawku,
150 miles from Tamale. The bank installed itself in a bar; the lease agreement was written on a piece of exercise book. We were allowed to use
half the counter until such time as the bar proprietor was ready to move
out.

In the midst of this feverish competition the two banks generally avoided setting up a branch each in any place that did not promise enough business for two branches. In a number of cases if one of them was first in a new spot the other promptly went elsewhere.

The pace of expansion was even more hectic for Barclays than for the BBWA. In Nigeria, between 1952 and 1962, the number of BBWA offices increased from eighteen to fifty-five and the number of Barclay offices from ten to fifty-seven. In the Gold Coast/Ghana the BBWA expanded from fifteen to forty-four and Barclays from twelve to sixty. In Sierra Leone Barclays had only a single office in Freetown until 1955 but in 1958 they had three in Freetown itself and seven upcountry. BBWA had started to spread out much earlier and had eight offices at the end of the decade. The figures must not be taken too seriously as a number of these offices were merely small agencies or sub-branches housed in light shacks, and not all of them survived.

Chapter Fifteen

ECONOMIC PROGRESS ACCELERATES

NEW MEN AND METHODS

IT was already evident in the early 1950s that a period of vigorous economic progress lay ahead in West Africa. For Nigeria this prospect was enthusiastically set out in the report of the World Bank Mission in 1954, which has already been mentioned (see pages 167–8). After a detailed study of resources and possibilities the Mission proposed 'an integrated development programme' which was, by and large, adopted by the government. The statistics of the period show a rapid growth of production, imports, and government revenues, even in terms of constant prices. On the expansion of the currency circulation the report comments: 'This has increased eightfold since 1939, partly because of higher prices but largely because of the growing use of money as a medium of exchange and larger cash holdings in the hands of Nigerians. The growth of Post Office Savings Bank deposits . . . represents a significant change in the habits of the population as a whole.'

Meanwhile in the Gold Coast – soon to be renamed Ghana – the output of gold, manganese, diamonds, timber and other export products was increasing and the efforts to contain the damaging disease that had attacked the cocoa trees were meeting with some success. The vast Volta River project which was to harness the water for irrigation and power and to develop important bauxite deposits for aluminium production was advancing from dream to reality. The extension of the port of Takoradi and the construction of a new harbour at Tema were under way. The railway system, regarded as the best in Africa, was being renewed and extended.

In Sierra Leone the great diamond rush of 1952 ushered in a period of greater prosperity; large iron ore deposits were being opened up and a new deepwater quay was built at Freetown. While the diamond boom hampered the output of the traditional export commodities because it drew men away from the land, the overall income was bound to benefit from the new trends.

There was a price to be paid for progress. The building of roads, railways and quays shifted trade out of its old channels. Many of the trading stations along the rivers closed down. Cargo ships which used to by-pass Freetown to enter the Sherbro River and anchor off Sherbro Island turned to the new city port. The flourishing Sherbro town of Bonthe with its jetties, warehouses, and fleets of launches and lighters became a ghost city almost overnight. The BBWA branch at Bonthe, opened in 1912, had been closed in 1940, and so – around 1958 – were the branches of the big trading companies. York Island nearby, another lively centre of the river trade, was entirely deserted except for dejected groups of Africans still hoping for the return of the golden days. More recently a little life has returned to Bonthe: the demand for piassava, a palm-frond product used for making brooms and brushes, has revived, and a few other products have found markets. BBWA opened a small new branch in 1956.

An interesting view of the profound economic changes that took place in the 1950s is given by A. G. Hopkins in *An Economic History of West Africa* (Longman 1973). It can only be summarised here; Professor Hopkins' interpretation is rather original and not undisputed. First, the expatriate trading firms fundamentally reorganised their activities by specialising on a limited range of trading functions and by introducing modern manufacturing industry. One reason was that expansion and diversification was making West African trade attractive to newcomers and presenting the expatriate firms with serious competition from low-cost operators, especially Indian, Levantine and African traders, and from overseas industrial concerns such as Imperial Chemical Industries, which set up their own local outlets.

The established, horizontally-integrated structure of U.A.C., C.F.A.O., and S.C.O.A. was ill-suited to do battle with specialised competitors. Engaging in trade in products such as motor vehicles and machinery put pressure on capital resources; selling and servicing new imports such as electrical goods required an expertise which the traditional firms did not possess; and stocking an increasingly diverse range of commodities led to a rise in handling costs.

By about 1950 the established firms had realised that the market was too large and competition too fierce for them to continue to dominate virtually all branches of the import and export trade as they had done previously. They began to transform themselves into specialists, thus reducing capital requirements and handling costs. The leading commercial firms reorganised their retail outlets and concentrated mainly on wholesaling activities. Direct retailing became centred on a few large department stores and supermarkets, such as Kingsway, Monoprix and Printania, and most of the established retail outlets were handed over to Africans. . . . In addition, subsidiaries with African directors were set up to import and distribute particular items such as motor vehicles, and finance companies were formed to enable independent African traders to develop their own businesses. The results were dramatic: whereas in 1949 the three leading commercial firms in Nigeria accounted for 49% of all imports, by 1963 this figure had fallen to 16%. One of the best examples of the process of Africanisation is provided by U.A.C. In 1939 Africans accounted for only 7% of the company's total management staff in West Africa: by 1957 the proportion had risen to 21%, and by the end of 1964 it had reached 43%. . . .

The second, and more radical, innovation was the introduction of modern industry. It is widely but incorrectly assumed that the expatriate companies were firmly opposed to industrialisation in Africa throughout the colonial period. That they showed little or no interest in modern manufacturing before 1945 is undoubtedly true. Their skills were those of general merchants, and as merchants they presided comfortably over commercial empires in which market-sharing agreements had blunted aggressive entrepreneurial drives. Moreover, industrialisation meant complications and risks. . . . By the 1950s the effective demand for manufactures had reached the point in some parts of West Africa where it could sustain at least a few firms of the size needed to produce the goods most commonly required. . . . The expansion of the market, by introducing a greater degree of competition, had reduced profit margins on many staple imports. The traditional firms not only countered this challenge by specialising, as has been shown, but also by becoming manufacturers in the hope that they could achieve sufficient savings in production and transport costs to undersell their rivals. It was no coincidence that the leading manufacturers in West Africa during the 1950s were established commercial firms, such as U.A.C., C.F.A.O., S.C.O.A., John Holt and Maurel et Prom, all of which had to undertake internal reorganisation and acquire staff with the necessary technical skills. By starting modern industries, as by specialising in trade, these firms also helped to further Afro-European cooperation during the final phase of colonial rule.*

Some of the changes described by Professor Hopkins occurred only towards the end of the 1950s, but it must have been plain quite early in the decade that a period of expanding activity had begun which was bound to call for greatly increased financial services.

At the Head Office of the Bank a new management structure took shape. During 1953 Frank Wright, the General Manager, progressively handed over the chief management functions to John Read who succeeded as General Manager on September 1, 1955, when Wright retired. Then Geoffrey Redmayne, who had been in London since 1945, and an Assistant General Manager since 1948, was given special responsibility for the Gold Coast, Sierra Leone, The Gambia and U.K. business. In 1955 E. J. McQuin was brought home from Lagos, where he had been District Manager for Nigeria, to become Assistant General Manager in charge of that territory. This triumvirate led the management team for more than a decade.

The drive for general commercial banking business in West Africa was successful. But it involved many adjustments in the Bank's aims and methods. To quote again from John Read's notes:

New savings accounts were coming in well and the idea of having a bank account was spreading among the Africans. Until then lending to Africans had been very restricted as the policy had been to require security, and owing particularly to the uncertainties of land tenure, this was rarely available. Some traders and produce buyers enjoyed credit facilities but they were comparatively few. In looking at this experience I found the best prospect was to extend the arrangement of lending unsecured for a month at a time. The idea was that a trader could borrow perhaps £1,000 on the understanding that he would pay in his takings regularly and this would more or less pay off the borrowing within the month. The scheme was acceptable to the African traders because they were accustomed to a very similar plan in their dealings with the large European trading firms.

*A. G. Hopkins, *An Economic History of West Africa*, Longman, 1973.

One difference was that the firms had usually tried to retain commissions with a view to building up security for their credit lines. Of course a bank advance gave the trader more freedom to shop around for the goods he wanted to buy. These advances were made by the branch managers under the guidance of the District Managers and were reported to London afterwards on a very simple form. We moved from one such form a day to seventy-five or more a day.

The range of experience was astonishing. There seemed to be a flash-point at £3,000. Traders handled increasing monthly advances very satisfactorily up to this point of £3,000; at that figure they were often tempted to close their business and depart with all funds. Another feature soon showed up: traders in traditional trading stations were much more concerned than those elsewhere to maintain a good credit standing with the Bank, and such points were therefore a much better risk. There was also a wide difference of experience between different tribal areas. The worst was in one upcountry area where an analysis showed two new borrowers out of every three became bad debts within two years.

One rather strange problem was to persuade young managers that they had to go out to visit their customers, so keeping in touch with their businesses, and seeing in a rough way that the Bank's advances were indeed going into stock-in-trade and not into other speculative ventures. However, I and my two colleagues visited the branches regularly to give guidance to the managers.

The spirit of enterprise was by no means as rare among young branch managers as these comments might suggest. In fact, some of those who had joined the Bank after the Second World War recall that 'the staff on the ground was far more enterprising than the head office and the board'. Among them were young men who had carried great responsibilities during the war and were more entre-preneurs than conventional bank managers. They did not take to the traditional system of central direction from London and did not recognise superior wisdom in the type of General Manager who preceded John Read. This kind of conflict was of course characteristic of business development at that time everywhere. A new kind of relationship between centre and operating points had become essential, and it was wanted as much by the men in West Africa as by the managers in London.

Some of the managers found scope for a good deal of initiative. In Northern Nigeria an Emir with considerable financial experience invited the Bank's branch manager, R. S. Woodward, to his palace and asked for help. He was president of the local horseracing club and this had suffered such losses that a bank credit was vitally required to keep racing alive. The manager offered to grant the credit on condition that he himself would take over the running of the club. The Emir agreed with relief and for the next few seasons Woodward was the president of the club, the manager of Barclays was in charge of the totalisator and the Chief of Police controlled the gate. A large profit was made at once and the Emir remembered many years afterwards (as he told me) how helpful the BBWA had been in this matter.

Personal relations between bank managers and eminent local Africans sometimes became so close that a European was elected a Chief. This is by no means a mere courtesy title. Only a man who has rendered important service to a particular African community and is completely trusted will ever be initiated. The ceremonies of election are long, colourful and exceedingly costly. The ritual robes alone cost a small fortune.

One member of the Bank's staff in Nigeria, Chief Elwyn Williams, told me how he came to be appointed. As branch manager at Oshogbo he was on good terms not only with the Oba (or Ataoja) of Oshogbo but knew many inhabitants of less respectable status, and he had learned to speak the Yoruba language. One night he was awakened to find a riot in progress and the Oba's palace, which was near the Bank building, surrounded by thugs who threatened to burn it down and kill the Chief. They asked for a ransom and the Oba sent a messenger to Williams asking for help. Williams knew the leader of the thugs and opened talks. Having cooled tempers he handed over a sum of money to be shared out among the crowd. They set the Oba free and Williams took him in his little car to a farm owned by a son. It was as a reward for saving the life of the Paramount Chief that Williams was made a Yoruba Chief, with the title Bobajiro of Oshogbo.

In order to spread the banking habit among Africans a large scale advertising and publicity campaign was launched. Norman Levy, who had joined the BBWA as a young clerk in 1928 and had later left for the Government service, becoming chairman of the Northern Regional Marketing Board in Nigeria, was persuaded to rejoin the

Bank as its public relations officer. For a time he was trained by a leading public relations agency and after that he soon transformed the Bank's publicity. Not only did the Bank advertise its services more skilfully and through a much wider range of media – press, radio, hoardings and others – but a professional analysis of results secured far greater value for the money spent. For several years the BBWA even joined with Barclays in a general publicity campaign which simply encouraged people to open a banking or savings account, rather than recommending a particular bank. At the same time the name of the BBWA was put forward in many other ways, and over a period its 'image' in West Africa was successfully changed from that of a staid Government bank to that of an enterprising commercial bank.

Such little things as the introduction of a new passbook just small enough to fit into the breast pocket of a T-shirt were part of the build-up. Special promotion schemes involving all members of the staff were very effective. This propaganda brought many African traders into the Bank who might at first merely want a savings account as a safe haven for spare money but would soon make use of current account facilities including short-term borrowing. During these years of deliberate expansion the Bank's commercial deposits increased so massively that they easily offset the loss of governmental deposits when these were transferred to the new African banks.

Besides running this campaign Norman Levy also produced regular studies of trade and economic conditions which the Bank circulated among traders and international bankers, where they were soon regarded as a valuable source of commercial information.

As the Bank went more directly into lending to African produce buyers it had to acquire more detailed knowledge of their operations. These advances soon rose to very large figures and the Bank could not always know whether the stocks of produce in outlying spots or in transit were sufficient to cover the loans. At the right moment the right man to solve this problem turned up. He was John Andrew Wright, who had joined the Bank in 1960 after a few years as a tea manager in East Africa. He quickly acquired a good knowledge of Hausa; he also had a fair command of Arabic, Swahili and French. Above all he disliked office work and loved to roam about the desert and its fringes. When his first home leave fell due he asked permission to travel by camel across the desert before continuing to England. John Read at once agreed and asked Wright to keep his eye open for business opportunities.

Wright was then at Maiduguri. He travelled north by way of Bosso, N'guigme, Tamanrasset and by the old *route du Hoggar* to Algiers. He arrived safely, took ship to England and brought home a good deal of useful commercial information. In 1964 Wright tried to repeat this journey and made elaborate preparations for crossing the Sahara by a different route: across the Tibesti mountains and northwards across the Libyan desert to the Kufra oasis and on to Benghazi. Among the equipment he assembled were three sun compasses lent to him by the Ministry of Defence. He also acquired three new camels. But he ran into the French-Algerian war and was turned back.

John Wright was generally known in the Bank as 'Camel Wright'. He certainly was the only officer ever to receive a camel allowance (£60 p.a.) granted in June 1962 'in lieu of car allowance'. When he was transferred from Gashua to Kano he was unable to sell his camel at a reasonable price and the Bank reluctantly agreed to pay the rail freight for the beast. Some highly coloured views have been expressed on the quality of his animals. In fact he obtained them from the Niger Republic where they were bred in the desert by Fulanis.

Wright was appointed produce controller; his duty was to visit the outlying towns and villages and the small markets in the bush to check the quantity and quality of groundnuts, cotton and other products purchased by the produce buyers under Bank credit facilities. The Bank explained this more politely to the buyers as an appointment meant to help them with their book-keeping and similar arrangements. Wright soon changed from camel to Landrover, taking off the windscreen 'to get more air and avoid the dust'. He would think nothing of spending a night in the open sleeping beside his car. While he caused grave concern to the man in charge of the Bank's motor vehicles, he became highly popular with the African customers and the Bank was commended in the Northern parliament for the help it was giving by this arrangement. John

Wright is now area manager in Northern Nigeria and looks like remaining a happy nomadic banker for the rest of his career.

MORE CAPITAL, NEW NAME

An early reminder that the status of Government banker could no longer be taken for granted came in 1954. In Nigeria a Federal Government with three autonomous regions had been set up. This change terminated the old agreements of the Bank with the Colonial Government by which the bulk of the official business was always placed with the BBWA. John Read went to West Africa and was able to negotiate a new contract with the Federal Government and with the Governments of the Northern and Eastern Regions. He reported that the Western Region had invited tenders for the Government account. It was expected that the Bank would obtain a large share, if not all, of the Western business though some part of it might go to the National Bank of Nigeria. This is what happened. Mr. Read also negotiated agreements with the Central, Eastern and Western Marketing Boards by which they would place their accounts with the BBWA. The Northern Board decided to have its account with Barclays.

These arrangements ensured that the Bank would continue to be the principal Government banker in Nigeria for some time yet. But the mere fact that the old relationship had been interrupted made the drive for commercial banking even more urgent.

The success of the expansion policy soon required an increase in the Bank's capital. In March 1955 shareholders received a circular letter from the chairman proposing that the issued capital should be increased from £1,200,000 to £2,500,000. 'In view of the remarkable expansion in the business of the Bank achieved in recent years', wrote Lord Harlech, 'and the correspondingly favourable opportunities for the employment of fresh capital, the directors are of the opinion that this is an opportune moment for increasing the paid-up capital of the Bank.'

A highly complex scheme had to be devised to satisfy legal requirements. The old nominal value of the shares – £10 each, £4 paid up – was reduced to £5 each. £300,000 was taken from the reserve fund to pay up another £1 of each share so as to bring the value of all shares up to £5 fully paid. This scheme was submitted to the Court as required, and sanctioned. Next, shareholders were invited to subscribe for two new shares of £1 each for every £3 of stock held. They duly put up the new money, more than doubling the paid-up capital and providing a handsome share premium which was used to raise the Reserve Fund to £1,900,000. The new shares were then converted into £1 stock units. The authorised capital was then restored to the previous figure of £4 million and the borrowing powers of the directors were increased to eight times the paid-up capital. In the process the old uncalled liability was extinguished. The scheme thus abolished an awkward handicap, which was common in the capital structure of banks at that time. In fact the B B W A reconstruction became a model for a number of other banks who adopted it to clear the decks for further expansion.

Evidently by the middle of the decade both the directors and the shareholders were confident that further expansion of the Bank's activities in West Africa was financially justified. Events proved that view to be right. Four years later, in mid-1959, the authorised capital was further increased from £4 million to £6 million and the issued capital from £2·5 million to £4 million. The latter change was made by capitalising £1·5 million of reserves to issue three fully paid shares of £1 each for every £5 of stock held. The dividend had been raised from 10% to 12 % for 1956–7; it was reduced to 8% on the increased capital in 1959–60, so as to maintain roughly the same total amount of dividend payments. The Reserve Fund was then restored to £2·5 million by the transfer of £1,250,000 from inner reserves.

By 1956 the name of the Bank was becoming a liability. 'Bank of British West Africa' reflected the colonial relationship which was clearly ending. The Bank had made its historic decision a few years earlier to remain in West Africa after the establishment of independent African states and to expand its banking business in the whole area with all possible speed. 'British West Africa' was not only an outdated concept but the term itself had begun to arouse political resentment. The question of a new name for the Bank was not settled as easily as the final solution suggests. Leading African politi-

P

cians were consulted in the course of 1956. The board set up a committee to study the problem. In February 1957 the committee recommended that the name should be changed to Bank of West Africa Limited, and this proposal was approved by an Extraordinary General Meeting in June 1957.

Oddly enough, the same proposal had been made, and almost accepted, as long ago as 1909. At that time the Bank wanted to spread its branch network into the French African colonies and found that the word 'British' in its name was a handicap. A formal decision was in fact taken then to make the change but the matter was dropped. A little later the Bank became known as 'the British Bank' and this turned out to be an advantage for many years.

The change of name in 1957 seems to have been quickly accepted by the public in West Africa and the Bank's business went on expanding. In May 1957 a representative of the Bank's auditors, Peat, Marwick, Mitchell & Co., attended a board meeting and observed that the board was to be congratulated on another record year. The internal position was 'infinitely stronger' than it had been.

THE GREAT DIAMOND RUSH

In 1949 the Bank's manager at Freetown, Stanley Patterson, wrote to London suggesting that a branch should be opened at Bo, a road junction 167 miles upcountry on the railway. There had been a branch at Bo once before; it was a collecting point for rice, cotton, palm and other products, and the centre of a densely populated district. During the retrenchment period the branch had been left to the United Africa Company to run as an agency of the Bank. Several large companies were established there: United Africa Company, Paterson Zochonis, G. B. Ollivant among them; and a number of Lebanese firms including J. Milhem & Sons who owned most of the modern buildings as well as stores. The Bata Shoe Company was turning over £10,000 a year. The Freetown manager was now being urged by Government officials to reopen fully at Bo because the administration of 'the Protectorate' was being shifted to the town, and the Government wished to have banking facilities on the spot. After Patterson had paid several visits to Bo which had to be kept a dead secret so that Barclays should not hear of the plan, a BBWA branch was in fact opened late in 1949.

The timing was fortunate. In 1952 a number of unusually large diamonds were found in the district by Africans digging illegally in the reserve areas of the Sierra Leone Selection Trust. Soon the surrounding villages were agog with the news and men left the land to seek their fortunes sifting sand. The rice fields were deserted and a serious shortage of rice developed. The growing of other foodstuffs was also neglected, and food prices soared. In 1955 a protest strike spread over large parts of the country and there was rioting in many places. Another aspect of the diamond rush was the spread of disease in the producing areas where many thousands of people crowded together without sanitation or safe water supplies.

'Bo and the surrounding towns and villages had a boom town atmosphere such as prevails in the Koidu area today' writes a former bank manager who lived through it. 'There was no accommodation, people slept in the open or on verandahs. Diamonds were sold on the roadside by the cigarette cup and even weighing was frequently done in the palm of the hand.'

Diamond mining had proceeded quietly since 1932 when the Sierra Leone Selection Trust obtained a mining concession for the area then recognised as productive. Between 1952 and 1956 the production of diamonds increased from about 200,000 carats to 2 million carats.* In the same period the number of diamond diggers is believed to have increased from 5,000 to well over 50,000. People came in not only from neighbouring parts of Sierra Leone but from other countries, particularly Liberia and Guinea, though many came from as far away as Nigeria in the east and Senegal in the west, either to dig or to deal.

Smuggling assumed enormous proportions and for several years the Government of Sierra Leone made strenuous attempts to suppress both illicit digging and unauthorised exports. Several times 'African foreigners', among whom Mandingoes, Marakas and Fullars from French Guinea were prominent, were expelled from the diamond zone, though many returned. Law and order was hard to maintain.

*H. L. Van der Laan, *The Sierra Leone Diamonds*, Oxford University Press, 1965, quoting an estimate by A. Moyar.

The temptation of robbery with violence was too great when a single African might carry a vast fortune in his pocket. Gangs offered armed protection to illicit diggers against the police, with the usual threats to those who did not pay up.

The BBWA branch at Bo found itself in the centre of the early diamond area, and it prospered. In 1956, when the Government decided to legalise both digging and exporting of diamonds, the Diamond Corporation, controlled by De Beers, was called in to take over the buying and exporting under licence. For a time both the BBWA and Barclays Bank (DC&O) were also granted export licences but in 1959 the Government Diamond Office (managed by the Diamond Corporation) became the sole exporter.

The BBWA branch at Bo actually bought diamonds in the early years, and so did the branch later opened at Segbwema, another boom town further up the railway line. At that time the manager of the Segbwema branch was Alex Barbour, who had been a successful diamond buyer for the Bank in the Gold Coast. He joined the BBWA in 1949 and became a branch manager in the following year. In 1954 he was sent to Tarkwa, where the branch had been active in buying diamonds for some time. Barbour quickly developed a sense for diamonds, and when he was transferred to Akim Oda, also in the Gold Coast, he became an expert in the sorting and valuing of rough stones. He went to Segbwema in 1957, and in September 1959 he was persuaded to join the Diamond Corporation of West Africa. He became manager of the Government Diamond Office at Kenema which the Corporation managed on behalf of the Sierra Leone Government. Several years later Barbour was called to London to join the Central Selling Organisation as a leading authority on rough diamonds and overseas buying procedures. He is now the director in charge of sales as well as an executive director of the Diamond Trading Company, the gem selling part of the Organisation.

The Bank did not continue diamond buying for long; it turned to financing the dealers.

As new rich diamond deposits were discovered the Bank opened further branches at Kenema and Koidu, and by the early 1960s it was handling the bulk of the diamond business. It was an adventurous period. Koidu branch was opened in July 1958 and the manager travelled seventy miles from Segbwema every day for a month until the building was ready. At that time there were only two licensed diamond dealers in Koidu; now there are several dozen, all Lebanese. The manager visited all the larger villages in person to announce the opening of the branch and to invite all Africans to open savings accounts. It was a great success. People who found diamonds gradually became highly skilled in assessing their value, and a simple villager might take a large sum of cash away with him when he sold to the dealer. With law and order still precarious, the chance of keeping the money safe in the bank was much appreciated. A dealer might easily pay out £100,000 for a handful of stones. Much of it was (and is) soon lost in gambling. Some of it is almost invariably spent in acquiring one of the large white Mercedes cars which abound in the neighbourhood. In fact these cars have become a kind of currency. Being forced at speed over corrugated mud roads their life is not long, and one can buy a used one, still looking spotless, for something like £500. The diamond dealers are said to have one of these second-hand cars always standing outside their door, and in bargaining with an inexperienced digger they will offer to 'throw in my white Mercedes' to cover a gap several times as large as its value.

The bank manager at Koidu may often be called out of bed in the small hours of the night to go to the branch and hand out a large sum of cash to a dealer who has just been offered a stone by a lucky digger. The local manager of Barclays arrived one morning to find that someone had been digging a trench right up to his back door.

It is still a rather lawless area. Helicopters are always whirring overhead to spot illicit diggers but most of the digging is done by night and is quite impossible to stop. Sierra Leone officials know that many diamonds are still being smuggled out of the country and shipped abroad from neighbouring countries where control is less strict. They point out that Nigerian statistics show a substantial export of diamonds although no diamonds are found in Nigeria. In the mining centres outbreaks of violence are frequent though in recent years nothing as big as the 1968 riots has been known in Koidu. As payment is still largely in cash these outlying branches have to be constantly supplied with large stocks of silver. This is nowadays carried by the small but reliable airline which links Freetown with the hinterland. Occasionally a van carrying cash from the airfield is ambushed and robbed, but losses have so far been modest.

To give some idea of the sums involved it may be of interest that in 1959 the branch at Bo kept a reserve of some £100,000 in coin in addition to £2,350,000 of coin and notes belonging to the West African Currency Board, which was kept as usual in a separate strong-room. An officer of the Board was by then stationed in the new bank building at Bo. It was here that the Queen came to pay a visit in 1959 to see something of the diamond fields.

Although the BBWA first moved in on the diamond boom by chance, it quickly rose to the opportunity and made good profits out of the business over the years. Diamonds became Sierra Leone's most important export commodity, representing almost half the value of the country's exports. By way of the substantial export duty, and despite continued large-scale smuggling to avoid it, diamonds produce a large revenue for the Sierra Leone Government.

While the bulk of the Sierra Leone production consists of fairly small diamonds some very large stones have been found there. In 1943 a fine stone weighing 530 carats emerged from the alluvial deposits of the Woyie River. In the same area a stone of about 770 carats was found in 1945; it was cut into thirty separate gems. The Selection Trust mine in the Yengema district threw up in February 1972 the third largest diamond in the world: the Star of Sierra Leone, weighing 936·9 carats. This was brought to England and put on show in the Geological Museum in Kensington, and eventually sold to a New York jeweller, Harry Winston, but the price was not disclosed.

Chapter Sixteen

THE RISKS OF GROWTH

BAD DEBTS AND FRAUDS

QUITE early in the expansion period Mr. Whitley-Jones, the deputy chairman, warned the board that with increasing advances the Bank's system of control would have to be constantly reviewed to ensure that local managers, in using their discretion, developed a sense of sound judgement. Translated from bank manager's language this means that the rapid rise of loans to new types of customers, and in many areas new to the Bank, could easily lead to losses. In fact, either these fears were overdone or the control system was sufficiently strengthened. In 1958 the auditors remarked that the ratio of bad debts to advances was 'not high'. The scale of lending at that period may be seen from an entry in 1958 that Alasan Dantata and Sons in Kano, Northern Nigeria, were granted new credit facilities of £900,000. It was found that lending was fairly safe in some areas and very risky in others. Thus in Onitsha, an old highly developed market place, the Bank had something like £1 million outstanding in unsecured loans in the mid-fifties, and it lost very little; at Port Harcourt losses were heavy and the same was true in Sierra Leone.

On the other hand losses through various kinds of fraud or forgery inevitably increased as the Bank expanded. The most frequent cases were forgery of signatures on cheques, raising the amount by altering or adding a figure, or removing the crossing with chemicals. Frequently, but not always, members of the staff were involved, and the amounts were often substantial. When an unknown person presented a cheque for more than £500 some suspicion should have been aroused, but sometimes he would produce a letter, also forged, purporting to give him authority to receive the amount. In some cases forged signatures were good copies; in others a false specimen signature card was put into the file. Unexplained cash losses occurred at least once a year. Sometimes cash disappeared from the reserve in the strong-room or from the manager's safe. In most cases the police suspected the cashier, and some were arrested and charged, but it was usually impossible to get proof.

Another form of fraud was the diversion of credit entries from the correct account to another, from which the money would be promptly withdrawn. This was done by destroying the first paying-in slip and replacing it with another crediting the account of an accomplice. When the vouchers were destroyed the police had no evidence on which to base a charge. Several times mail transfer advices from another branch were forged and payments were made as a result.

One of the most intricate and expensive series of frauds in the history of the Bank occurred in Kano around 1959. A Southern Nigerian who had joined the Bank in 1935 became a cashier. He was highly regarded and in 1957 he was selected as one of a group of African clerks who were sent to London for a six weeks course at Head Office. On his return he was appointed manager of a small branch. About a year later he became involved in an intricate series of irregularities which continued for nearly two years before they were discovered. No evidence was produced that he gained any personal benefit from them. It seems that he paid cheques drawn by a customer who had no funds. The customer's account was not debited because such an entry would have to appear in the fort-nightly returns to Head Office and lead to immediate questions.

To conceal this overdraft, and others later, various internal accounts were debited and sometimes the current accounts of custo-mers who had no connection with the fraud. The false entries would be reversed a few days later and switched to another account. The main accounts used to hold false entries were the clearing accounts of other banks. The balances on these accounts were reported to Head Office twice monthly, and the manager was careful to falsify these accounts at the middle and end of each month so that no awkward questions would arise in London. After nearly two years of these manipulations he slipped up; the return for July 31, 1961, showed that the Bank of the North was supposed to owe £87,136 and this was questioned in a letter from Head Office to the executive director in Lagos. Two inspectors were sent to Kano to investigate.

The manager tried hard to avoid discovery. He removed a blank double page with the correct folio number from an old ledger and instructed the ledger clerk to re-write the customer's account with new figures. He then removed the corresponding page of the current ledger and called in a bookbinder to sew in the substitute page. This was discovered through a technical process known as 'balancing the legs' which is no longer possible with mechanised accounting. It was found that eighty-eight cheques had been held over and that thirteen customers were concerned. The total debt was over £160,000. The manager was charged with criminal breach of trust and falsification of accounts. The customer and 'nine Alhajis' were accused of abetting him. The principal culprit was sentenced to seven years, one customer to five years, seven others to four years and the remaining two to two years. The manager was dismissed by the Bank in October 1961. The General Manager at the time, J. C. Read, affirms that the case had no subsequent effect on the promotion of other Africans.

A more spectacular crime occurred in 1962 when about twenty Africans attacked a bank lorry carrying notes and coin from Benin to Sapele. £60,000 in notes was stolen but £20,000 was recovered. A clerk and an escorting policeman were slightly injured. Seventeen people were arrested and charged with highway robbery. As the movement was insured the Bank suffered no loss. The Bank had been paying a premium of £17,500 a year to insure such cash movements. After the Benin incident it was decided that the Bank would carry the risk itself, setting aside £15,000 each year. In the event, armed robberies and hold-ups were remarkably rare in West Africa.

THE RISE OF AFRICAN BANKS

African complaints that the BBWA was not helpful enough began as early as 1912, when the absorption of the Bank of Nigeria revived old objections to a banking monopoly. A pamphlet published in Lagos in that year – *An appeal from the native traders of Lagos to the financiers of Great Britain* – alleged that the BBWA was reluctant to 'finance natives' and charged too much for its loans. African traders continued to believe that the British banks discriminated against them in favour of the European firms and later in favour of the Levantines.

The real grievances of the African traders were not concerned with the British bank or banks as such but with two aspects of the financial system. First, African savings, private and public, were already substantial in the inter-war period, but the greater part was held or invested in London rather than converted into lending in West Africa. This was true of private deposits in the banks as much as of the reserves built up by the West African Currency Board, and after the war of the surplus funds of the produce boards. Secondly, the great bulk of the lending activity in West Africa was carried on not by the banks but by the European trading companies, which naturally lent to their produce buyers and distributors rather than to independent African competitors. In any case lending was largely done on the security of produce in store or in transit; the problem of obtaining collateral security from African traders for general credit was a real obstacle to change.

It was for these broader reasons that Africans found it difficult to finance their business, and their intense commercial zeal was frustrated as the volume of trade expanded. A demand for new African banks sprang up. The first attempt was the 'Industrial and Commercial Bank', set up in Lagos in 1929, only to be liquidated a year later. It was found to have made large loans to the managing director and other investments that could not be recovered. Then came the 'Nigerian Mercantile Bank', founded in 1931, with the same managing director; it had great difficulty in attracting deposits or capital from the public and made losses every year until it closed down in 1936. Such failures and irregularities are, of course, common in most countries in the early stages of organised banking.

A far sounder enterprise was the National Bank of Nigeria, founded in 1933. It had a prudent African management. Its deposits grew from £2,000 in 1934 to £10,000 in 1939 and continued to rise during the war years, to reach £173,000 in 1946 and £871,000 in 1951. Profits were at first very small but increased steadily.

In 1947 an important competitor appeared on the scene: The Nigerian Farmers' and Commercial Bank. This grew rapidly. By 1951 it had an office in London and some thirty branches in Nigeria. Yet it went into liquidation in 1952.

The early experiences with African banks led in 1948 to an enquiry into Nigerian banking by an official of the Bank of England, G. D. Paton. He recommended that a banking ordinance should be issued to regulate banking practices and protect depositors by laying down minimum capital ratios. This was in fact done in 1952. But the general drift of policy was fully known before, and it can be assumed that fear of coming restrictions was the main reason for a rush to establish new banks. A separate enquiry into banking services was held in the Gold Coast (where no private African banks existed at the time) under the chairmanship of Sir Cecil Trevor whose report was published in Accra in 1952.

Both reports suggested that there was a gap in the financial services provided in West Africa – a gap that might be filled either by Development Corporations or by banks that could call on Government funds. But both concluded that the economies were not ripe for fully fledged central banks to act as issuing and reserve banks for the currency and as lender of last resort; for Nigeria the question of a central bank was then more fully studied by J. L. Fisher of the Bank of England whose report was published in 1953.

'In the fifteen months from February 1951 to May 1952 no less than eighteen indigenous banks were registered', writes Charles V. Brown in his *Study of the Nigerian Banking System*, published in 1966. Some of these 'mushroom banks' never really opened for business, and 'with one exception, the Merchant Bank, they had all ceased operations by 1954'. The Merchant Bank itself lost its licence in 1960 'as a result of misuse of Government funds'.

It was not only the National Bank of Nigeria which survived the confidence crisis of the mid-fifties and went on expanding, based on political support in the Western Region. In the east the African Continental Bank began operations in 1948, led by Dr. Azikiwe, the prominent politician. For a time this bank served mainly to finance the activities of the 'Zik Group' of companies controlled by Dr. Azikiwe himself, but it expanded well beyond that base. Its close connection with the Eastern Region Government led in 1955 to the purchase of some £800,000 of its shares by the regional finance corporation; between 1960 and 1962 the Eastern Region Production Development Board invested a further £3 million in the bank.

Without the injection of public funds this bank would not have survived. The way in which that support was obtained by Dr. Azikiwe, who was by then Premier of the Eastern Region, led to allegations which had to be publicly investigated. A tribunal was set up by the Colonial Secretary in July 1956 under the chairmanship of Sir William Foster-Sutton. It found that the bank had been insolvent more than once and had been able to continue owing to the political influence of Dr. Azikiwe whose enterprises were financed by the bank. However the tribunal also conceded 'that Dr. Azikiwe's primary motive was to make available an indigenous bank with the object of liberalising credit for the people of this country' – and the African Continental was granted its licence.

In his defence, conducted with all the publicity he could muster, Dr. Azikiwe sharply attacked the Bank of British West Africa, suggesting that it had put the Colonial Office up to the allegations against him because it feared the competition of his well-run African Continental Bank. The BBWA had of course disliked the way in which large Government deposits were channelled into this bank. At that time correspondence between London and the Coast was still sent by mail steamer and to guard against letters being lost in transit duplicates were always sent by the next mail. But in 1956 one such duplicate, a letter from Frank Wright, the General Manager, to J. C. Read who was then visiting branches, and bringing him up to date on the London view of the Azikiwe affair, followed him around the country and finally landed in a waste-paper basket. Heavily marked 'Confidential' it attracted the attention of an African clerk who passed it along to Zik. It was published in a local paper. The letter no more than confirmed the poor opinion which the BBWA management had formed of the African Continental Bank and its handling of government funds; but Dr. Azikiwe brilliantly turned it into evidence that his bank was being unfairly persecuted.

Moreover his version was reported in *The Economist* and the BBWA directors grimly took Counsel's opinion on what action they should take. In fact *The Economist* was simply asked to apologise and did so. The legal adviser, Mr. Christmas Humphreys, was then sent to Lagos with a watching brief to attend the tribunal, and he promptly reported that Zik was 'unlikely to make any further attacks on the Bank'.

The report of the tribunal contained nothing unfavourable to the BBWA, but it led to a proposal that the Bank should do more 'to keep the Nigerian people informed of its activities and services to the country'. The need for organised public relations was soon taken seriously.

The third substantial Nigerian bank was also closely linked with official operations. The Agbonmagbe Bank was founded in 1945 and developed slowly until in 1959 it received a deposit of £200,000 from the Western Region Marketing Board.

In 1959 three 'mixed' (Nigerian and foreign) banks were licensed and began operations. They were the *Berini Nigeria Bank* (Beyrut Riyad, Lebanese-Nigerian); the *Bank of the North* (also part Lebanese); and the *Bank of Lagos* (Swiss-Nigerian). They made an impression on particular areas or communities. The Bank of the North, especially, managed to get many Levantine and Mohammedan accounts away from the two British banks. However, its turnover was of quite modest size.

This brief sketch of indigenous banking ventures until the late 1950s indicates that the leading position of the European banks was not seriously affected until the approach of national independence led to the establishment of central banks. No doubt the rash of bank failures did much to discourage public confidence in African banks for some years. But it is also true that the rapid expansion of branch networks by the European banks after 1950 went a long way to fill the long-felt gap in West Africa's financial services.

The first of the new Central Banks came into being when the Gold Coast became independent in 1957 under its new name of Ghana. The Bank of the Gold Coast which had been set up by the

Government in 1953 with Alfred Eggleston as the first managing director was now split into two: the Bank of Ghana, to be a bank of issue and to grow into a complete Central Bank, and the Ghana Commercial Bank, to be the Government's commercial banking instrument. Alfred Eggleston was appointed the first Governor of the Bank of Ghana in July, 1957. As expected the Bank of Ghana took over the management of the currency in July 1958 and soon issued a separate national currency. The Ghana Commercial Bank assumed the function of government banker and in time took over the finances of most Government and semi-Government corporations.

In Nigeria Mr. J. L. Fisher of the Bank of England had suggested in 1952 that a central bank in Nigeria should be built up in three stages: one, the transfer of the West African Currency Board to Africa; two, the establishment of a Nigerian Currency Board; three, the setting up of a Bank of Issue which would gradually develop into a fully fledged central bank. The World Bank Mission in 1954 agreed that it would be 'premature' to establish a complete Central Bank but thought that 'the timing should not be as cautious as Mr. Fisher proposed'. The World Bank said that a state bank should be set up soon and that its first task should be to issue a new Nigerian currency. After that, when an adequate staff had been assembled and gained some experience, the state bank should take over governmental and other funds. In August 1957 followed the report of Mr. J. B. de Loynes, another adviser of the Bank of England. This became a basic textbook for new central banks in the developing world. It contained the drafts of a banking bill and a central bank bill, both of which were adopted in March 1958. A central bank was established by stages between September 1958 and July 1959 when it became fully operative.

A NEW EUROPEAN COMPETITOR

In 1948 a new French-owned bank was established in Nigeria. French banks were, of course, operating in all the French colonies surrounding and dividing the British territories. Apart from the government bank, Banque de l'Afrique Occidentale, the largest commercial bank was the Banque Nationale pour le Commerce et l'Industrie. In 1947 its London manager M. Hervé Laroche, visited Nigeria, judged that it had great prospects, and wrote a book about it. It was a time of change: the bank had been nationalised in 1945 and in the following year it had converted its London branch into a new UK company, the British and French Bank for Commerce and Industry. It was decided to launch the Nigerian venture as a subsidiary of the London company and to give it the same name – British and French Bank for Commerce and Industry. (In 1956 the last four words were dropped both in London and in Lagos.)

At first the new French bank in Lagos secured mainly Lebanese and Syrian customers, many of whom were French-speaking. The two large French trading companies remained loyal to the British banks for some years, although one of them later gave a share of its business to the French bank, which was also successful in gaining a number of British accounts because, as a newcomer, it worked harder than the old-established banks to get business. In the late 1950s came an influx of Indian traders, mainly Sindhis who had been made homeless by Indian partition and had first gone to Hong Kong, where the French bank was strongly established. From there some of them went to West Africa, chiefly as textile traders, and looked for assistance to the bank they had known in the east.

In February 1961, the British and French Bank in Nigeria, which by then had ten branches, transformed itself into the *United Bank for Africa*, incorporated as a Nigerian bank with an issued share capital of £1·5 million, soon afterwards raised to £2 million. This was subscribed by five international banks – British and French Bank, Banca Nazionale del Lavoro, Monte dei Paschi di Siena, Bankers Trust Company of New York and Amsterdam-Rotterdam Bank. Expansion continued. The Dutch bank later withdrew. In 1971 UBA had 24 branches and a staff of 945. It then made a share issue to the Nigerian public – like the other two expatriate banks – and obtained some 2,500 Nigerian shareholders for 11% of the capital.

In 1966 the French parent bank amalgamated with the Comptoir Nationale d'Escompte de Paris to form the Banque Nationale de Paris, the largest bank in France. The two London companies were also merged, and the Nigerian bank remained under London control.

This has continued despite the shareholdings of the American Italian and Dutch banks in the United Bank for Africa; and even after the Nigerian Government, in 1973, acquired 38% of the bank's capital.

Having established good relations with the Nigerian Government and public and a network of international banks to act as a catchment system for new customers the UBA became one of the major banks in Nigeria. Its expatriate staff is usually about half British and half French, and the general managers have been at times French, at other times British. It gradually obtained a fair cross-section of business and became a serious competitor of the Bank of West Africa.

Early means of promoting
the banking habit – a Bank
home safe (about 1930)

(*Above*) Loading cash at
Kano, 1974

(*Opposite Top*) Loading
cash at Ikeja Airport, 1955

(*Opposite Bottom*) Cash
transport by head-load

Lorry load of metal specie
boxes

Chapter Seventeen

INDEPENDENT STATES EMERGE

CREATION OF NATIONAL CURRENCIES

A COMMON currency had been one of the few unifying elements during the period of British rule in West Africa. Almost all other aspects of civil administration had been developed in the form of four separate countries. The organisation of production and trade, though conducted in recent times by trading companies that were large enough to span the whole area, had to be sub-divided in many ways to fit the administrative separation. But ever since silver money was effectively introduced and the British silver currency became legal tender, it penetrated the whole of British West Africa.

From the outset the care of the currency had been one of the principal functions of the Bank of British West Africa. The anxious struggles of its early directors to obtain and retain the sole right to import silver coins from the Royal Mint have been described in previous chapters. In 1912 the English shilling was superseded by a new currency and the West African Currency Board was set up to issue and supervise it. But the Board was only a small body meeting in a single office in London, and the BBWA was its sole agent on the Coast. Its local managers, in conjunction with colonial civil servants appointed as currency officers, handled the distribution of coin and notes throughout the British territories in West Africa as well as the withdrawal and repatriation of worn or surplus coin. Since 1942, when Sir Roy Wilson died, the Bank had not had a member on the Currency Board, but relations had remained close and friendly, as the file of correspondence between Board and Bank shows.

It is true that the Bank at times became concerned about the weight of work and responsibility which its agency position entailed. When John Read first went to West Africa in 1952 to tour the branches he was appalled at the amount of time spent by managers on the Currency Board's business, moving coin and notes in or out of the strong-room, checking large consignments of money, or dealing with accounts and correspondence. 'All this time they ought to be talking to customers', Read said unhappily. Clearly the annual agency fee of £4,000 which had been fixed in 1927 had long ceased to compensate the Bank for the work done, even when the commission for transfers within West Africa was added.

In November 1952 the directors were so impressed with the vast amount of cash the Bank was holding on behalf of the Currency Board – it had risen between March and September of that year from £31 million to £53 million – that they asked the General Manager to examine the relationship with the Board and to obtain a legal opinion on it. This had last been done in 1938. The directors not only wanted to be sure of the Bank's liability in the event of any losses but they asked 'what advantages or disadvantages accrued to the Bank in its capacity as agents for the Board'.

The solicitors of the Bank, Lawrence Jones & Co., went into the matter carefully and gave a reassuring opinion. With regard to the money held by the Bank in safe custody, at that time about £60 million, the lawyers found that the responsibilities of the Bank had been clearly defined as long ago as 1924; and that the Bank was almost entirely relieved of any liability for losses. 'We can see no reason to advise the Bank to ask for any change in the terms of its relationship with the West African Currency Board', the lawyers concluded.

Armed with this opinion the General Manager pointed out that the strong-rooms provided by the Bank for the storage of currency were 'undoubtedly the best built and protected strong-rooms in West Africa'. Armed guards, police or military, were provided by the Government for duty at strong-room points. All running expenses incurred by the Bank were met by the Currency Board. And quite apart from costs and rewards, 'an immense amount of prestige accrues to us as Currency Board agents and, although its value is difficult to measure, our standing in West Africa has gained immeasurably, especially where Africans are concerned'.

The directors were satisfied and no further action was taken. But the amount of currency handled for the Board continued to grow fast. In February 1954 it had reached £92 million and the directors noted this high figure 'with some concern'. They requested Mr. Becker and Mr. Wright to look once again into the terms of the agreement with the Currency Board and to make sure that the Bank's responsibilities were clearly defined. A few points were discovered on which there might be some uncertainty, and the Currency Board willingly gave fresh assurances. Again there was no need to change the relationship, although the amount of currency at the end of April 1954 had risen to £101,824,428.

With approaching independence the colonial territory was going to be split into four new countries. That is how political and administrative trends had developed. One of the first attributes of national sovereignty was bound to be the right of each state to issue its own currency. In April 1955 the Minister of Finance of the Gold Coast announced that a national currency would be issued as soon as this could be arranged. It was not done overnight. In 1957 the Gold Coast became independent as Ghana. The new central bank, the Bank of Ghana, opened its doors in July 1958. During the next twelve months the new currency was issued, at first almost entirely in the form of notes. The Currency Board worked closely with the Bank of Ghana to ensure a smooth withdrawal of its own notes and coin so that they could be replaced by the new currency without a hitch. The old currency was accepted by the Bank of Ghana in exchange for the new, and in turn the Board took the withdrawn currency for redemption and paid out sterling cash, pound for pound. Its notes and coin remained legal tender until July 1, 1959, and were then progressively demonetised.

In Nigeria a Central Bank was established in March 1958, well before independence. It opened for business in July 1959. Almost at once it began to issue a new Nigerian currency. Again the West African Currency Board gave every help in easing the change-over.

The process is described in *A History of the West African Currency Board* by J. B. de Loynes (first published 1962, revised 1974):

This was a large task. Over the years Nigeria had absorbed vast quantities of coin. As late as 1952 coin probably preponderated by value in the total currency circulation. It seems likely that in 1959 nearly one thousand million pieces of the Board's coinage were held in the country, though this estimate must admittedly be reduced, as an effective circulation figure, by the unknown quantity of metal lost, destroyed or gone out of circulation in other ways. Some of these 'other ways' were unusual: for example, with rising prices many Africans had found that the one-tenth penny and even larger coins made convenient and inexpensive metal washers for corrugated iron roofs, etc. . . .

It was inevitable that the replacement of the Board's coinage in Nigeria should take a long time. Both the Board's notes and coin remained legal tender until July 1, 1962: and to avoid hardship to holders in remote places the Board continued to redeem its notes without commission in Lagos until 30th September 1962, and its coin until 31st December 1962.

The main burden of exchanging the old currency for the new fell on the commercial banks, and particularly on the BBWA. Fortunately the new currencies were first established at parity with the pound sterling so that the exchange could be made pound for pound and shilling for shilling. Gradually the two central banks set up their own currency agencies in the main centres but in many smaller places the BBWA, which by then had changed its name to Bank of West Africa, and Barclays Bank (DC&O) continued to act as agents. The old notes had to be disposed of by cutting machines, 'the staff wearing face masks against the clouds of dust which arose'. The old coin was sent back to England for melting. Not all of this could be done at the Royal Mint in London, and some coins were melted down in Germany and the USA. To reduce the security risk coins were cut in half when despatched for melting.

In Sierra Leone the new national money was not issued until August 1964 and the Board's currency remained legal tender until February 1966. A new note issue was made in The Gambia in October 1964 and coins of the Gambia Currency Board began to be issued in November 1966.

As the old currency was withdrawn the Board began to distribute its reserves. In September 1960 £6 million was credited to the

Government of Nigeria and £3·5 million to the Ghana Government, both in sterling. The return of currency continued for several years more; indeed in 1966 the Board (according to de Loynes) 'noted that the currency which had been returned from Nigeria far exceeded the total recorded as issued there. It had long been recognised that money crossed the frontiers. . . . In October 1966, in the light of this discovery . . . the Board paid the Federal Government of Nigeria a further sum of £4 million. At the same time a provisional payment of £950,000 was allotted to the Government of Sierra Leone.'

The Board had in fact started making payments to the West African Governments as early as the fiscal year 1919–20, when the first £100,000 was distributed from the annual income yielded by its reserve investments, as laid down by its Constitution in 1912. From then onwards distributions were made each year, rising to £1 million in 1954–5, £2 million in 1957–8 and £4 million in each of the two following years. Altogether between 1920 and 1968–9 a total of £33,100,000 was distributed to the West African Governments from the Board's annual income; in addition payments from the reserves (1960–1 to 1971–2) – including those mentioned above – amounted to £20,676,016, and a final distribution of £4 million was made on October 16, 1973 in the form of interest-free loans. This brought the grand total distributed by the Board to £56,776,016.

The circulation of the Board's currency had reached its peak of over £125 million on December 31, 1956. By then the proportion of notes to coin had steeply increased: in 1951 the total of £79 million was composed of 48% notes and 52% coin; by mid-1957 when the total had fallen back slightly from the peak to £107 million notes accounted for 65% and coin for only 35%. In the following years the circulation declined rapidly as it was replaced by the new national monies. By November 1, 1973, this process had reached a stage where it was decided to bring the Board itself to an end. Its residual assets were transferred to the Crown Agents who continued to manage the funds and to redeem the remaining currency.

A great deal of work was done by the Bank's staff in carrying out the exchange of the old currency for the new national currencies. In 1960 the Currency Board's annual report paid a courteous tribute: 'The redemption of the Board's currency caused much additional

work for the Board's agent, the Bank of West Africa Limited. . . .
The Board wishes to place on record its appreciation of the cooperation of the Bank in carrying out a task of this magnitude, a
typical example of the helpfulness shown by the Bank throughout
the forty-six years of its association with the Board.'

By that time it was clear that the Bank's services to the Board were
no longer needed except for the final withdrawal of the old currency. The Bank was left with the strong-rooms it had built over the
years at its own expense for the exclusive use of the Board. It had
received an annual rent roughly equivalent of 5% on the capital
expenditure, but the capital itself had never been repaid. After some
discussions the Board, while not accepting responsibility, agreed in
June 1961 to make an *ex gratia* payment of £30,000 to the Bank. A
new agreement between the Board and the Bank covering only
Sierra Leone and The Gambia was made on January 1, 1962. Under
this the Bank was to continue handling the currency until the function was taken over by a central bank or national currency board. A
handling charge was to be paid in addition to actual expenses for
transport, police escorts, porterage and so on, as well as the rent for
the strong-room.

MORE CHANGES IN THE BANK

The expansion of the Bank's organisation and business which began
in the early 1950s led to many changes in the board of directors and
senior management. Throughout this period the board met fort-
nightly; it had no established committee structure, though *ad hoc*
committees were formed each year to consider provisions for bad
debts and the remuneration of staff. In 1954 Mr. William Antony
Acton was elected a director. He was an experienced and active
banker with much influence in the City: a former managing director
of Lazard Brothers & Co., the merchant bank, he also held seven
other bank directorships. Although his role was that of a part-time
board member, his counsel was important at times. It was decided
that two deputy chairmen should be elected annually and Mr. E.
Whitley-Jones and Mr. W. F. Becker were appointed joint deputy

chairmen. Sir Sydney Parkes, who had been a director for ten years and a deputy chairman for six, resigned. Soon afterwards Sir Frank Baddeley, who had also been a director for ten years, resigned on reaching the age of eighty. To fill the vacant places G. Y. Hinwood and Sir Eric Miéville were elected; the latter resigned in 1957 because of his duties with the Westminster Bank.

Lord Harlech who had been chairman of the Bank since 1951 and paid a number of visits to West Africa between 1954 and 1958 retired from the chairmanship (though not from the board) at the end of 1958. He ceased to be a director in June 1961 and died in 1964.

On January 1 1959 Mr. Sylvester Gates was elected chairman.

Sylvester Govett Gates was a lawyer by training. After education at Winchester and New College, Oxford he practised as a barrister from 1928 to 1939. During the war he was called to the Ministry of Information (as controller of home publicity) and when peace came he was invited to become a director of the Westminster Bank. It was this bank which in 1949 nominated him for the board of the BBWA, where he served for nearly ten years before being elected chairman on January 1, 1959. At that time he was also a member of the Royal Commission on Taxation and a member of the Port of London Authority. His experience was thus spread over law, banking and public affairs. Legal habits of logic and method remained strong in his attitude to BBWA affairs. Coming to the Bank's chair after a succession of imperial consuls, Gates provided the right leadership for the post-colonial era. He was able to work smoothly with the strong management that was now running the bank.

In 1959 W. F. Becker did not stand for re-election as a deputy chairman and E. Whitley-Jones became the sole deputy chairman.

In 1960 Sir Eric Tansley was elected to the board. This was an interesting acquisition for the Bank. Sir Eric Tansley was probably the world's leading authority on the cocoa trade. He had joined the London Cocoa Market in Mincing Lane in 1920 and had gone to West Africa in 1924 as a cocoa buyer for John Holt & Company. In the time he worked for John Holt he gained an intimate knowledge of the complex process of cocoa buying, from the farmers in the villages by way of the middlemen, the produce buyers, agents and brokers, to the main buying centres and on to the ports by rail or road. From 1926 to 1937 he was back in London with Frank Fehr & Co., trading in cocoa.

When war broke out in 1939 and John Cadbury was appointed Cocoa Controller Tansley became his deputy; in 1940 he joined the Colonial Office to run a new scheme under which the government purchased all West African cocoa and later all groundnuts, palm kernels, palm oil and cotton. From 1948 he was managing director of the Nigerian, Gold Coast, Sierra Leone and Gambian Marketing Companies and he frequently acted as adviser to the West African governments and the marketing boards. He was on friendly terms with Dr. Nkrumah in the years when the independent state of Ghana took shape. When he joined the BBWA board in 1960 he retired from the trading world but his experience, wisdom and far-flung contacts were of immense value.

Tansley's personal impressions of life on the BBWA board are rather different from those of the professional bankers. He noted (with approval) that the General Manager carefully selected the matters on which the board was asked to consider policy. Very few papers were circulated. But all opinions expressed were taken seriously. The atmosphere was that of a family business in which all parties trusted each other. In his view this applied to the BBWA throughout its operations. Its managers on the spot were given more discretion, apparently, than those of Barclays, the chief competitor: as a result the Bank could make quicker decisions and was less hampered by Head Office delays.*

A number of changes were also made in the senior managerial appointments. In 1953 the Secretary, S. J. Andrews, retired and was succeeded by E. J. D. Kewley. In Lagos E. J. McQuin was appointed District Manager, a post he retained until the end of 1955 when he was called to London as Assistant General Manager. W. E. Sells, the Lagos manager, succeeded as Nigerian District Manager at the beginning of 1956. Still in 1953 D. H. Medcalf was made District Manager for the Gold Coast. S. Patterson, who had been manager at Freetown, Sierra Leone, was brought home and made Assistant Manager and later Manager of the London office. In 1954 W. J. Haymes was appointed

*Sir Eric Tansley in a talk with the author.

Accra Manager. The principal change in 1955 was the appointment of J. C. Read as General Manager from September 1, taking the place of F. G. Wright who retired. In 1956 G. W. Smith and L. C. Hawkins were made joint Lagos managers. The chief accountant, A. Walker, retired in 1958 and was replaced by R. J. Kimmis. This incomplete list indicates that the senior staff was being moved around a good deal as a matter of policy.

About this time it became the custom for directors to pay frequent short visits to West Africa. Besides the visits of Lord Harlech already mentioned, Mr. Whitley-Jones went to Lagos in 1955 to open the new Bank building. In 1958 he went together with Lord Milverton on a more extended tour. Sylvester Gates paid a number of visits to Nigeria and Ghana and so did W. A. Acton, who in 1959 also visited the Ivory Coast, The Gambia, Senegal and the Canary Islands. Major General Spears went to Ashanti, where he had his goldmining connections, in 1956 and later he visited Ghana, Nigeria and Morocco. Frequent visits were also made by senior executives. By the end of the decade contacts between the centre and the branches had been sufficiently strengthened for people to know each other and to understand the nature of the business as a whole.

Perhaps it was a part of this growing understanding that a fresh salary review for Coast staff was undertaken in 1955. All European salaries had been raised by 15% at the end of 1952. In September 1955, following the report of an official committee which recommended new scales for Nigerian civil servants, it was decided to introduce new salary scales for both European and African staff of the Bank in all West African territories. For example a European going to West Africa for the first time was to be paid £785 a year (previously £690) for the first year, rising to £925 in the fifth year. Added to this were duty allowances of £120 a year on salaries up to £924, and £145 on higher salaries. Instead of three months leave at the end of each tour it was decided to allow six days leave for each completed month of overseas service during one tour. A new salary scale was also introduced for staff serving in England. This was the beginning of a regular series of increases which took different forms in the succeeding years and included considerable improvements in other benefits such as an education allowance for children, travel grants and facilities for children to join parents in West Africa.

Salaries and other benefits for African staff were also improved from 1955 onwards. Thus a junior clerk then started at £214 per annum and rose to £284 per annum. First class clerks would start at £560 and rise to £780. A number of higher appointments for Africans would carry £785 per annum, rising to £1,100. African staff were not fully satisfied with the new terms and after consultation with the Union in Lagos further improvements were made. The Bank also decided to offer three scholarships each year to its own African staff for training in London. Further scholarships were agreed for trainees who would come to London and work in one of the Clearing Banks rather than in the BBWA. This was the start of an important venture in training Africans in banking practice in England.

By that time some Africans had already been promoted to senior positions. In Lagos, for example, Mr. J. K. Agbaje was a branch manager in the early 1950s (he is now a director). The slow pace of Africanisation at the higher levels which has often been criticised was not just a matter of reluctance on the side of the Bank. As the African staff of the civil service and other institutions was expanding very fast and a large proportion of the trading business was moving into African hands it became difficult to recruit and retain suitable African staff. The decision to bring some of them to London for specialised training raised new problems, for when the men returned they expected immediate promotion in spite of the lack of practical experience. If this did not happen a number left.

Yet another symptom of approaching national independence was the decision taken in 1960 that the most senior officers in each of the West African countries should in future be given the title of 'Executive Director'. This was done after the chairman, Sylvester Gates, had visited Nigeria and Ghana and found that the previous title 'District Manager' was outdated in view of the enormous growth of the Bank's business. The first two executive directors were D. A. MacLeod for Nigeria and D. H. Medcalf for Ghana.

The expansion during this period of radical political changes is illustrated by the following table. While deposits fell off for a time as public funds were transferred to African banks, they soon recovered; lending activity increased very strongly, and profitably.

Year ended March 31	Deposits	Advances (in £ millions)	Liabilities for Customers	Profit after Tax, etc. £	Dividend %
1954	79·4	14·4	9·6	244,712	10
1955	78·8	11·4	10·2	290,374	10
1956	68·0	16·5	13·1	351,381	10
1957	62·0	18·6	11·7	387,047	12
1958	67·6	24·2	7·5	386,044	12
1959	73·2	23·2	7·4	385,525	12
1960	65·9	22·0	9·6	403,274	8 (increased Capital)
1961	62·8	36·8	9·0	445,426	9
1962	65·8	32·7	10·8	438,294	9
1963	70·4	34·0	14·8	466,083	9
1964	74·9	35·6	14·1	535,212	10
1965	85·0	43·2	15·1	611,630	11

Another aspect of the Bank's expansion in its last decade of independent existence is brought out in the following table showing the number of Branches open in the years mentioned.

Bank of British West Africa Ltd./Bank of West Africa Ltd.
Number of branches open at 31st March

Year		Year	
1896	4	1932	51
1899	5	1935	45
1902	9	1938	40
1905	10	1941	39
1907	12	1945	30
1911	18	1948	33
1914	30	1951	39
1917	38	1954	51
1920	48	1957	82
1923	51	1960	110
1926	53	1963	118
1929	55	1965	112

A DIFFERENT KIND OF BANKING

Seen from the centre, the most significant change of policy was a massive shift of the Bank's resources from the London money market to West Africa. It is not certain that the BBWA was any quicker than the other British banks to wake up to the disastrous decline in the value of British Government securities as the post-war attempt to keep interest rates artificially low was failing. But the Bank's investment records reflect this trend so plainly that it must have been difficult not to see the signs. Various Government stocks were frequently bought and sold in an effort to make the best of a falling market, and one sale in March 1956 resulted in a loss of £473,365 (some of which may have been offset against a tax liability).

Against this experience the obvious risks of investing more heavily and for longer periods in West Africa must have appeared less daunting than they had done in the past. A beginning had already been made with long-term investments in various development projects since 1947. Some typical investments of the new kind after 1954 may illustrate this trend. In 1954 the Bank began to tender for ninety-day Treasury Bills of the Gold Coast Government. This continued until May 1957, when a further £250,000 such Treasury Bills were purchased and the Bank agreed that up to £2 million might be taken. (This was done and in 1963 the Bank had to convert the Bills into 5% five-year stock). In Nigeria the Bank agreed in 1955 to invest £10,000 in ordinary shares in a new company formed to erect and operate a hotel in Lagos. In the same year a credit facility of £50,000 was granted to W. Bartholomew & Co. to finance consumer 'hire purchases' of durable goods. The Bank and the company shared the risk equally. This turned out to be a good business and the credit line was increased to £350,000 in 1963.

In 1958 the Federal Nigerian Minister of Finance, Chief Festus Okotie-Eboh, visited the Bank in London to discuss finance for the extension of the Nigerian railway system. He was on his way to Washington to arrange a World Bank loan of $28 million for the purpose, and he proposed to raise an additional local loan of up to £3 million, to which he asked the BBWA and Barclays to subscribe. The Bank agreed to participate to the extent of £1 million for not more than ten years.

In 1959 a Development Corporation of Nigeria was formed and the Bank subscribed £50,000 to its capital. In subsequent years a series of development loans were launched in Nigeria to all of which the Bank subscribed considerable amounts. In 1961, when the Government of Ghana took over the mines and required £5 million of new finance a syndicate of banks was formed in the City of London to raise the money and the B W A agreed to put up £500,000.

Similar changes are apparent in the Bank's record of advances. Many new names, both European and African, are listed and the credit facilities authorised are for increasingly large amounts. In 1958 the directors decided that the figure above which credit applications should be submitted to them was to be increased from £5,000 to £15,000. In practice amounts of £100,000 advanced to a single customer became frequent. Advances against produce in store remained important: in the five years from 1958 to 1963 they reached a total of more than £1 million at the height of each season. For 1964-5 overdrafts against groundnuts reached £5,390,000 and against cotton £2,105,000. The borrowers were fifty-two Africans. More risks were being taken: in 1962 the record shows three loans for undefined purposes at Sokoto in Nigeria; two were for £100,000 each and one for £70,000.

Loans to Governments and Marketing Boards were expanding fast. In several years a credit of £250,000 was granted to the Sierra Leone Government for the purchase of rice. Various loans of similar proportions were made to the Federal Government of Nigeria without specific purpose. A loan of £1 million was made to the Ghana Government in 1963 for building a road from Tamale via Yendi to Bimbila. Overdrafts were of course regularly granted to the Nigerian Regional Governments against the security of federal revenues. Substantial credits were opened for the Nigerian Ports Authority, the Nigerian Electricity Supply Corporation (several), the Lagos Executive Development Board, the Cameroons Development Corporation, the Nigerian National Shipping Line, and even for the Bank of Ghana. In 1961, when it proved difficult to arrange finance for the Western and Northern Region Marketing Boards a guarantee of the Federal Government was obtained; then an overdraft of £1·5 million and a discount facility for Bills up to £5 million backed by contracts for the sale of cocoa were approved. Similar arrangements were made for the sale of groundnuts. To raise some of the large sums required for the following season a consortium of twelve London banks was formed to assist with cocoa financing, with the BWA acting as managers. It was a successful innovation.

The position of the Bank in Ghana was becoming less secure. Some time before independence, in 1955–6, a protracted strike in the goldmines had forced one of the oldest mining companies to close down and upset one of the country's main industries. In the same year, as the chairman reported, 'the termination of our diamond exporting licence has forced us out of an industry which we had been largely responsible in developing'.

At the end of 1960 the Deputy Governor of the Bank of Ghana stated that the expatriate banks would be gradually phased out. The Minister of Finance, K. A. Gbedemah, affirmed that this was not the policy of the President or the Government of Ghana and, in fact, the President had confirmed this in a Press Statement on January 11, 1961. The Minister of Finance went on to say that he was 'watching with interest the progress of the development programme' which the Bank was undertaking. A little while later Mr. Gbedemah ceased to be a Minister and left the country. Evidence of some hostility to expatriate business in general and the British banks in particular remained. This was not really supported by President Nkrumah. At any rate the Executive Director of the Bank, D. H. Medcalf, called on the President a number of times and found him reasonably well disposed towards the Bank. Indeed in January 1962 he reported to London that the President wished the expatriate banks to remain in Ghana and thought there would be adequate business both for them and for the indigenous banks.

In practice the business of the Bank in Ghana had already been seriously affected by the Exchange Control Act of July 1961 which impeded the free flow of money to and from London. It was decreed that 60% of net profits had to be re-invested in Ghana. This in itself raised no immediate problem as there was abundant demand for capital in the country. But in 1963 the chairman reported 'a further serious contraction in some of our normal commercial banking operations in Ghana, not due to any lack of initiative on our part, but as a result of restrictions on lending and official directives excluding us from handling export transactions in our capacity as international bankers'.

In Nigeria oil was beginning to appear in the Bank's records even before the presence of oil and natural gas was firmly established. Throughout 1952 the Bank was discussing with the Anglo-Iranian Oil Company a proposal to set up bulk oil storage plants at Lagos and Port Harcourt and distribution centres throughout Nigeria. This would require a credit of £400,000. Afterwards a similar operation was to be undertaken in the Gold Coast. The financing plan was agreed. Then came the turning point. In the course of 1953 the Shell/BP Development Company which had been prospecting for oil in Eastern Nigeria ever since 1937 confirmed the discovery of commercial quantities in the Opobo and Aba areas. In the next four years plant and equipment for the production and transport of oil was steadily assembled, the Bank being frequently involved in financing. On February 17, 1958, the first shipment of crude oil left Port Harcourt. This was the beginning of a dramatic transformation in the economic prospects of Nigeria.

NEW PREMISES AND HOUSES

From 1950 onwards large sums were set aside each year out of profits for the building of new Bank premises in West Africa and of new houses for the staff. Between 1950 and 1960 well over £1 million was earmarked for this purpose. Much larger sums were approved for building purposes in 1960, and again in 1962. Some of the earlier works, such as the replacement of the main Lagos branch and the building of many staff bungalows and flats, have already been mentioned. As business expanded the pace of new construction quickened. Some delays were caused by the fact that the European staff had previously lived over the banking premises. When this custom was changed new accommodation had to be built or at any rate leased before a bank building could be pulled down and rebuilt. Even more difficult was the question of carrying on the Bank's business during the reconstruction. Sometimes temporary premises were found, as at Accra; the new building might be put up on an adjoining plot as at Kumasi, or construction might be in stages so that the old and new buildings could be in use at the same time, as at Lagos.

Between 1950 and 1965 virtually all the Bank's premises in West Africa were renewed and many new buildings constructed in additional places. A large number of houses, bungalows and blocks of flats were built. Nearly all the new buildings were designed by Ronald Ward & Partners who had become the Bank's regular architects after the second war. Building costs were of course constantly rising. In the early part of this period substantial bank branches could be completed at between £10,000 and £20,000 but later on the figures were much higher. By comparison, the interesting pre-war bank building at Kano with its famous dome which became a landmark for pilots was constructed between 1927 and 1929 at a cost of £18,000. The designer of this striking edifice which survived until 1974 was the Bank's staff architect, H. G. Holt.

A few of the more interesting new buildings constructed during the period are worth mentioning. In Freetown the old premises in Oxford Street were demolished in 1959 and a handsome modern three-storey block designed by Ronald Ward & Partners was erected. First came the installation of enormous new strong-rooms – still much the biggest and heaviest in Sierra Leone. Then the bank was virtually built around the vaults. It was air-conditioned throughout. On the third floor the British High Commissioner established his offices. The building was opened by the Prime Minister on April 24, 1961, and its striking façade is still one of the finest in the business quarter of Freetown.

An interesting experiment was made in Jos, where the Market branch had to be replaced on a site which suggested a circular structure. This was erected to a height of thirty-seven feet with a radius of forty feet and a dome constructed of aluminium panels. It cost £31,100 to build, and the low price was a mistake. The dome panels were joined together with a rubber-like material which soon began to let in water. The branch was opened in January 1963, and in the same year leaks from the roof became a nightmare. The

(*Top*) Drying cocoa beans
in the sun, after fermentation
(reproduced by courtesy of
Rowntree Mackintosh Ltd.)

(*Bottom*) Preparing logs for
export in Takoradi Harbour

(*Above*) Volta River dam at
Akosombo, Ghana, during
construction

(*Opposite Top*) Alluvial
diamond winning in Sierra
Leone

(*Opposite Bottom*) Building a
groundnut pyramid in Nigeria
(the method of storage pending
railment to port)

Loading groundnuts
into a lighter on the
River Gambia

Hides and skins
drying in the sun in
Northern Nigeria

trouble was eventually cured but the noise of rain drumming on the metal dome remained a serious disadvantage. In the end, however, the Jos Market building – always beautiful to look at – was considered a success and served as a model for a much larger round building at Ibadan.

Rebuilding at Ibadan was begun in 1964 and completed in 1969, at a cost of £375,000. Like the prototype at Jos it was designed by Ronald Ward & Partners. The main banking hall is circular, 150 feet in diameter, with a reinforced concrete shell domed roof, without any internal supporting columns. On the underside the ceiling is finished with an acoustic treatment intended to last the life of the building. The exterior is faced all round with adjustable vertical aluminium louvres twenty feet high. Seen from the outside these produce a constantly varying pattern of light and shade, as the sun moves around the building. Internally the louvres screen the windows against direct sunlight. The hall is raised above a large parking area underneath, which also includes four drive-in cubicles where customers can do banking business from their cars. The entire building is air-conditioned by a central high-velocity system. Behind the main hall is a separate building with four strong-rooms and a security loading bay for Treasury vehicles. The dome in Ibadan has given no leak trouble.

Gradually during the 1950s the supply of electricity spread to many parts of West Africa and transformed the way of life. It became possible to abandon the use of paraffin lamps. Only then were electric fans, refrigerators and water heaters installed; from about 1954 onwards the first air-conditioners appeared in some offices and houses. A drinking-water cooler was purchased for the Accra office in June 1964 at the request of the staff. Piped water supply was a novelty in most places during the 1950s, and the water tanks fed by rain water from the roof were increasingly abandoned. Another sign of progress was the provision of fully furnished accommodation for the European staff, including carpets, curtains and cushion covers to match the decorations, and good furniture made locally of hardwood. In the past the term 'furnished room' usually meant bare floors and walls with a bedstead, a small table and one or two chairs – and no more. In 1959 the first drive-in bank was

R

established at Ikeja and various other branches were then equipped with this American device.

Rebuilding continued of course after the period here described. To mention a few examples, the rebuilding of the bank at Bathurst (now Banjul) was completed in 1965 at a cost of about £100,000. An imposing new building was constructed in Accra between 1966 and 1968 at a cost of about £700,000. It is 200 feet long and has five banking floors besides two floors for car parking. Incidentally, the London Head Office at 37 Gracechurch Street had been reconstructed in 1958–9.

Expansion and modernisation has been a continuous process.

Chapter Eighteen

JUSTIFIED BY EVENTS

THE TRANSITION YEARS

WITHIN ten years the choice made by the Bank in the early 1950s – to expand rather than retreat – was proved right. Independence had come but mutual goodwill had stood the test. The British banks survived the decline and fall of the British Empire. Naturally they had to face many difficulties and to adapt themselves drastically to new conditions. They could not expect, and they did not expect, the newly independent nations to leave the management of their financial affairs largely in the hands of the strangers from across the sea. Certainly the control of the national currencies and the regulation of banking practices was bound to become the prerogative of the African governments. But beyond that these governments would inevitably want their nationals to have the main say in domestic deposit banking. The bankers in London took a long view and met the wishes of the West African governments more than half-way. A new relationship was worked out which loosened the direction of the banks from London and made them more responsive to the needs of each West African country. On this basis they prospered.

But there was a long transition period to be passed. Central banks were set up in the new States to issue and handle currency. They soon assumed the control of commercial banks and laid down fairly strict regulations. African banks acquired much of the Government and semi-government business. Yet the demand for British banking services remained strong. The main difficulty arose in Ghana, partly owing to the severe financial strains which appeared after 1960, and partly because of a more nationalistic attitude. West

Africa had entered a period of vigorous economic development. Not only was capital investment from abroad urgently needed, but a variety of banking services such as was offered by the far-flung branch network of the British banks was essential for the mobilisation of domestic savings and the financing of the widely dispersed production of crops. Their close links to the London money and capital markets were equally useful for the provision of development finance.

These views were not universally accepted by African leaders in the transition years. Some of them would have preferred a system of socialist planning and direction in which privately owned banks had no place. Others placed their hopes in the African banks that had survived the confidence crisis of the 1950s. What mattered in the end was that the British banks, whatever their shortcomings, had built up a viable banking system which made a solid foundation for the new kind of financial markets and services, quite apart from providing the main training ground for the indigenous monetary institutions. In time these advantages helped the expatriate banks to make their position in West Africa once more secure. While other banks, European, American and African, played an increasing part from the late 1950s onwards, the two British banks – always hotly competing for first place – remained in the lead.

By the time the withdrawal of the European trading companies from produce buying and general retail trading was complete the vacuum of banking services created by this move had been filled by the expansion of the two British banks. Everywhere the Bank of West Africa had established good relations with the fast expanding African business community as well as with the new political leaders. A symbolic occasion was the opening in 1957 of the new bank building in Kaduna by the Sardauna of Sokoto, then the most eminent public figure in Northern Nigeria.

Lord Harlech, the chairman, was present. Many such ceremonies followed in the succeeding years. Indeed the Bank's annual review began to have uneasy references to 'growing official enthusiasm for industrialisation'. Clearly the encouragement from the African side owed much to a keen desire for finance to feed ambitious development plans, and the Bank had to husband its resources.

In 1959 the authorised capital was raised from £4 million to £6 million and the paid up capital from £2·5 million to £4 million. The Reserve Fund, which had been used for the capital increase, was still healthy at £2·7 million after the operation. In 1960 the total deposits of the Bank dropped moderately because of the transfer of further Government accounts to the new central banks in Nigeria and Ghana; but by 1963 they had fully recovered and in the following year they began to expand again, reaching £85 million on March 31, 1965. The published net profits also showed the impact of the transition period. From £445,000 in 1960–1 they dipped to £438,000, recovered to £466,000 and then rose briskly to £535,000 for 1963–4 and £611,000 for 1964–5. In the same way the dividend was held steady at 9% for the first three of these years but then rose first to 10% and finally to 11%. These figures bring out clearly how the Bank managed to live with the political problems of the time and to re-establish its business in a new role (see table on page 233).

It may be useful to recall the enormous range and size of the development plans that were taking shape around this time. In Nigeria, where a federal system had been established since 1955, the First National Development Plan 1962–8 contained among other large projects the start of the Niger Dam at Kainji with power stations and an electricity distribution grid attached; iron and steel plant, extensions to roads and railways, enlargement of ports, modernisation of telecommunications, etc. Meanwhile manufacturing industry was spreading rapidly to products previously imported.

Ghana had launched a National Development Plan some time earlier, and it had been given a good start by the spectacular rise in the world price of cocoa which allowed large overseas assets to be accumulated. However these conditions did not last long and financial difficulties soon slowed down development. The Volta River project, the centrepiece of the plan, was officially launched in 1961 with the help of large loans from the World Bank, the American and British Governments and some private investment. The new port of Tema which formed part of the Volta scheme was completed in the same year. Finance was also flowing in from the Soviet Union and other communist countries including China, based largely on the purchase of cocoa. By 1962 there were already ninety industrial undertakings in Ghana and plans for twenty-one further new industries had been announced, including iron and steel, fertilisers, cement, oil refining and pharmaceuticals.

In Sierra Leone diamonds had become the greatest source of wealth, but owing to large scale smuggling much of the revenue did not benefit the country. Other mineral production, particularly of iron ore, was becoming more important. Many small industries were started ranging from breweries and flour mills to paint and cigarettes. The greater part of the early development expenditure however was devoted to infrastructure and social services.

This is not the place to assemble a long list of new public utilities, ports, roads, bridges, railway lines and industrial plants established in West Africa in the first decade of independence. Some of the more ambitious early projects naturally dropped out or took longer to accomplish than expected. What was crucial for the fortunes of the Bank of West Africa was that the entire area of its business was humming with activity – construction, transport, enlargement of towns and cities and ports, modernisation of every kind of equipment. All this needed finance; and even where the resources came from governments or from overseas they generated more banking transactions.

Nigeria was by far the largest of the former British-ruled territories and had the richest resources to develop. It was also the BWA's strongest base. The Central Bank of Nigeria had been set up in 1959 on a British model, and the BWA did not find it difficult to adapt itself to the new regime. The earliest regulation was a minimum amount of specified liquid assets – 25% of deposits – to be held by all commercial banks in Nigeria. Next, all banks had to be licensed by the Ministry of Finance after consultation with the Central Bank. Expatriate banks had to have a paid up-capital of at least £200,000. Limits were laid down for the amounts lent to any one customer and especially to employees and directors. Full returns on these and some other requirements had to be made regularly to the Central Bank. None of these rules presented any difficulty to the BWA.

Although the Central Bank of Nigeria opened branches at Kano and Ibadan this did not seriously affect the business of the BWA. Meanwhile a short-term money market was being built up in Lagos. The first Accepting House was set up with help from London in 1960 and soon the first Treasury Bills were issued. A Bankers' Clearing House was established in Lagos in 1961 and the first Stock Exchange was opened in the same year. Further legislation in 1962 raised the minimum paid-up capital for Nigerian banks to £250,000 and ruled that expatriate banks had to keep assets of no less than £250,000 in Nigeria at all times. The Central Bank was given explicit power to define which foreign assets might be counted as 'liquid assets' by any licensed bank. This was clearly meant to induce the expatriate banks to retain more of their spare funds in Nigeria. Another new rule by which the rates of interest charged by licensed banks were to be linked to the Nigerian bank rate (and no longer to the London bank rate) served the same purpose. But Central Bank control did not inhibit the expansion of commercial banking. By 1963 there were seventeen licensed banks in Nigeria.

Events moved differently in Ghana. When the Bank of Ghana was set up in 1957 it took many of its senior staff from the old Imperial Bank of India. They had no previous connection with the commercial banks and introduced some features of the former Indian system. For instance, official 'currency agencies' were established in a number of centres to reduce the physical movement of cash. Some of these were in fact taken on by the BWA. In January 1961 the banks agreed to base their interest rates on the rediscount rate of the Bank of Ghana instead of London bank rate. Their difficulties stemmed far more from the stringent exchange control measures of July 1961 than from the banking regulations as such. But they had also to face state-owned competition in their own field. The Ghana Commercial Bank which had taken over the commercial business of the old Bank of the Gold Coast had for a time only three offices, in Accra, Kumasi and Takoradi. After 1960 many more branches were opened; there were forty by the end of 1962 and the GCB had taken over the accounts of Government and public corporations wherever it was represented.

In Sierra Leone the Central Bank opened for business in August

1964, more than three years after independence. Its first task was to issue a new currency and soon afterwards it made an issue of Treasury Bills. For a time BWA and Barclays were the only two banks. Then in 1961 the Intra Bank SAL, which was based in Beirut, opened a branch in Freetown. This bank had been established in the Lebanon in 1951 and achieved a rapid expansion, opening branches not only in the Middle East – four in Lebanon, three in Syria, five in Jordan one each in Iraq and Qatar – but also in France, Germany and Switzerland. In Sierra Leone further Intra branches were opened in Bo and Koidu, both places with Lebanese business communities. But in 1966 a run on the bank in its homeland forced it to suspend payments, and all its overseas branches were closed. In Sierra Leone all bank customers were repaid in full. The BWA took over a number of Intra customers.

In The Gambia where BWA had been established at Bathurst since 1902 it remains active. A Gambia Currency Board was set up in 1963. Since then a Central Bank of The Gambia has been formed and a French commercial bank is operating.

SERVING NEW MASTERS

Looking back, one must give credit to the Bank for the smooth manner in which it adapted itself to the political changes. Those who lived through this period must have wondered at times whether the organisation could withstand the strains that were put upon it from so many directions at once. They had to devise effective working arrangements with the new national rulers, the new central banks and the many influential African businessmen who were emerging. They had to adopt lending techniques first developed by the trading companies, to which the Bank had not been accustomed. They had to set aside cherished London banking traditions by subscribing to long-term local loans and making capital investments in unproven development projects. Competition was increasing, and new methods of publicity had to be found. The rapidly growing number of Africans in senior positions, including branch managers, threw extra responsibility on the remaining European staff.

Throughout this period the Bank was guided by the same board of directors and management, with only few changes made necessary by retirements or deaths. Sylvester Gates remained chairman from 1959 to 1965. Sir Eric Tansley, appointed in 1960, also stayed on for some years. In 1960 G. Y. Hinwood died. He had been a director since 1955 after being Chief General Manager of Lloyds Bank. In 1963 Field Marshal Lord Harding was nominated to the board by one of the shareholding banks. While the famous soldier had no financial experience his judgement of people and situations was found to be invaluable. At the same time the Earl of Inchcape resigned owing to pressure of other duties after serving on the board for eleven years. Lord Runciman was nominated by Lloyds Bank in 1963 and elected deputy chairman in 1964 but left the board in the following year.

In 1964 E. Whitley-Jones, who had been with the BBWA in Egypt for seven years before joining Lloyds Bank where he became Chief General Manager, retired. In the same year F. G. Wright, who had given many years of service to the Bank and had been its General Manager in a critical period before joining the board, resigned on account of ill health. Two others who remained on the board through this period were W. A. Acton and Major-General Sir Edward Spears. As for the management, John C. Read was the General Manager who saw the Bank through the transformation, assisted by E. J. McQuin and G. Redmayne. Stanley Patterson was manager of the London office, E. J. D. Kewley was secretary and L. C. Hawkins chief accountant. In West Africa the team was led by D. A. MacLeod, executive director for Nigeria in Lagos, and D. H. Medcalf, executive director for Ghana in Accra.

The vigorous expansion of the branch network had slowed down around 1960 although some new offices were still being added; at mid-1964 the Bank had sixty branches in Nigeria, forty in Ghana, eleven in Sierra Leone, one in The Gambia and one each in the two Cameroons, a total of 114. Only eight of these had been added since mid-1960. It was a formidable organisation to supervise from the distant London Head Office.

Tensions developed at times where the man on the spot was a strong personality and claimed more independence than the General Manager was prepared to delegate. The balance between central control and regional discretion is, of course, an eternal problem in all large organisations (without it, business consultants would not make a living). Expert knowledge of banking and wide experience rested in London; the men on the Coast had a closer acquaintance with local situations and people. In West Africa in the early 1960s this normal division of authority had another aspect. The Bank, like all other European businesses, was under strong political pressure to free itself from Head Office control and to become a genuine part of the national structure in the new countries. It was a delicate task to respond to this perfectly natural demand while retaining sufficient power at the centre to ensure prudent banking.

The problem was tackled by a fuller use of steadily improving communications, by increasingly frequent inspections and numerous short visits to West Africa by directors and managers. Fully mechanised accounting was introduced in the main branches from 1969 onwards. On this basis a gradual dispersal of decision-making took place as the Bank, as a matter of policy, increased its advances – with the twin results of larger profits and higher bad debts. Between 1959 and 1965 nearly £2 million was set aside as provisions against bad debts, and only just over £500,000 was recovered in that period.

The Bank became increasingly involved in the social and educational progress of West Africa. The records show a long list of donations to such institutions as the University College of Ibadan, Fourah Bay College, Freetown, the University of Zaria, and various hospitals. Donations to the Liverpool School of Tropical Medicine, which the Bank's first chairman had helped to set up, also continued.

While in Nigeria the Bank's problems were mainly the natural results of expansion and political change the situation was more difficult in Ghana. The restrictions imposed on commercial banking in 1961 under pressure of foreign exchange difficulties have been mentioned. Even stricter controls were introduced in 1964. The Bank of Ghana, armed with a new Act of 1963, directed the commercial banks that they must no longer keep working balances in foreign currencies. All imports into Ghana had now to be financed by documentary credits on a sight or acceptance basis.

Another order issued in April 1964 required the banks to observe new liquidity and other regulations. A cash ratio of 8% was introduced; liquid assets of at least 48% were to be kept from March to August of each year and 54% from September to February. In addition to the liquid assets at least 5% had to be held in 'special deposits' with the Bank of Ghana. The order also laid down that any advance to an individual customer in excess of £5,000 must have the prior approval of the Central Bank.*

The new liquidity rule was inconvenient to the BWA as its ratio of liquid assets to deposits in the balance sheet of March 31, 1964, had been only 40·5%. Altogether the chairman stated in May, referring to Ghana: 'We are still finding it extremely difficult to operate there. Further regulations and controls have been introduced which will clearly tend both to restrict still further the volume of our business and to increase operating costs.'

In fact the Bank was losing money in Ghana. It had spread its branch network in the hope of sound economic expansion, but conditions had changed. Running losses in Ghana were estimated at around £100,000 a year, and it was found that eight branches accounted for most of this drain. The eight branches were closed down in the course of 1964. This seems to have suprised the Ghanaian authorities which at that time believed that all banks made vast profits. Some time later a regulation prohibited the 'opening or closing of branches' by all commercial banks without prior permission of the central bank.

Banking restrictions were only one aspect of the financial pressures which descended on Ghana after 1960 as a result of over-ambitious government expenditure and balance of payments deficits. However, the economy of Ghana showed some encouraging aspects as well. When a Mission from the International Monetary Fund arrived early in 1965 it found that the main Volta Dam, the keystone of the National Development Plan, had been completed; electric power was about to be produced and work had started on the aluminium smelter at the new port of Tema. Moreover cocoa production had been well maintained and even increased, and this more than compensated for the fall in the world price of the commodity. These must have been the kind of considerations which made the Bank look to the longer term for its own prosperity.

*Commonwealth Banking Systems, edited by W. F. Crick, Clarendon Press, Oxford 1965.

MERGER WITH THE STANDARD BANK

Towards the close of 1964 the Bank of West Africa was approached by the Standard Bank with proposals for a merger. Bank mergers were much in vogue at that time, and for good reasons. As the corporate customers of the banks, the industrial and commercial companies, grew both larger and more international, their financial requirements were often greater than an existing bank could prudently meet. With the rapid expansion of world trade and international investment, more and more business firms needed finance and related services in a number of countries, and if their usual bankers could not offer this they had to go to other banks in other territories. These were the basic reasons which induced many banks in the 1950s and 1960s to amalgamate, both inside each country and across the frontiers.

The British Overseas Banks had a special problem: with the ending of imperial and colonial power their specialisation on a single country or group of countries became a liability. They needed a wider spread over several different parts of the world so that they might balance risks and losses in one part against positive returns in others. Moreover, the end of British political power was bound to lead the independent new nations to taking over the monetary functions carried out by British banks before. And what room for commercial banking activities remained would certainly soon be challenged by American, European and other competitors.

This thought had occurred to the management of the BBWA as early as 1955, when John Read suggested informally to the board of directors that the Bank's future might be more soundly assured if it joined with another British overseas bank operating in a different area. At least one bank was mentioned which was then regarded as having poor leadership but a good branch network and able senior staff. In the course of these studies a possible later association with the Standard Bank seems to have been considered. The plan came to nothing because the directors disliked the idea of the Bank 'losing its identity'.

It was nearly ten years later that the Standard Bank's proposition came along. The prime mover was Sir Cyril Hawker, who had

spent forty-two years at the Bank of England, eight of them as an
Executive Director, before becoming chairman of the Standard
Bank Limited in 1962. Hawker was concerned about the future of
the British Overseas Banks. With the disappearance of the British
Empire which had made London the centre of trade finance for vast
areas of the earth, banking business would no longer come to British
banks automatically. In some of their traditional territories they
might be partly or wholly prevented from operating, and in others
they would soon face strong foreign, especially American, competition. In Asia, where they had usually concentrated on financing
trade, they might perhaps continue in that field if they were well
enough managed; but in other parts of the world where they had
gone into deposit banking and domestic lending they would come
up against very strong political obstacles. They would have to
work wholeheartedly with the new independent governments to
gain their trust.

This kind of reasoning led straight to the conclusion that what was
needed was not a large number of localised overseas banks but a few
big banks based on London, each with large capital resources and
covering a large part of the world.

The general idea (which I have summarised here from talks with
Sir Cyril Hawker and others) was known inside the Standard
Bank as 'the grand design' and Sir Cyril was regarded as its chief
protagonist. The Standard Bank was then operating in several
parts of Africa but had no foothold in West Africa. What he was
aiming at, as a first step, was to form a British bank that would be
able to offer services as far as possible all over the African continent.
The Bank of West Africa seemed a natural partner.

He first consulted the chairmen of the three clearing banks which
had large shareholdings in the BWA – Lloyds, Westminster and
National Provincial. He explained his 'grand design' and asked for
their views on a merger between Standard and BWA. The chairmen
of Westminster and National Provincial were strongly in favour of
the scheme, but Lloyds Bank had a delicate problem. It was also a
large shareholder in National and Grindlays Bank, which had long
before spread from its Indian base to East Africa where it competed
strongly with the Standard Bank. National and Grindlays might

perhaps have solved the problem by joining the proposed new group, but it would not give up its independence.

Lloyds Bank decided, therefore, that it did not wish to impede the merger but could not remain a shareholder in the Bank of West Africa if it merged with Standard. Hawker then approached the chairman of the Midland Bank and asked if the bank would be interested in taking the place of Lloyds in a new Standard–BWA group. Rather surprisingly, Midland agreed. This was a change of policy for the bank, which had always avoided international capital involvements but had maintained worldwide relationships entirely through a network of correspondent banks.

A share was also offered to the Chase Manhattan Bank of New York, with whom Standard already had some association. Chase had started to operate in Africa on its own account, attracted by the growing business of American firms based on US aid and capital investment. That was presumably too small a basis for developing an expensive branch network all over the continent. A link-up with Standard and, by way of the proposed merger, with BWA may have seemed more promising. For some years the participation of Chase was a great advantage, as it introduced some new banking techniques and a spirit of aggressive competition which involved high-pressure marketing and publicity. After a few years, however, Chase withdrew for its own policy reasons, but that occurred after the close of this history.

Throughout the preliminary discussions in 1964 the Governor of the Bank of England was kept informed and gave his support to the plan. Before placing the merger scheme formally before the directors of the BWA Hawker tried to take the idea of a single British bank in Africa one step further. He discussed informally with the chairman of Barclays Bank (DC&O) the possibility of joining forces. Like his predecessor in 1934, the chairman was unable to agree. He would welcome some cooperation in general policy, particularly with regard to relations with African governments; but banking competition was to go on. So it was a more limited proposal that was put to the Bank of West Africa early in 1965.

The chairman of the Bank of West Africa, Sylvester Gates – who was also a deputy chairman of Westminster Bank – had been consulted at an early stage. Though he had some reservations both he and the General Manager, John Read, favoured the merger scheme.

'The purpose of the merger', said a letter sent to shareholders of the BWA on March 26, 1965, by two London merchant banks, 'is to bring together two complementary banking institutions operating in Africa in order to form the basis of an overseas banking organization with particular interest in that continent but centred in London and with international connections.'

The Standard Bank (the letter explained) had been a shareholder in BWA since 1920 and had always had a nominee on its board. Three London clearing banks, National Provincial, Westminster and Lloyds, had also been long-standing shareholders and associates. In the course of the merger talks these banks had been consulted and Lloyds Bank decided not to join the new group. The Midland Bank had agreed to take over Lloyds' stake. Standard had already formed an association with the Chase Manhattan Bank of New York, which had established itself in Nigeria and South Africa and decided to participate in the group.

'With these connections, and its widespread interest in Africa,' the letter from the merchant bankers went on, 'the new organization will be able to do much to stimulate and finance trade, not only between the many developing territories in Africa itself, but also between those countries and the rest of the world. Furthermore, it will be able to collaborate more effectively with important international development organizations in arranging finance for the development in Africa of natural resources, existing industries and new ventures. . . . The new organization, with a network of over 1,100 branches, will operate in some 16 separate African territories.' It would benefit from its close links with the world financial centres of London and New York.

Seen from the board room of the Bank of West Africa Sylvester Gates, the chairman, put it to his shareholders as follows:

Good management and careful husbandry have enabled your bank to grow steadily over the course of time, but your directors have been conscious of the fact that further progress might be restricted both by its comparatively small resources and by the rate of growth in the limited area in which it operates. Your board believes that to add momentum to development in overseas territories it is essential that banking units should be created with larger coverage and resources and with international backing. For this reason the approach by The Standard Bank Limited and the proposed association with The Chase Manhattan Bank are welcome as a means of securing immediately some of the objectives which your board had in mind. The broadly based new banking organization will be better able to serve the needs of developing countries in Africa and elsewhere which, whatever their political philosophies, have very similar economic problems.

Standard was the larger of the two banks, both in resources and in geographical spread. Its issued capital before the merger was £11,650,000 compared with the £4 million of BWA. Its deposits were £467 million compared with the BWA's £85 million. Published profits had risen in the previous year from £1,200,000 to £1,900,000 while those of BWA were shown as £535,212. Net assets were £30·8 million against £8·2 million. Standard shares were also a more popular counter on the London Stock Exchange: in the six months before March 1, 1965, when the merger plan was first announced they had varied only between 54s. and 59s., while those of BWA had risen from 29s. to 44s. 6d. Those were the main published figures but they did not tell the whole story. BWA had built up very strong inner reserves, and when these were disclosed to the accountants, as were the inner reserves of Standard, the relative values shifted. BWA was able to insist on a price that would have seemed unduly high on the basis of published figures alone. BWA shareholders were offered one £1 Standard share for each £1 BWA share, and any holder who did not wish to accept the exchange was offered 58s. per share in cash.

As part of the merger Lloyds Bank disposed of its BWA shares for cash. The other two clearing bank shareholders, Westminster and National Provincial, accepted Standard's share offer. The cash for paying off Lloyds Bank was put up largely by Midland and partly by Chase.

To implement these offers, Standard issued £3,600,050 of new shares to meet the share exchange and allotted a further £2,250,000 for cash to Midland and Chase. Its issued capital was thus raised to £17,500,050 of which the three London clearing banks and Chase were to hold about 22%. In addition Standard Bank purchased from Chase its Nigerian branch and Chase's bank in South Africa was merged with Standard; some further shares of Standard were issued to Chase in that process.

The merger proposals were accepted by the shareholders of all the banks concerned; in the case of the Chase Manhattan the sanction of the Federal Reserve Bank of New York had to be obtained. In working out the terms the Standard Bank had been advised by J. Henry Schroder Wagg & Company and Lazard Brothers & Co., while the Bank of West Africa had as its financial advisers Baring Brothers & Co. All three merchant banks had expressed the opinion that the terms were fair to the shareholders of both banks.

It was agreed that the interests of the staff of both banks would be safeguarded. The day-to-day business of Standard and BWA was to continue separately until the 'necessary studies' on integration had been completed. In fact integration proved to be a fairly lengthy and difficult process, as it usually is. On November 1, 1966, the BWA formally changed its name to 'Standard Bank of West Africa Limited'. But long before that, on November 4, 1965, the com-position of the board of directors of the BWA was extensively changed. The boards of the two merging banks became, in fact, identical in membership and met as a single group, though for legal reasons separate boards remained in existence for a time.

Sir Cyril Hawker, chairman of Standard, also became chairman of BWA. Sylvester Gates resigned as chairman and was appointed a deputy chairman of both banks; a second deputy chairman was Michael Robson who had already held that position on the Standard board. At this point a human problem emerged. Sir Cyril Hawker was no part-time chairman who left the running of the bank to the managers. He was doing the running himself, and he wanted to set out at once to visit all the new territories of the group. He needed a full-time deputy chairman at home. Gates was not able to give his full time to the task but agreed to remain a deputy chairman of the group. Cyril Hamilton, another ex-Bank of England man whom Hawker had brought into the Standard board some time before, was appointed senior, full-time deputy chairman of both boards.

Lord Milverton and Sir Edward Spears resigned from the BWA

S

board and received a tribute for their valuable services over the years. The reconstruction was then completed without further difficulty.

Merging the banks themselves with their separate managements and staff and different ingrained ideas was a much longer task than the reconstruction of the board of directors. It involved many shifts and changes in appointments at all levels. A few basic ideas were firmly kept in mind throughout this period. Above all, the senior men had to establish good relations with the governments, officials and business communities in the countries where they operated. This was an overriding policy: the Bank had to involve itself in the affairs of these countries, to ride with the trend of history, not to resist it.

Next, a more positive policy of looking well after the staff was developed – salaries were raised more easily, complaints looked at more carefully, and so on. High on the list came the appointment of Africans to all grades of job up to directorships. The problem of finding really suitable men was tackled in an unconventional manner. The chairman would call on a Minister or Central Bank Governor and say something like this: 'You want us to take on more of your people; very well, produce them! Release some of your really best men from their present jobs and allow them to join the bank. We shall soon push them all the way up if we find they are good.' That is how the three successor banks found some first-class Africans to take senior jobs, and the process is still going on.

Yet another new policy was not so successful. John Read, having become Joint Group General Manager, spent a considerable time trying to get a foothold for the Bank in 'French' Africa. He got as far as holding serious discussions with one of the leading French banks in Paris about a possible joint venture – but the French backed out.

In the four years following the merger separate financial statements were still issued for the Bank of West Africa, with the change of name to Standard Bank of West Africa in late 1966. Deposits were rapidly expanding: from £85 million at March 31, 1965, to £95·5 million, £109·5 million, £123·6 million and £163·4 million in 1969. In the same period the reserve fund grew from £4 million to £5 million and loans and advances from £43 million to £60 million. After that the business was divided between four distinct new banking companies.

Having seen the merger and the change of name carried through John C. Read went on to wrestle with the problems of integration until he retired in 1969. He was succeeded by L. C. Hawkins, who became a Senior General Manager until he, too, retired in 1974. Around the same time the entire management team which had led the Bank successfully for more than a decade reached retirement age: in London the Deputy General Managers, E. J. McQuin and Geoffrey Redmayne, as well as the London office manager Stanley Patterson; in West Africa the Executive Director for Ghana D. H. Medcalf was succeeded on retirement by C. P. Johnston, who had joined him as assistant director in 1964. D. A. MacLeod remained Executive Director for Nigeria until he retired in his turn in 1971, to be succeeded by C. P. Johnston.

Several other members of the staff of the Bank of West Africa took an important part in the head office administration of the new Group. E. J. D. Kewley retired as Assistant Staff General Manager in 1970 and R. N. Thompson as a Regional General Manager in 1975. At the end of 1975 L. R. Bishop was Joint Secretary; R. J. Kimmis was Financial Controller and H. J. Maltus was a Regional General Manager.

The history of the Bank of West Africa comes to a gradual end during the eight years following the merger with the Standard Bank. On June 20, 1969, a separate company was incorporated in Nigeria under the name Standard Bank Nigeria Limited; on October 1, 1970 a similar change was made with the establishment of Standard Bank Ghana Limited, and on April 1, 1971, Standard Bank Sierra Leone Limited made its appearance. These are the successor banks which exist and flourish to this day.

One further step towards establishing the three banks as local institutions was taken in the course of 1971. The Government of Nigeria acquired 36·1% of the share capital of the Standard Bank of Nigeria, and a further 12·9% of the equity was offered to the general public and was taken up by Nigerian investors, raising the African stake in the bank to 49%. In Ghana, 12·5% of the share capital of the Standard Bank of Ghana was offered for public subscription and taken up. In a similar offer, 7·92% of the capital of the Standard Bank of Sierra Leone went into the hands of local investors.

The business of the old BWA in the United Kingdom was transferred to The Standard Bank Limited on January 1, 1973. The branches at Duala and Victoria in the United Republic of Cameroon were closed in 1974. This left the 'Standard Bank of West Africa Limited' with two branches at Banjul (formerly Bathurst) and Basse in The Gambia. That is still the position. Standard Bank of West Africa continues as a small separate company with an issued capital of £300,000.

The development of the Standard banks in the separate countries of West Africa in the ten years since the merger is not part of this history. It is sufficient to say that the structure built on the foundation laid in 1891, when Sir Alfred Jones founded the first bank on the Guinea Coast, has proved its endurance. A successful business was created in constantly changing conditions, and the Bank not only dealt with commercial and political problems as they arose but rendered solid services to West Africa. No one seeing the successor banks in action today, with their gleaming modern office buildings and their far-flung branch networks, can doubt that this history has been a success story.

INDEX